All My Meadows

All My

Meadows

Patricia Penton Leimbach

Illustrated by Jack Homesley

PRENTICE-HALL, INC., Englewood Cliffs, N.J.

Book Design: Linda Huber
Art Direction: Hal Siegel

All My Meadows
by Patricia Penton Leimbach

Copyright ©1977 by Patricia Penton Leimbach
All rights reserved. No part of this book may be reproduced
in any form or by any means, except for the inclusion of
brief quotations in a review, without permission in writing
from the publisher.
Printed in the United States of America
Prentice-Hall International, Inc., London
Prentice-Hall of Australia, Pty. Ltd., Sydney
Prentice-Hall of Canada, Ltd., Toronto
Prentice-Hall of India Private Ltd., New Delhi
Prentice-Hall of Japan, Inc., Tokyo
Prentice-Hall of Southeast Asia Pte. Ltd., Singapore
Whitehall Books Limited, Wellington, New Zealand
10 9 8 7 6 5 4 3

Library of Congress Cataloging in Publication Data

Leimbach, Patricia Penton.
All my meadows.
1.   Farm life—United States—Addresses, essays,
lectures.   2.   Meadows—United States—Addresses,
essays, lectures.   3.   Leimbach, Patricia
Penton.   4.   Farm life—Addresses, essays,
lectures.   5.   Meadows—Addresses, essays,
lectures.   I.   Title.
S521.5.A2L438   973.92   77-24352
ISBN 0-13-022525-8

For Gertrude Dieken and Laura Lane who persuaded me that I had a vocation; For the farm women of America who encouraged me to define it; And for my farmer who is indispensable to it all.

FOREWORD

In the past four years I have been an overnight guest in more farm homes than the proverbial traveling salesman (my first book, *A Thread of Blue Denim*, has involved me in a surprising love affair with the farm communities of America), and I have made a pastime of studying the features these homes have in common with my own. I notice that the view from the kitchen window is of no small significance to farm families—to the women in particular.

Sometimes it's the barnyard, sometimes a pasture, a distant mountain, an orchard, a panorama of corn fields and sky; oftentimes, as at End o' Way, it's a meadow that one looks out upon. Whatever that view, it's a tangible link between the life within the house and the farm work without.

The meadow at End o' Way slopes sharply behind the barn, then levels into an upland plain beyond which the wooded banks fall steeply to the wild and unspoiled valley of the Vermilion River flowing northerly five miles to Lake Erie. I haven't retained option to my meadow view without a struggle. On a long ago afternoon Aunt Clara came by to find the bride crying. Making light of my protests, the men were moving an old chicken coop in a direct line between kitchen and meadow. She read them the riot act and they moved the coop forthwith.

In the intervening years my meadow has become the ground of my dreaming as well as the earth of our solid accomplishment. Most of the essays that comprise this collection took form at the kitchen counter with the meadow as backdrop, so it seems an appropriate symbol for these gleanings.

The meadow now is far more to me than it was the day Aunt Clara "saved" it. So many of the dreams I spent upon that meadow have grown to fruition in our quarter century here. Our sons have grown almost to maturity, our land holdings have expanded, our crop yields have improved, along with our standard of living. We have gained, often painfully, the insights of twenty-five years of marriage. And we have had opportunities to extend our experience that could only come to farm people in the last half of the twentieth century.

My intimacy with other farm homes has broadened the dimensions of my meadow. I see it now as the spiritual acreage I share with farm families everywhere. Their "meadows" have become my "meadows," and mine I would lovingly share with them—or with you—or with anyone who needs a spot to dream over.

Traditional farm life has always focused on the production of a meadow, never found much time for the field flowers thriving there.

My own focus is more frequently on the bloom of the thistle, the sunflowers, the daisies flourishing on the fringes—a picnic in the woods stolen from the high noon of May, a fool's adventure at the wheel of a semi, a journey into a startling book, a new friend, a reprieve from a traffic cop, the splendid moment of calm at summer's end when the last bean picker has gone down the road—ah, there's the nontaxable profit! (Strangely enough, the reverse migration of our city cousins is showing us more clearly than rural isolation ever did that ours is a precious environment.)

For more than two decades now I have been wielding my subversive influence at End o' Way farm and I note that frivolities once unheard of or dismissed as "damned foolishness" have been quietly accepted as routine. This book is a collection of the "daisies" I've gathered in these middle years of my life as a farm woman. I hope you'll find that some of them bloom also in your "meadows." Oh, not daisies *alone*, of course. I've noticed that a bunch of daisies is much more fetching when it's interspersed with stalks of wheat and accented with random weeds. . . .

Pat Leimbach

CONTENTS

IN DOUBLE HARNESS

Farming was already a Mom and Pop operation when Adam and Eve left the Garden of Eden. Pop may ever since have been wary of Mom's involvement, but the fact is that the partnership between a farmer and his wife grows more vital with the passing years and the growing complexity of the business. It may concern questions as involved as marketing agreements, labor disputes, investment credit, and E.P.A. standards. It deals with financial decisions reaching into the hundreds and thousands of dollars.

Yet the farmer-wife partnership meets its crucial tests in the same old daily irritations: sorting pigs for market, driving vehicles in tandem, herding loose cattle, coping with the great unanswered question, "What happened to the odd socks!"

Not Another Farm! ─────────────────────

The way of farm life today is by acquisition. One man dies or moves to town and his neighbor buys up the property. Every farmer knows the pattern and every farmer's wife agonizes with it.

Paul always coveted the Schuster farm: "Best soil in the area." His father had said the same thing of "the Schuster place," and his grandfather and his great-grandfather. In an era when land was cheap and tilling a field something of an extravagance, some Schuster forebear had dug up the place and painstakingly and properly drained it. The heroics of the effort were not lost on the Leimbachs.

Paul never drove past the place in midsummer without assessing the abundance of the crops, and the envy in his remarks was ill-concealed. He really took spiritual possession of that farm years ago. Farmers are a matter-of-fact lot, and they don't rhapsodize about it, but good land means more to them than almost anything else.

When the three old Schuster brothers worked it no longer, Paul was vexed at the disuse of good cropland. It was painful for him to watch it grow up in thistles and glory vines. He was prompt to respond to a request by an heir to come over and mow the place. I should have known then that he wouldn't be happy till he owned it.

Farmer's wives, who are inclined to measure wealth by fluid assets, don't get as carried away by this drive for land acquisition, so when the property was finally offered for sale, I fought the purchase all the way.

"We already have more land than I've found time to walk over," I protested. "Don't you realize you're going to be ninety and ten years dead when that property's paid off?"

Paul had found himself an ally in his farming partner, Ed. They sat down with their record books and Ed's little calculator and figured that they could make it.

"What are we gonna do with another old house and all those barns?" I argued.

"We'll sell them. Just keep the land. People are dying to get a little place in the country that they can fix up."

"The only way you could fix up that house is with a bulldozer!" I said. I might as well have saved my breath. I was a voice crying in the wilderness. With farmers the land instinct is deeper than reason.

They discussed the matter with their lawyer, who shared their optimism. "You can't go wrong," he said. "You'll struggle for a while, but in the end you'll make out." All they heard was the "make out." All I heard was the "struggle."

So we bought the Schuster place. Paul and Ed are as happy as clams. They go with their shovels and repair the drain tiles; they mow and trim and lay out plans of the crops to come.

I stay home and wring my hands and think of ways to increase the income to meet the payments. But life inflicts its irony upon hard-working men like Paul and Ed. I have a feeling born of long observation that in the end they will have the "struggle"—and their widows will "make out."

One Man's Junk

With the present mania for recycling, "getting rid of" may soon be an idiom gone from the language. Certainly getting rid of anything down on the farm these days is next to impossible.

For years now Paul has been wanting to burn the kettle house, a little vine-covered shack in the backyard, containing a great kettle built into a brick fire pot used once for rendering lard and making apple butter.

"Don't you dare touch that!" I say. "It's a period piece—irreplaceable!" And besides, I need it. It's crammed with old newspapers and pop bottles and flower pots and push lawn mowers and dozens of other things awaiting recycling.

Forty feet south of the kettle house is the ice house crowded with antique tools and household implements and Great-great-grandfather Leimbach's gilt-framed portrait. The seed house, forty feet to the north, houses a wealth of old doors and windows and lumber and porch swings and butter churns and discarded appliances "somebody might need sometime."

The horse barn, in addition to motorcycles and bicycles, shelters old harnesses and horse collars and wagon wheels.

That's just the beginning. There's also the granary, the chicken coop, the hay barn, and the "big barn"; then there's Newberry's barn (when you buy a neighbor's farm his fields and buildings traditionally carry his name ad infinitum); Newberry's milk house, and Newberry's toolshed. And every weathered building has its cache of farm treasures.

For a hundred years the Leimbachs have prevailed on this site, enlarging, expanding, acquiring, with neither a sale nor a fire. The accumulation is overwhelming.

Every time I get ready to do a good cleaning job, some yahoo comes around blabbing, "Don't throw THAT away! They're paying fabulous prices for that stuff." Where, I ask, are all these people paying "fabulous prices" for barn siding, mason jars, old bottles, rusty nails, wavy window panes, hand-hewn beams, and—are you ready for this one?—worn and faded blue denim?

Yup! I was just fixin to go down cellar and make a clean sweep of those dusty old overall jackets I inherited when we bought the Newberry place, and then I read it right there in *Time:* Saks Fifth Avenue was selling old denim jackets for twenty-six bucks! And bikinis made of old denim go for twenty. Wow! If Nelson Newberry thought his overall jackets might be resurrected as bikinis, he'd have himself reincarnated!

Odd as it seems, there's justice in placing such value on genuinely faded blue denim. (It seems they try to simulate the faded effect, but imitations don't command the price of the real McCoy.) In order to achieve the desired quality, blue denim needs to do a lot of bending in the sun and whipping in the wind. It needs to be dunked in farm ponds and ground into the slag of playgrounds. It needs to fall from horses or motorcycles or bicycles a few dozen times, and be forgotten on a fence post for a while. It should kick around in a dusty pickup truck a couple of weeks. Most of all it needs to be soaked repeatedly in sweat. It has to lie in dirty laundry piles on damp cellar floors and hang for long spells on clotheslines. It needs to be shortened and lengthened again and mildewed in the mending, nursed back to health with patches.

Then, and only then, does a garment of blue denim have integrity. And believe me, it's worth more than any city slicker's money can pay.

I wonder idly, while I'm pondering the new values, if there's any market for a retread farmer's wife in her late forties who can bake bread in an old black stove, make apple butter in one of those old kettles, can tomatoes (she raised herself) in those old mason jars, make butter in a stomp churn, and manufacture faded blue denim as a matter of course.

Stonepicker

I have been apprentice and journeyman stonepicker, and I think I am now stonepicker first class. It's May and I'm again mounted behind the potato planter watching the seed pieces drop into the hopper to be caught by sharp picks which transfer them to the ground. The few stones which have survived previous sortings fall into the potato slots and play hob with the picks. My job is to remove them.

It is nice up here behind the planter on a May morning, a really sensual trip. The world is all green and gold and blue; the birds call, the air caresses. There's a new planter this year equipped finally with the padded seat I've been teasing my husband about these many years.

But sometimes hours, even days, go by between stones! Feature what that can do to your self-concept. After a while you get the disturbing impression that you are expendable. I am not by nature a slacker, and I feel a need to be fulfilled in this job. Oh, I operate a couple of levers and hold the fertilizer hose when we fill the planter, but that's nothing my husband couldn't manage without me. The stones are my real reason for being. So is it surprising that there's a fiendish joy in me at seeing an alien stone boil up in that potato hopper?

I think a great deal about the psychological impact of that stone, of this job, which is in a sense one of safeguarding and prevention, like so many other jobs.

We of the stonepicker classification depend for our fulfillment upon an undesirable commodity, and however perverse it may seem, there has to be a secret sense of rejoicing in the evil that makes our jobs meaningful.

How would it seem to be a fireman without fires, a policeman without crimes, a doctor or nurse without illness, a body-fender man without accidents, an undertaker without deaths, a soldier without a war?

Field Trip

"It's supposed to rain on Thursday, and if it does, we'll ride down to Lisbon and pick up those seed potatoes," says Paul along about Monday or Tuesday. He doesn't have to ask if I want to go. There's a special tradition of pleasure about a day stolen midseason from farm routine by a farmer and his wife. From then on you naturally gear the week toward that "field trip." If you have any zest for life at all, you don't let routine interruptions interfere with the plan.

Thursday dawns wet and gloomy as promised, and all systems are go. Dressed in his newest blue jeans, a light jacket, and the cleanest of his peak hats, Paul goes out to gas the pickup. I scrawl a note for the boys to find when they return from school, scoop up my knitting and a writing tablet, and we're off.

Conversation is minimal. The immediate territory is familiar and we've long since said all there is to say about it. After twenty-five years there's a thought pattern couples share that supplants words. We wave to Mel Niggle and George Reinhard and know they'll be saying at lunch, "I see Pat and Paul went off on errands today."

"George's oats are up," says Paul tersely. "Pretty nice stand." Then more silence.

We drop off a bag of potatoes for an elderly cousin and chat briefly about our day's plan.

"Wish I could ride along," she says.

"Glad to have you," we say in unison.

"No, I've got this floor to wash," she says, and we know it's futile to argue with eighty years of rigid schedule.

The freeway lulls me to sleep, and I settle my head in Paul's lap for a postbreakfast snooze. I am awakened by the sound of his humming loudly to himself to stay awake. Then it's my turn. As soon as he drops off, I rev up the truck to a speed I know he wouldn't approve, and the miles pass.

I amuse myself by studying the vehicles in the traffic flow—a U-Haul truck towing the family car, followed by another auto driven by a woman and crammed with plants and fishtanks. Station wagons with college logos on the rear window, packed with clothes and skis and sundry junk. A customized van which seems to fade away into its own sunset (painted on the rear window). Rolling eastward are flatbeds of farm machinery—tractors, combines, balers, Ford blue, International red, Case cream, John Deere green.

We leave the freeway and Paul wakes in time for lunch at a truck stop. Fun to sit there and appraise the pairs of men who straggle in and out, wonder where they're going, where they've been, eavesdrop on their travelogues. They can't know I'm a frustrated truck driver, nor I that they are frustrated writers, dreaming of writing books to tell their incredible tales.

What Paul and I enjoy most about these jaunts is passing through farm country making deductions about what goes on in the shadow of the silos, figuring out who runs the show. A great stand of prosperous barns and a mean, neglected farmhouse always give me pause. When the reverse condition exists, one assumes that the farmer has an off-the-farm income or an unusually ambitious woman. Saddest are the places where both are neglected and one resents such poor stewardship.

A chicken yard on a scraggly hillside evokes thoughts of a time when every farm plot supported a flock, when Saturday morning was surrendered hatefully to cleaning the chicken coop.

There is the mild surprise of coming upon a farmer's landing strip, the revulsion of passing a hovel set about with abandoned cars, old tires, and all manner of junk.

Country churches inspire a range of thought. Some speak forcefully of an enduring tradition. Others tell a story of theological progressions from Congregational to Methodist, to Baptist, to Pentecostal. How, I wonder, do the spirits in the weedy cemeteries adjacent find peace in the changing climate?

There are little towns strung along the way, Welcome Wagon towns where the Kiwanis meets Monday, Rotary Tuesday, the Lions on Thursday, and St. Joseph blesses them all Sunday morning.

Each has its town square with a sleepy main street: postoffice, bank, hardware, and all manner of struggling emporiums. Alongside the railroad stands the grain elevator and the feed store and lofted over all the water tower painted in the high school colors endorsed by the "Class of 1977" and the "Class of 76" and Kilroy.

And so the day passes peacefully and too quickly. We dispatch our errand and meander home retracing the miles. Driving back into the township my eyes fall on Harry Stick's Mail Pouch barn. "Treat yourself to the best," it says. And, by golly, that just about covers it.

Subterfuge

You can "smell" a new tractor coming two or three years ahead. The first thing a wife notices is that the thrill is gone. (The thrill of the old tractor.) He no longer fondles the fenders, caresses the hood. No more does he run in the face of a storm to get 'er under cover. A crumpled muffler may lean into the wind for months on end. The vinyl seat splits and he seems not to notice. Foam oozes from the rupture and is carelessly obscured beneath a feed bag. Gone is the pride that once moved him to slyly detour visitors through the tractor shed. It doesn't seem very important anymore who drives the old thing—the wife even gets a crack at it.

"Give you any trouble?" he'll ask casually at lunch. Then as he chomps down on a cob of corn he'll move into phase two of the buildup: innuendo and suggestion.

"Been startin' a little hard lately. Thought maybe you'd notice. . . . Shifts a little rough, don't you think?" You can agree or disagree. The psychological workup is in progress. The seeds of disturbance have been sown.

"D'ja notice how much oil that tractor's been burning?" he'll say to his son one day, making sure you're within earshot. And then he'll interrupt his bookkeeping some early morning by walking into the kitchen (ostensibly for a snack) and remarking, "Guess how much we spent for repairs on the 706 last year?" And then go on to name a figure half again as high as the household budget.

"What!" you shriek. "On that new tractor?"

"That 'new tractor' is ten years old."

"You're kidding!"

"I am not kidding. We bought it the year the willow tree fell on the outhouse. Remember? I'll tell you how long we've had that tractor. We've had it so long it's paid for."

The next thing you know, there's a tractor dealer coming by on trumped-up charges, hanging around the gas pump, leaving slick four-color brochures in your kitchen, "giving" your husband the kind of time he's charging ten dollars an hour for back at the shop.

Someplace in the campaign you'll be treated to the "poor lil' ol' me" routine.

"Russ and Chuck traded their John Deeres in on a coupl'a 4-wheel-drive Cases two years ago. Don, Lenny, George, and Bob—they've all had a complete tractor turnover since we bought that 706. . . ."

Then there's the scare technique: "Parts are gettin' harder and harder to locate for that machine. Wouldn't surprise me a bit if they quit making them altogether."

About this time you'll find a list of figures on a scratch pad conveniently placed to catch your eye—over the sink next to the telephone, on the back of the john. You think at first it's an inventory of all your holdings.

"Is this anything you want to keep?" you ask.

"Oh that—that's just something the tractor dealer jotted down for me. Uhhh . . . Some figures on a tractor—and a plow. New tractor takes a new plow. Says he'll take my old tractor on trade and give me just what I paid for it ten years ago. That takes'er down to about fourteen thousand."

"Fourteen thousand dollars! Holy cow! We don't want to buy the business. We just need a tractor!"

You realize suddenly that it's all over.

Disking Dilemma

As tractor work goes, disking is about as low on the skill scale as you can go. Any ten-year-old can do it, and that's my problem. Every time I begin to think I've developed some proficiency at the business, I have a ten-year-old growing up to take over the job.

The disk and cultipacker operation aims to break up and smooth the soil immediately ahead of the planting. It isn't essential that it be done in perfectly straight passes, but why do my swaths always curve at the ends like fetal backbones? Why do I always finish with a pie-shaped wedge at the land center? How is it that I only remember the turning brakes when I've made three curvaceous rounds that resemble canoe paddles?

Paul drives past and shakes his head. I know he's hoping nobody from the Soil Conservation Service will come over for aerial photography until he gets a chance to straighten out the kinks with his planting.

It's a complex business of throttling down, raising the disk, applying the turning brake, and turning simultaneously. It really shouldn't be too challenging for a woman who has driven in a kindergarten car pool with an old stick shift. All I know is that it's a lot simpler for a ten-year-old with an uncluttered mind than a romantic in middle age who gets carried away with the scent of wild blackberry.

By the time I've coordinated all four actions I'm three feet into the adjacent wheat field. If I'm lucky, it's the neighbor's wheat field; more often it's my own.

That's just the routine part of the job. It's the less routine things that defeat you, like looking back and discovering you're carrying along a boulder, your disk is riding four feet off the ground, and you've piled up what amounts to an Olympic ski jump. You *know* it's gonna take three years of fitting and planting to level that hump.

You hop down to deal with the problem and dirt sifts into your shoes. Sometimes you have to dig through a mass of weeds and cornstalks with your hands to free it from the disk. I wouldn't be caught dead lifting that rock if there were anyone within half a mile, but with all the grace and grunt of a TV wrestler I hoist it up onto the disk. These are the times when you ask yourself why you didn't marry a bookkeeper, or why you married at all.

Overconfidence is an ever-present hazard. Get absorbed in studying cloud patterns, and you're likely to "awake" to find you've ripped out three fence posts and a mile of barbed wire.

The supreme aggravation is looking back to discover that you lost the cultipacker someplace in the last round. I have even heard tales from women who said they were approaching something big and black in the field and discovered it was the disk. At all events, this involves passing around again, backing up the disk, and hoisting the half-ton cultipacker into place. This may be child's play to a ten-year-old, but I seldom accomplish it without an "(expletive deleted)."

Without that little shot of adrenaline provided by the expletive, no woman could ever move the tongue of the son-of-a-gunning culti-packer three inches to the left without getting a hernia. Then . . . when herculean effort has finally accomplished the miracle of bringing one hole above the other, you realize that you forgot to look for the connecting pin!

There is one hazard about this disking business which I have not yet faced. The thought of it often wakes me up nights in a cold sweat. On the occasion when I turn too short and hang the whole rig up on a telephone pole, I'm going to hoof it for the barn and turn in my Slow-Moving Vehicle sign.

And what do you suppose runs through the mind of a farmer's wife when she's out there on that tractor disking for endless hours? Ah, she has her dreams. And one of them, I suppose, is of being some day a truly liberated woman. But I can promise you one thing—after twenty-five years of bouncing up and down with a disk across a rutted field, I'm not going out and burn MY bra!

Rye Is Renewal ————————————————————

A field is a field is a field, I suppose, until you've planted one and tended it and seen it yield in such abundance that you know the mysteries of the universe are working together for your increase. And then a field is a quiet miracle.

I knew it tonight as we came down the lane in the November twilight. All afternoon I had turned under with a disk the last of the spent potato fields while Paul followed with the grain drill. Vegetable ground is sown with a cover of rye as we finish with the crops from early September through early November. Most of our fields are already secured under its lush carpet.

All along the lane the staggered plantings are in varying stages of emergence. If the weather is warm and the soil damp, it comes through in four or five days, first in a haze of reddish-brown shoots almost indistinguishable from the soil. Then the scattered shoots become yellow-green rows. It's a thrill to watch, especially if you have been party to the sowing.

The secrets of the sower are soon evident in those ever more distinct drill rows. You see where he doubled over, or ran out of seed, or skipped a little teardrop section in turning. As the shoots thicken and grow longer the sower's errors are obscured in the mass of chartreuse.

Sun shining on rye against a frame of flaming woods or fencerow is magnificent, as it was tonight. The last of the gold light washed over the rye fields. The long shadows fell over the newly sown field, neatly grooved by the grain drill, like chocolate frosting scored with fork tines.

I thought back to the spring when Paul and I came out with our seed potatoes and fertilizer to tackle this last field. There it lay with those same orderly grooves, formed by the disk that time, ready for the commitment of seed.

How much work has gone between that day and this—the planting, the harrowing, the spraying, the hilling, the weeding, the irrigating, the harvesting. The barns are full to overflowing, truckload after truckload has gone down the road to the city. This last planting will emerge under the warmth of snow, put down a root structure to hold and aerate the soil, then nourish and loosen it when plowed under as humus in spring. The earth gives up its fullness, the farmer takes his yield, and rye is renewal.

Farm Wife in Drag

A farmer doesn't beat his wife; he just calls her out occasionally to help him tow something. The circumstances dictating this course of action assure its being a dismal affair.

If it isn't 5 degrees below zero, it is at least very early in the morning. Unless you're a dairyman's wife (in which case you'll already be in the barn), you may well be ripped from the womb of sleep and ordered to get on your coat. Before you can say, "Today is the first day of the rest of my life," you'll be sitting zombielike on something with a bad set of points or a dead battery.

The important thing to remember is that you have not been called out here to think. Fred Farmer will take care of that end. (Thinking is to be discouraged in any situation where you're working in double harness with Fred. He's the head horse, and don't you forget it.) The only reason you were chosen for this catastrophe is that there was no choice.

If you are the "tow-ee" as opposed to the "tow-er," as is usually the case, there are several things to remember. Deep troughs in my slag remind me that it's very difficult to tow something when the brake is on. Take that one liberty where using the brain is concerned; release the brake. If the objective is to start the cursed thing, you will be told which gear to put 'er in and when to release the clutch. The tricky thing is getting stopped when the motor starts. Ramming the rear end of the towing tractor is frowned upon, to say the least. It takes a bit of fancy footwork with brake and clutch and accelerator, especially when your nightgown is tangled in the gear shift.

If you happen to be the "tow-er" (which is to be regarded as status position), there are also important things to remember. If you forget, you will be reminded.

Rule One: "Don't slip the !?&#! clutch!"

Rule Two: "Don't jerk the !?&#! chain!" A farmer is a rock in the face of real calamity, but he has an unreasonable affection for a length of good chain. Breaking one is tantamount to burning his barn.

Rule Three is also important, but you won't hear him when he shouts it: Keep your eye on the rear vision mirror so you know when you've lost him 100 yards back. Fred Farmer's very testy about sitting there helpless as Clarabelle speeds up the lane. (Which is probably why she is more often the "tow-ee.")

If you happen to get involved in a long-distance tow along the highway, still other rules apply. Remember that there are going to be a lot of "stupid you-know-whats" out there. It's your job to see that you are not one of them.

A lot of rubber has been laid on country roads by wives who forgot to take a towed vehicle out of gear, and a lot of clutches have been sacrificed to the same stupidity. Let's get that rule perfectly clear. Take it out of gear.

The advice that will be shouted back to you at the first crossroad is "Keep your foot off the !?&#! brake!" Of course, he doesn't mean this in the strictest sense, which you will learn when your machine climbs the tailgate of his pickup at the second crossroad. Going around curves in tow is another very tricky business, as you will discover when you wrap the tow rope fourteen times around the axle.

Make up your mind that there are going to be some smart remarks in the neighborhood: "Well, will you look there at Fred and Clarabelle! I do declare, that's the first time since he married 'er that he's held 'er in tow!"

Work Is for Women and Horses ————————————

Part of the traditional conditioning of growing up female is acceptance of the admonition that a woman shouldn't do any heavy lifting. This, of course, is a bunch of hooey, and goes a long way toward locking women into the "helpless little female" image.

It goes without saying that nobody, man or woman, should do any heavy lifting if he or she has never done any. The man who lifted the cow, after all, went out and lifted the calf every day. And each body has a physical limit that is not too difficult to ascertain. I learned at the age of sixteen that I could not lift a 100-pound sack of cement, though I'm sure there are women around who could work up to the job.

Girls who grow up on the farm are often exempt from the weight-lifting stigma. They get a steady diet of lifting experience on fertilizer bags, hay bales, feed sacks, tomato baskets, and cabbage crates. In my own case (growing up in apples, marrying into potatoes) the transition was a simple one. Moving down from crates (which weigh seventy-five pounds) to bags (which weigh fifty) was no trick.

So because it is a job I can manage and enjoy, I spend a lot of my days on the highways delivering potatoes. The men who run supermarkets and roadside stands are often thrown into panic when a woman appears with a load of potatoes, until they realize that I can hold up my end of the unloading detail.

I always feel a bit sorry for the guys with genuine problems. "Gee, I'd like to help you, but I've got a bad back," or "I wish I could help, but I'm recovering from a heart attack" are apologies I hear often. Considering the stereotype of the physical superiority of men, it has to be humiliating for a man to watch a woman unload a truck of potatoes.

That isn't my intention. If I ever felt sorry for myself as a workhorse, I have long since revised my sympathies. And as I push on into middle age and hear more and more of these back and heart reports, I feel better and better.

One day it was a woman who gave me a heart-attack story with apologies. Then she stood there smoking as I unloaded my fifty bags of potatoes.

"You poor kid," she mumbled.

"Gosh," I said, "You don't have to feel sorry for me. After all, it isn't everybody who can do this work!"

Left After Taxes

"Hey, make me up a list of what you earned last year," hollers my husband from the next room where he's winding up his six weeks' dalliance with the income tax.

Well, let's see. What did I earn last year? A skilled homemaker should be worth at least $3 an hour, and she invests about 12 hours a day. Of course, I wasn't here every day and Sundays were light. . . . Say 300 days at $36 a day. That's $10,800 to start with. And then a farmer's wife has "hired man" tasks to lengthen most of her days. I went to work with my thinker and my eighth-grade math and I drew up my list. Amount earned:

Skilled homemaker	$10,800.00
Labor foreman (equally skilled)	1,280.00
Tractor driver (mediocre)	450.00
Truck driver (fantastic skill)	450.00
Purchasing agent (reputation—"Scotch")	500.00
Sales clerk, real estate agent, phone operator, social secretary (gracious, knowledgeable, witty)	300.00
	$13,780.00

I laid it on the bookkeeper's desk and left. In a calculated few moments there was a roar. "That's not what I wanted!"

"But you asked me what I earned. I thought my estimate was conservative, considering my education and experience."

"Would you please make me up a list of what you actually got," he said in exasperation.

"Ohhh . . . what I actually got . . . Well, that's something else . . . ."

Much later I slipped in and laid my second list on his desk: Payment Received for Services Rendered:

sunrise over the valley about 300 times (No failure with the sun.
    I was absent a few times.)
sunset over Schmalz's barn
a picture frame of barn siding
picnics in the pasture
two dogs working a woodchuck hole
rain coming across the potatoes in August
new peas on counter, June 10
sweet corn on counter, July 10
new potatoes on counter, August 10
a banana cream pie (from scratch) from a son on Sunday
    morning
swamp buttercups in May
rural free delivery
an oriole in the pear tree
hot buttered rum by a hearthfire in a blizzard
a wrought-iron kettle restored by a son
lunch alone with my honey on weekdays
sons coming in to supper from working with their father
a golden gingko tree in October
little kids in leaf piles
impromptu visits with neighbors
a chipmunk on the back steps
one perfect coal bin full of wood, coal, and a neat stack of
    kindling (Beautiful!)
walking down the road on a starry night
bare branches against the moon and the winter sky
wheat emerging under snow
more love, support, concrete assistance, and encouragement
    than I deserved

Total value: Incalculable.

And to it I affixed the following note:

   I found it impossible to assign a value to these things, and I suppose it's just as well. If the IRS figures a way to tax our real wealth, we'll be bankrupt. No matter how you slice it, "Payment Received" exceeds "Amount Earned."

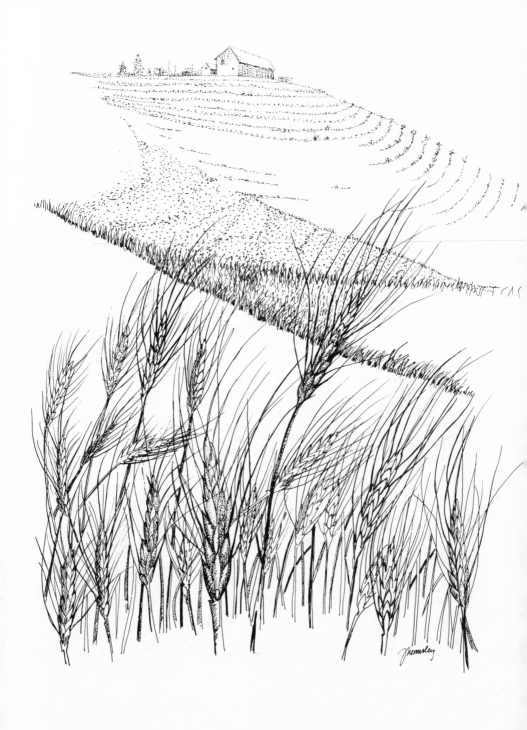

FOCUS ON THE FARMER

*"We marry what we need. . . ."** I married a farmer, and indeed it would seem to have been my destiny. For all-around, everyday, all-season wear, farmers can't be beat. They are inclined to chafe under the burden of leisure (a minor vexation on the farm), but they thrive on neglect and adversity. They are not given to flights of fancy, which was probably the attribute that most commended mine to my needs.*

Plow Pointers ———————————————————————

In his peasant heart, each farmer longs to be the first to dip his plow in the earth come spring. But each is disciplined by the condition of his soil, and a man gains no respect from his neighbors for jumping the gun.

How many times I've heard Paul mutter over a never-prosperous rube struggling to pull a plow through a too-wet field, "Damned fool!" Oftentimes it's a boy (sent to do a man's job) who hasn't mastered all the warning signs; and there's a certain sympathy extended for his poor instruction. But the boy's father does not escape the criticism of his neighbors.

A field plowed too wet, left lumpy and hard to fit, is a plague throughout the season. The stand will be poor; the cultivating and the harvest rough. The only hope for improvement is a succession of freezing nights and thawing days or a long "soft" rain.

Where farmers gather—in the yard after church, at the corner store, over at the elevator, down at the hardware—some poor devil's bad tillage will come up for discussion, and there'll be a nodding of heads and agreement all around that you just shouldn't try to push it too fast in the spring. "Doesn't pay," they'll say, as their fathers and grandfathers before them have said.

*"We Marry What We Need" from I Marry You, John Ciardi.

Striking the lands properly is also crucial to the tillage which follows, and it isn't delegated to just anybody. When a farmer's son has finally merited the responsibility, it's as good as a partnership. When I meet a farm wife who "strikes the lands" I know I have met a bona fide partner in the farm enterprise. (My solitary effort at plowing was judged deplorable, and I was very soon relieved by a twelve-year-old son.)

Paul is seldom the first on his land in spring. The farmers on the sandy ridges of this Great Lakes region have the lightest soil and always beat out the rest of us. On the morning when Paul drives home along North Ridge to comment "George Reinhard's plowing," I know how the fever mounts; the longest days of spring are ahead.

Most good farmers till so many acres that they have both early and late ground; Paul knows George will be working away on some of his acreage when the crops have emerged from our sandy loam. But that doesn't seem to lessen today's frustration.

He hauls out his plow, runs to town for points or belts or a tube of grease. He stops by the house and as he reaches for the Gelusil remarks that now Don Northeim's plowing the Baird place. He just can't wait to get out there and have at it.

When this northern Ohio area of the nation was settled, the English farmed all these rich and fertile lakeshore lands. The German immigrants came later to the heavier, less valuable acreage to the south.

Somewhere in an old church history I read the lament of those latter-day Englishmen that the industrious Germans were moving up, fraternizing, and slowly taking over.

Eventually the Northeims, the Kneisels, the Leimbachs, the Kishmans, the Reinhards, the Schmalzes or some other ambitious German family absorbed nearly all the old English farms.

I think of that today à propos Paul's agitation at that plow poised and ready. I suppose Helen Reinhard's out washing windows and Dorothy Northeim is planting sweet peas. Golly! I haven't even taken down the Christmas wreaths! My forebears, alas, were English.

Seasons in the Sun

When Ted comes in and shouts "Hurry up and change your clothes,

Orr, Dad's mad!" you know that down at the barn everybody's doing the goose step, keeping his mouth shut and his ears open. The imperative of the planting season has made itself manifest.

A farmer awaiting the perfect ambience for committing seed to soil is a sprinter on the line. When the gun goes off, anyone who doesn't want to be trampled had better be running alongside. When the soil is damp and loose, the wind has died, and the temperature hovers around 55°, Paul doesn't care whether there's an F.F.A. banquet or not. He's not concerned with scrap drives or choir practice or 4-H meetings or track meets. If there's a social event that involves him, you commit him only tentatively and spring the news on him at the psychological moment—five or ten minutes ahead of the affair.

A farmer who fathers a son, through all the years of the boy's childhood, subconsciously plots the action of May days when his boy will be fourteen, fifteen, sixteen, or seventeen. They'll work in tandem, these two, one fitting ground, one planting. And his son will understand instinctively the urgency of May and the hunger of soil for seed.

Somehow it never occurs to him that this boy will be a boy among boys who sit languorously in school on May days dreaming of two-thirty and changing into a baseball uniform for a game across the county . . . or of taking a blue-jeaned doll for a joyride in somebody's jazzed-up Jeep.

He doesn't recognize in advance that few of his son's friends will be programmed into agriculture and that a whole bevy of Mickey Mouse activities (the farmer's judgment) will be deemed essential to his son's social development.

"First things first!" are a farmer's priorities. The optimum growing season for a given area is pre-determined and any deviation from it can mean reduction in crop yield. Weather is such a variable that those perfect hours for planting are numbered. "Says right here in the *Vegetable Grower,* 'A farmer's labor in planting time is worth $200 an hour,'" says Paul smugly over lunch, as if to put an end to a silent argument we've waged since the first of his three sons was fourteen.

But there is an optimum season for living to be considered, and a goodly portion of it falls when you're delicately balanced between your change of voice and your first shave. How many poetic May days are there in the life of a boy? How long are you young enough to go tripping barefoot through wet grass or sneak down to the reservoir for a few fast casts?

"Hey, Dad," says Ted one night, thumbing through an old photo album, "What's this picture of you and this other kid sitting bare-naked down by the river?"

"Mike Tansey and I the year we graduated. We played hookey one afternoon and went swimming," says Paul.

"No!" says Orrin in mock horror. "Not you, Dad!"

Slipping into the mood of a vanished May, Paul goes on to describe that special day. Should I remind him that there are certain hours in a boy's life that are beyond price?

"Rain, Rain, Go Away"

Formal education for me began with a two-line verse on the flip chart in the front of the first-grade room, "Rain, Rain, go away. Come again some other day." It's a rhyme that has run through my head daily for a month now. Today Orrin dramatized the childish emotion that inspired the lines when he slumped into a chair at the kitchen table, crossed his arms on his baseball mitt, put his head down and cried. His baseball practice had just been cancelled for the fourth time.

"It seems like every time I want to do anything it rains."

Even as I said "Think how your father must feel," I realized that grief is never lessened by comparison. Sobbing was the catharsis Orrin needed and I had no right to try to take it from him. He isn't yet burdened with his father's concern for getting on the land to work his crops. He has never gone to bed hungry, and a mortgage is a nebulous thing that has nothing to do with him.

Then, like Job, he lashed out at God. "If God is good, why does He let it rain like this?"

Nor was I any consolation in replying, "That's one of the great unanswered questions religion poses." I'm sure Orrin concluded that God and I were both cop-outs.

At least I have lived through hot, dry summers peering into the sky for weeks on end in hope of a cloud, a balance in experience to tell that one man's flood is another man's drought. At least I have schooled myself to pleasures and preoccupations that go with rainy days.

Many the pleasant days when we have awakened to the sound of the rain falling through the maples, sent the children off to school, lingered late over breakfast compiling a list and a shopping itinerary. Then, like teenagers on a date, we bounced off in the pickup to do our rounds at the bank, the Farm Bureau, Sears, and the Farm Credit office, stopping at the tractor dealer's for plow points or transmission oil. Every place there was farmer talk about weather and crops and you sized up your situation in relation to hearsay of the others.

Or we made our own appraisal of the state of things as we drove through the countryside, noting where the tiles flowed and where the water was standing and how the crop was coloring or how much hay was down and being rained upon. You dream and plan and think out loud to one another; you have lunch out or stop for coffee with a neglected relative, then hurry home to beat the school bus.

But we have done all those things now several times. We have spent more money on shopping trips than the present state of things ever promises we can pay. Time together almost ceases to be fun, because it represents the tragedy of not being in the fields. The deadline for corn planting is long past.

The optimum date for soybeans is fast approaching.

A farmer's wife turns all her talent to distracting her husband from the essential problem—too much water. I watch with an aching heart as Paul walks up the lane, his hands in his pockets and his shoulders almost slouched. He's going out to check the state of the few vegetables that shiver there in the cold and damp. He'll size up the possibility of getting back on the land tomorrow or the next day or God knows when.

The little boys are the lucky ones, who can put their heads on their arms and sob out their grief.

Amber Waves of Grain

Today the wheat will go. Paul will haul out the combine and in a fury of whirring and clanking and blasphemy will put the old machine in operation for its twenty-fifth summer. The growing of a little wheat is incidental to our vegetable and potato farming and doesn't justify investment in a new $35,000 machine, air-conditioned and self-propelled.

Paul claims these acres of wheat are a vital link in the chain of crop rotation he prefers for good potato production. I wonder sometimes if they aren't more vitally a link in his chain of farm heritage, a link he's reluctant to surrender, as he and his father painfully parted with first the orchards, then the sheep, the cows, the swine, the poultry, and the beef cattle. There was no longer then any need for field corn or hay.

No small farmer can afford the specialized machinery that belongs to so many enterprises—the planters, harvesters, packing equipment, and so on. There isn't enough time to pursue the technology involved in each, or energy to establish marketing connections for such diversity.

But Paul clings to the wheat, and I understand that. Wheat is elemental and fulfilling. There's a rush to get it planted early in the fall, and the vigil begins. Comes a day when a farmer sits to lunch and as if in blessing says, "Wheat's up." You watch it throughout the fall shining green, green against the autumn orange and gold. And all through the winter, wheat is hope, supine and thick upon the land. Then spring. And it's suddenly upright and tall, inviting little children to wade in and tunnel. The heads begin to form tiny green braids pushing out from a sleeve of grass, green and then yellow, then gold, and finally warm tan-wheat-colored—no other name for it.

These are the days of anxiety, the vulnerable days when heavy rain or hail or strong winds play havoc. Always the wheat gets a pelting or two and a farmer grows apprehensive. But a resilience is there, an irrepressible will for life, and it rises again. The grain matures and the heads arc under the sun of midsummer.

I sit on the knoll with my dog and look across the fruitful mass of bowed heads, and I, too, feel the thrill of being part of an agrarian heritage that predates the pyramids and stretches into the present to the massive modern tracts covering the American prairies.

I see Millet's gleaners under the blue skies of France, and the black Africans on the velds of the Transvaal. I see the peasants of the Ukraine, the sturdy blonds of the Northlands, family groups on tiny plots in the subdivided fields of the feudal lands—and the wheat, the lovely waving wheat, the arching ripened wheat—the common bread of our humanity.

Yes, I understand the wheat, and my husband's tenacity. I hope the old combine will make it again this year.

Having a Corn Ball

A "stampede" is by definition a "wild, headlong rush," and that pretty well describes the situation created by a seemingly innocent little "pick your own sweet corn" ad in the paper. My phone rings off the hook, my front yard is trampled, dust hangs in the air, and there's somebody at the front or back door or both at the same time. Chaos!

Brother Bill, who has been retailing corn for thirty years and knows the business better than most, describes sweet corn as an "emotional vegetable. People get more uptight about sweet corn than any other item of produce we sell," he says. "Everybody is a self-appointed expert on sweet corn."

The critical factor in the production of good corn is achieving and maintaining a high sugar content. Corn varieties mature at differing rates from sixty to ninety days; the generally accepted theory is that the longer it's in maturation, the sweeter. The warmer the weather, of course, the higher the sugar production.

The earlier corns must be very hardy varieties capable of surviving in snowdrifts, "but some of them are really terrible," says Bill. "Of course, these fanatics with their sweet corn tongues hanging out really think they've struck gold, which confirms my opinion that flavor is more of the mind than of the palate." But, if you've been eating week-old supermarket corn all winter, I presume anything fresh and local will taste good.

Our own struggle as wholesale growers is to get the corn to market sweet. Ideally corn should be picked in the cool damp of the morning before the stalks are warm. (Believe me, on most days that's a cold wet job!) The ears should be cooled to 40 degrees and maintained at that temperature. At the very least, they should be loosely packed and well ventilated. Close corn in a tight bag in an unrefrigerated truck for a few hours, and the heat given off by this still live plant builds up intensely. The sugar turns to starch and that fresh farm flavor is gone, gone, gone!

All the "experts" have their favorite varieties. Golden Bantam has long since been replaced by hundreds of improved hybrids, but it has taken twenty years of hard talking to dispel the mystique. Just about the time you wean the consumer off one variety onto a better one, some new strain emerges and it has to be done all over again. The contemporary rage is a white-yellow hybrid (created by cross-pollinating white corn with yellow) marketed as "butter and sugar," "Sweet Sue," or any of several other fetching monikers. Varietal names are assigned by the seed companies, and corns with identical characteristics may be marketed under differing names.

The fact is that varieties which survive are those which prove to be the best producers. There really aren't any bad corns any more, Bill claims. "What about this Seneca Chief people seem to want?" I ask my husband.

"About as big around as your finger with six or eight rows of kernels," he says, dismissing it as a nostalgic fetish. Paul favors large-eared corn which detaches easily from the stalk and has a close-fitting husk to discourage birds and ear worms.

The principal adversaries of the sweet-corn grower are the corn borer, which afflicts early and late corn, and the ear worm, more prevalent in late corn. The corn borer lays its eggs on the leaves and the stalk and is easier hit with pesticide; but the ear worm infects the silk and is very difficult to reach with control agents. Late corn, therefore, is usually wormier than early corn.

But borers or blight, worms or weevils, everybody is hungry for a bargain, and the rush is on. They're out there snatching corn from the beaks of the grackles.

No doubt about it, in the cornball index of American passions, sweet corn ranks right up there with mother and apple pie. People remember the good old days and the good old flavors, and the good ol' corn patch out back. You can even find a few souls who'll swear that the best roastin' ears they ever ate were gleaned from the field corn early in the season. "Now that was good eatin'," they'll tell you. Where flavor is concerned, I agree with Brother Bill: the memory is more highly developed than the palate. I can understand, however, why folks will drive twenty miles out to the country to find a patch of ——Excuse me a minute. The phone's ringing, and there's somebody at the door. . . .

Hail! Hail! And What's All the Good Cheer About? _____

If the fog comes on little cat feet, then hail comes on wild pony hooves—in terrifying cadence. Nobody suspects. In the prestorm rush of putting away machinery, battening barn doors, snatching up blowing baskets, and dashing indoors to close windows, you rejoice that a damaging drought is about to end. The front of white advancing across the western fields is a welcome sight from the haven of the living room.

Then it strikes, and a kid on a side porch hollers to his brother, "Hey, Orr! Come and see this stuff!" and the sound catches up with you and you know suddenly that you have taken a viper to your bosom.

But hail never hurt you before; why worry now? Think of your friends who are in fruit. Niggles' plum orchard down the road, ripened almost to perfection!

And hail never looked like this before. There were always a few stones you could run out and gather for the freezer to brag about later as "big as golf balls!"—well maybe marbles? But these are clattering down on one another, flat pellets as big as half dollars, and thousands of them!

The boys are fascinated. It's an intriguing natural phenomenon and they pay no attention to the fervent "Oh no's!" you utter over and over and over through the interminable minutes.

Out on the prairies of the Midwest I have met and chatted with salesmen of hail insurance. It seemed amusing to me that anyone made his living selling hail insurance like the Music Man selling "big brass bands to the kids in the towns."

On this July afternoon looking out at the ice piling up on the lawn, hail insurance ceases to be a laughing matter. All you can think of are those acres of prime potato vines stretching in full and perfect rows to where they escape the eye beyond the knoll. What is happening to

25

them out there in that cascade of ice? The money and time and work invested—your whole hope for surmounting the fiscal impasse—will it all come to nothing?

Finally the hail ceases, and your menfolk go out to assess the damage. About seven minutes it lasted, some of the longest minutes of your life. The crop report is optimistic. There are some vines cut, and the stems are scarred and Paul thinks the half inch of water will help us more than we've been hurt. The boys' pumpkins look bad, but we can live without a pumpkin crop.

Christine Niggle calls in deep concern, and I give her Paul's assessment. "But what about those plums?" My good neighbors sold their farm and retired this year, retaining only their pretty little plum orchard, a delight to the eye in all seasons. It was going to provide a bit of the luxury retirement seldom affords.

"Oh, we've written off the plums," she said, with a resignation implying that they had already rotted a month ago, "but our garden is just a ruin. It's a good thing we enjoyed those nasturtiums last week. They're flatter than a pancake now."

It was a garden tended with all the expertise and love of retired farmers. I had enjoyed its beauty and variety and abundance with them, and now. . . . Well, Mel and Christine are the sort who shrug their shoulders and smile and set their minds to figuring new solutions. Their concern was for their neighbors.

Nearly twenty-five minutes the hail had pelted down on a narrow area east and west of the river valley. We were south of the worst of it. Schmalz's corn was in ribbons and looking severely wilted when I saw it later that afternoon. Beverly was out puttering in her cabbage minus her customary good cheer, it appeared. I hadn't the heart to stop and make small talk.

Across the river at Miller's the peach crop which had been all but in the baskets was a salvage operation. Late in the week I stopped over to see my vegetable-farming friend Bob Aufdenkampe. "How goes it?" I asked, implying an awareness of calamity.

"Well, I shaved today," he said "I didn't shave for three days. Do you want to see the fields?" he asked. "Not that I'm crying in my beer. . . . "

"I know," I said. "There's always next year."

"Yes," he said, "there's always next year. Although you look out there and you know how much you borrowed to make that possible and now no income to pay it off. . . . You don't know whether you have the courage to do it again, or whether you want to. But, darn fool that I am, I planted another field of squash yesterday, and the boys are out there throwing good money after bad." He indicated where several sun-bleached boys were broadcasting fertilizer on the devastated tomato vines with the forlorn hope that maybe with a good rain, sun, and time. . . . "We only picked them once."

We wandered over to where a vast field of cabbage heads were split open and turning grayish. "Know anybody that wants to make a lot of sauerkraut?" he smiled.

And then he showed me how the mutilated squash plants were generating a cluster of new growth.

That's what I keep remembering from my sad, sad field trip with Bob, those furry little triangular leaves pushing out from the ends of those seemingly dead plants . . . the persistent miracle that binds us all to this hazardous business.

Country Lane

Ron Zaleha comes zooming on his trail bike through the arch between the hickory and the sumac hedge. He lifts a hand quickly in greeting, grips his handlebars and bounces on, happy possessor of a precious hunk of real estate—our country lane.

You can put up all the gates and wires and "no trespassing" signs you want, but you might as well understand that if you've got a country lane, the kids in the neighborhood don't think the impediments are meant for them.

Of course, strangers now! That's something else, and suddenly you find the neighborhood kids the fiercest defenders of your privacy. They don't, after all, want "their territory" infringed upon.

A country lane may not seem like a high road to adventure, but you have to consider how a country kid of thirteen or fourteen looks upon it. It's a large part of his experience of life. He made his first trips out that lane on the tractor snuggled securely in his dad's arms. He trudged out there in search of his mother when he awakened from preschool naps. He rode his tricycle there, later his pony, his horse, his bicycle, now a tractor, an old jalopy, then the pickup, finally the car.

The lane in winter led him to frozen ponds, to coasting hills, on hunting and trapping expeditions, testing ice on the inevitable mud holes of country lanes. The spring mud of country lanes leads to a hundred recurring miracles, none finer than the mud itself.

Bloodroot and trillium and jack-in-the-pulpit come home in wilted handfuls from the fencerows and meadowsides and spring banks where he scared out a rabbit or woodchuck in the process of his picking. Routes to fishing streams and swimming holes, to picnic spots and camping groves, follow country lanes.

There's a point in every farm kid's life when the lane is the thorny path to romance. When the house is suddenly stifling with your relatives, where else to escape with the love of your life, than the lane? You'll want her somehow to understand what this lane means to your life, but how can she? She may fake it, but it won't be her lane till she has lived it a few miles.

Up past the open fields where our lane leaves the riverbank and enters the woods to terminate on the back road, it was already a lover's lane when you could give the horse her head and she'd take you clean back to the stable. In recent years we put up a gate to discourage such dalliance, but love will find a way. . . .

A farm lane is a quiet discovery of hundreds of country joys. It usually meanders along the unproductive fringe of things—the creek, the pasture lot, the woods, a power line, a drainage ditch; in our case, the river gorge—all places where wild flowers flourish and wild game seeks cover—the fringe benefits of the lane.

Some folks whip open the bar when you visit, challenge you to a game of Ping-Pong or a swim in the pool. At Leimbach's you get the farm tour, complete with crop report and a large dose of rural chauvinism. Nobody enjoys it as much as the farmer and his frau, but if folks are really your friends they'll suffer through the field trip up your lane, next time remembering to bring old shoes.

Oh Tannenbaum!

"Of all the joys of rural living, one of the most exquisite is cutting your own Christmas tree . . ." or so it says here in *Reader's Digest*. The author didn't have to explain that she was a new arrival on the rural scene. Nobody who has lived in the country forever, who regularly tramps about a cold feedlot, carries heaters through snowdrifts to outlying barns, or bounces over frozen ruts after firewood with a tractor and wagon, describes the ordeal of struggling down to the pasture with a saw and an ax and dragging home a tree as an "exquisite joy."

Those are clearly romantic notions engendered by old Christmas card scenes, and the idealistic breed of back-to-the-landers swallow them hook, line, and sinker. Something tells me, too, that all those city papas coerced into driving twenty-five miles into the boondocks to a "cut it yourself" place would describe the whole ritual as something less than exquisite. Probably take two bourbons to recover! Those guys aren't all that handy with an ax; and they soon discover that the trees in the meadow aren't any more perfect than the ones the Odd Fellows are selling on the corner.

This is not to imply that we farm folk think of our woods and fields and trees as ho-hum. On the contrary, Paul would cheerfully slaughter anybody who laid a hand on one of those white pines he planted over on the river bank. Cut them for Christmas trees? Never!

We do have native cedar trees aplenty, and many a lean year we were forced to settle for one of them. Nobody who knows cedar trees is going to describe them as exquisite on either end of the trek. Cedar trees in shelter belts have been a great boon to the American prairie, but blue spruce they are not! A cedar is a dark grayish-green blob of tree which grows lovelier as you recede from it. Up close it looks like a fugitive from a pulp mill. Each branch has tiny barbs which prickle and scratch and carry an odor reminiscent of dog urine. The only way to camouflage one is to spray it liberally with paint and pine oil. The price is right, but everything else is wrong.

Out front in the snow a spare Scotch pine leans against a bright red picnic table looking as much like a Christmas card as it's likely to look. Dad brought it home and the kids have registered their complaints.

"Scrawny-looking thing!"

"You call that a Christmas tree!"

"That's not tall enough!"

As far as I'm concerned, it's "exquisite." As for Paul, he too has a clear memory of what it was to trek to the pasture with an ax, bring home a cedar, and struggle to make something lovely of it.

No Christmas tree that ever came into the house was tall enough, short enough, full enough, shapely enough, or green enough to suit our kids. Nor did we ever decorate a tree with our accumulation of trinkets—ancient and new, made or remade, elegant or rinky-dink—that we didn't appraise finally as splendid.

The fact is that a Christmas tree, like the holiday itself, is pretty much what you make it.

Farm Midwinter

It's the time of year when one takes stock of things.

The Chancellor of the Exchequer has been sitting at his desk trying to figure out where all the money went. I can look out my window and see all too clearly where it didn't go. It didn't go for barn repairs. "Too far gone," says Paul. "Just pouring sand down a rat hole." The barn roof is a tar paper patchwork, torn and curling, several big doors hang askew on their sliding tracks, and there are gaps in the siding you could ride a motorcycle through.

Last week's all-night gale pruned the dead wood from the maples and it litters the front yard along with old shoes and grease rags and tin cans hauled out by the dogs. Summer's tired picnic table across the road still leans into the wind. The dogs nestle among the leaves blown into the bushes.

Besides the "Clean up, Paint up, Fix up" that waits on the spring, there's a drainage problem in Newberry's woodlot that's giving Paul and the Soil Conservation fellows fits—a ditch 20 feet wide and 150 feet long with broken tile and sinking sand at the bottom. There's a nagging worry about nitrogen, which none of the salesmen will promise. Oil supplies are rumored to be fickle, but so is the weather, and a farmer can't afford a nervous breakdown worrying about either.

Superficially it appears things are forlorn and neglected down on the farm. But, ah, things are not always what they seem. Over in the office where the Chancellor struggles with his computer printout sheets (Yes, even farmers are computerized today) he finds he's not so far in the red as he had feared. He contracted for his potato seed and fertilizer before the price of both skyrocketed. His corn and bean and melon seed has been delivered.

Those beat-up barns yonder house a stock of handsome machinery worth more than the structures. The grain bins hold a generous quantity of wheat and soybeans for speculation. The potato barn, snugly insulated against the elements, will keep us solvent till summer.

Stretching south and west and north, the fertile land lies dormant beneath the thick growth of rye. Below ground the water table is high. The tile runs freely. Promise for another fruitful year is good.

And in the house, life is equally secure. The fruit jars and the freezer are full. There's bread in the oven, soup on the stove. There's coal and wood aplenty in the coal bin, a roaring fire in the furnace. The farmer, weary of bookkeeping, stretches out in a lounge chair and falls asleep. The state of the farm—steady and holding.

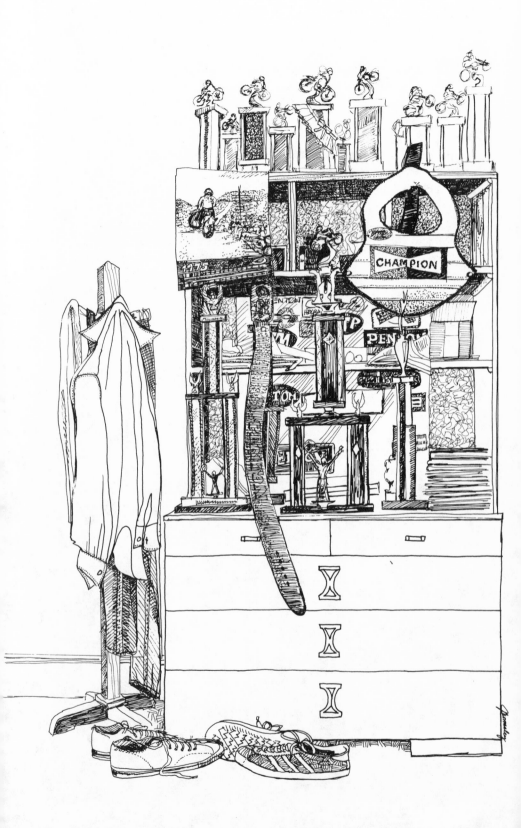

SONS AND SO FORTH

We have never been martyrs to parenthood. We survive as parents mostly on the dictates of hard work and common sense. The farm continues to be our best discipline. Our highest achievement is synonymous with our deepest satisfaction as parents of three boys in the young-adult phase—we are sympathetic friends.

Visitation

Paul reports evidence that a deer has been nibbling the young corn up next to the woods. In some parts of the nation that would be cause for alarm, but deer are not so numerous here that they cease to be creatures of wonder, and we just chalk up the loss to aesthetics. In our supper conversation about the vandal, Orrin recalls his discovery of deer. . . .

He was three and I had taken him out on the tractor with me one early morning, as I often did, to drag the potato fields (weed control just ahead of plant emergence). As we climbed the knoll on the way to the pond I was startled to see a huge buck loping as in slow motion across the meadow. I stopped the tractor, and drew Orrin's attention to him in hushed tones. The dog who had been tailing us down the road also caught sight of the buck and took off in pursuit.

The buck, unaware that he was being chased, stopped suddenly and began munching alfalfa. Peppy, startled, likewise stopped. The deer walked on, and Peppy guardedly followed, stopping as the buck stopped. Finally, with relief, Orrin and I saw him standing regally against the backdrop of woods and riverbank, safety in easy reach. We watched until our vision blurred, and then I went on about my dragging.

Orrin, caught up in my excitement, wanted to chase to the woods and get a closer look, but I knew better than to try to extend a mystical experience. All morning, however, my eye followed the path the buck had taken.

Where had it come from, this sense of wonder? From a mother who, thirty years earlier, awoke a little girl from sleep with excited cries of "Quick, Patty, wake up! A deer!" And the little girl was wide-awake, peering under the half-drawn blind at the entrancing sight of a deer and her fawn in the morning mist over the asparagus bed.

Orrin grew drowsy then with the droning of the tractor and the monotony of crossing back and forth over the potatoes. I carried him over to the wheat field, where I fashioned a nest of my quilted underwear jacket, and he fell asleep. I could have presumed that the memory would vanish with the nap, but I didn't reckon with the power of a "vision." Orrin remembers. . . .

Pumpkin Prowess

If you want to teach a farm boy private enterprise, you give him an odd piece of ground and tell him to make something of it. So it was that we spawned a couple of pumpkin tycoons.

Ted and Orrin are not at harmonious ages; it has been a long season of disagreement. But out behind the barn on a hillside sloping toward the river lies a picturesque field of great orange moons, and the boys are united finally in their success.

Because it was a lot more appealing than picking peas, Teddy fit the ground without complaint on a morning in early June. Then, in his unsubtle way, he dragged Orrin out of bed by one leg to "get out there and help plant the seed."

Two or three arguments followed when the leaves were through the ground and it was time to cultivate. There were green beans to be picked and, given a choice, each decided he would rather cultivate (a job for one). On the day they went out to hoe the crop they effected their first good compromise. There was solid agreement that neither of them wanted to hoe. And as I went up the lane that morning in July they presented an amusing illustration of how great inventions are born. Teddy straddled the rows with the tractor while Orrin sat on the drawbar dragging the hoe. As he approached each plant he lifted the blade, dropping it again just past the plant. It wasn't a perfect system but it did the trick, and in a few days a jungle of pithy vines crowded out the remaining weeds.

I remarked about the unusually lush vine growth and Ted explained with no small measure of self-congratulation: "Dad sent me out to empty the fertilizer hopper so I whipped around that pumpkin field a couple extra times" (a classic demonstration of why agriculture flourishes so much more under free enterprise than it does under socialism).

The only part of the pumpkin business that the kids can't handle alone is the marketing, and I frequently get roped into the trucking detail. Pumpkins are sold by the ton to groceries and roadside markets. You wouldn't believe how many pumpkins there are in a ton until you've unloaded ten thousand pounds into grocery carts in a pouring rain in the dark of night.

The last gasp of the pumpkin season around here is what Paul refers to as the "blood bath." The boys early learned that the key to success in business lies in cutting down on overhead. By saving the biggest and best of their crop for seed they could retain a larger share of the gross.

Seeing fifteen huge pumpkins outside the back door to be cut and emptied of seed prompted me to suggest a jack-o-lantern party for the kids of the neighborhood. With my usual disregard for caution I herded them all into my cellar (like an evil witch), gave them knives, and told them to go to it.

Luck was with me the first year. We only had a couple of Band-Aid cases. But the second year we sent two kids to the emergency room and bandaged a couple of cuts at home, while Teddy collapsed on the floor with a sympathetic nosebleed. Now the mothers of the neighborhood put a sheltering arm around their children and turn away when they see me coming.

When the Great Pumpkin smiles down on End o' Way on Halloween he surely has dollar signs in his eyes. I've never had the energy to stay up and see.

Anybody Wanna Buy Marvin Gardens?

There is a place in the "heartland" of America where inflation has not hit, where the bank will never go broke, where you can buy the best lot on the poshest street for $400 and erect a hotel for a thousand and retire and make a bundle. It's a wonderfully democratic place where even you can win a beauty contest or be elected Chairman of the Board, where the ordinary citizen supports the opera, where one can have a broken leg set for $50 and get out of the hospital for $100. It's a place where the bank now and then makes errors in your favor, where income tax is stabilized at 10 percent and never exceeds $200 and you sometimes get a refund. It's the wonderful world of Monopoly, where nothing has changed since 1936. The Boardwalk has not grown shabby, the Pennsylvania Railroad has no fiscal problems, the Water Works is not stormed by irate citizens screaming "Pollution!" and the Electric Company dispenses power without fear of future shortages.

The Community Chest seems capable of supporting the poor with an occasional poor tax of $15. Justice is swift and definite and favors no one: Go directly to jail! Do not pass Go. Do not collect $200! (Or does it? Some people get out of jail free, and others are obliged to pay 50 bucks.) Repairs to a house (general repairs, mind you) can be made for $25 and wages are both equalized and (glory be) stabilized at $200.

Yes, I have been there recently and found everything the same, including the eager gang around the board. Hopes rise and fall; tempers flare and subside. Somebody always invokes Ma. The banker is still accused of being a "dirty double cheater." Egos are bared. And the game seldom ends.

It stretches from morning, through lunch, into the afternoon; and then somebody comes by to go skating and the economy grinds to a halt. A world lies abandoned as by an act of God—money scattered about, houses drifting over from Atlantic Avenue onto the B & O Railroad, "Get Out of Jail Free" cards discarded carelessly. Investigation indicates that the guy with hotels on the cheapies, Mediterranean and Baltic Avenues, was on the verge of winning, while the guy who overextended on Boardwalk and Park Place is mortgaged and nearly broke.

Solacing to know that some things do stay the same? Well, don't take too much comfort in the fact. Ted comes home to report that his social studies teacher has the classes playing Monopoly as an exercise in economics. At specified times in the course of the game, Mr. Buehner declares inflationary periods and all the costs double.

Fie on you, Mr. Buehner! Go take a walk on the Boardwalk!

Soft Soap

It started as a minor irritation a week or so ago. "I think I'd like to make soap for my history project this month." I ignored it, thinking surely it would go away. Monday he said it more positively. "I'm gonna make soap for my history project this month."

"Orrin, I don't know anything about making soap. Forget it!" I had always looked with scorn upon my mother-in-law's soapmaking. It didn't seem to me that we could be that hard up, all those cans and jars of icky rancid fats. Ugh! It might have worked fine for her with her soft water, but ours was hard and that soap congealed on the surface like the grease it was made from.

Tuesday there was a sign on the mirror: "LEVER BROTHERS— Why not LEIMBACH AND SON?"

"Orrin, why don't you just make a little oral report on soapmaking and let it go at that?"

"But I never made soap. How'm I supposed to report on it?"

"I never made it either. With all the failures I have to my credit, why must I add soapmaking? Mr. Buehner would just love to flunk me at soapmaking. He's had it in for me ever since my world map was better than his last fall."

"Don't be silly, Mom. If he'd wanted to flunk us he'd have done it last month when our telegraph set wouldn't work. Remember? *Somebody* must know about making soap. Call them."

By the mirror on Wednesday it said, "If Fels and Naptha can, we can!"

"Get a can of lye, Mom, and call somebody."

All day Wednesday I tried to think of alternate projects. Ordinarily Orrin would go down to his uncles' machine shop and with $25 or $30,000 worth of equipment turn out snazzy little replicas of guillotines or cotton gins. Why not something simple like that? Why soap? . . . I suppose Mary Smith or Elsie Schmalz would know how to make soap. . . .

"Tomorrow's the day we need the soap," said Orrin Thursday morning. "Don't forget the lye."

I called Mary Smith. "The recipe's on the can," she said, and then proceeded with precautionary advice on working with lye, enhancing the very fears that had been dissuading me all the while.

As I lay in the dentist's chair that afternoon I tried to figure out how (and where) I was going to collect five and a half pounds of grease and get it made into soap between 4:00 and 6:00 when I was supposed to speak for some posh affair at the country club.

Aunt Mabel had a pound or two when I stopped at her house enroute home from the dentist's. I got on her phone and called likely prospects. "You got any fat over there that you can spare?"

"Yeah, I've got about ten pounds around the middle that you're welcome to," was the good-natured reply. I finally arrived home at 5:00 armed with a can of lye, an enamel kettle, and assorted cans, bottles, jars of fat.

When I should have been storming the country club at 6:00, I was up to my elbows scraping lard and tallow and bacon drippings from smeary containers, melting it, straining and squeezing it through my jelly bag.

"Just lay out the recipe," said Orrin as though we were talking about chocolate pudding, "and I'll make it."

"No," I said, remembering the lye bit. "You wait for me."

So there we were at 11:00 P.M., Mr. Procter and Mr. Gamble, out in the backyard checking the fat temperature with the only thing we could find, a rectal thermometer. Procter poured and Gamble stirred and the elements were combined, grease and lye water.

"Supposed to get like thick honey, it says on the can."

"Looks more like thin sewer sludge," says Orrin.

"Smells like soap," said I, encouraged.

"Smells like grease to me," said Orrin, discouraged.

"I think we've gone about as far as we're going tonight," said I. "You tell Mr. Buehner that if we flunk soapmaking I'm not ever going to loan him my *How to Win at Monopoly* book."

But in the morning, Eureka! Our brew was like "thick honey." Gamble poured and Procter spread the mixture in a cardboard box lined with an old flannel nightgown. Orrin carried it off to school with an air of "I knew it all the time."

"Just think," I said to Paul, as we quietly ate breakfast, "only six more weeks and four more days and I'll be finished with eighth grade and Mr. Buehner forever!"

I Think I'll Take My Marbles and Go Home _____

Leslie raps excitedly at the door and hurries in, bubbling over with her latest enthusiasm, marbles. "You got any I can have, Aunt Pat? I'm making a collection. Lynn made me a marble bag. See!" she says, holding up a pretty drawstring sack with its familiar lumpy form. It stirs a lot of memories.

"Do you play marbles, Leslie," I ask wistfully, "or are you just collecting?"

"Yup," she says ambiguously, "Do you got any?"

I went off to look, hopeful that Leslie might succeed where I had been so inept.

Oh, I used to play the game. We had a corner of the dining room where we would chalk a circle on the rough pine boards and kneel at marbles by the hour, but I never understood what was going on.

I remember hollering "Nothin's on ya!" and "Any's on ya!" and "No hunches!" but it didn't mean a thing. My brothers gave me a few chipped, lackluster marbles which I carried around in a dirty sack and prized like eggs in a bird's nest.

What a precious thing a marble was and, in the subconscious, remains. Who can come across a marble, spading in the garden, or swept up with the dirt from the cellar floor—and not drop it into one's pocket with a certain sense of "treasure"? There were the "aggies" and the "puries," the cat's-eyes, and the wondrous boulders. There were in the early Depression years, I remember, some cheap little clay marbles known as "kibbies." They came in dull pastel colors and were easily chipped by the sturdier "glassies." There was always some wiseacre who showed up with a bunch of "steelies" which were in reality just steel balls from a ball bearing race he'd hammered apart. These things were a real threat to all the glass marbles and were much coveted by the knicker set who crouched at recess around the rings under the fire escape.

My personal failure at marbles always rankled. When Teddy was seven and came home boasting of marble conquests on the playground or of how in that most active of the world's trading centers, the back of the bus, "Some kid swapped me a 'purie' for a pencil sharpener," and "Ain't it a beauty!" the old itch returned. Surely mastering marbles shouldn't be any trick at this point in life. I was pushing forty and had quite a string of achievements to my credit.

"Would you teach me marbles, Teddy?" I asked.

"Sure," he said, fishing a handful of marbles from his pocket and going on to explain the procedures. To my astonishment the game had changed completely. No longer did you take a stick and scratch a ring in the dust. Nor did you get down on your knees. Skill with marbles seemed to consist in tossing your marbles at your opponent's marbles from a standing position. Patiently he explained the lingo involved.

"This is what you call 'tops.' And this is 'sides.' When you hit 'er from this angle it's 'bombs' . . ." but my eyes had glazed over, and an awful understanding began to come. Marbles has nothing to do with the wisdom of age or accumulated knowledge, nothing to do with French idioms or the life cycle of the butterfly, the properties of matter or the Malthusian theory. It is unrelated to ironing shirts or cooking ragouts or plowing a field. It relates only to being a boy and being seven years old.

Scholar's Lament

As a student long ago I was straight "A"—not a brain but a grind. It was a fantastic ruse to spare me household drudgery. My mother was so glad to have an eager student that she didn't even notice she was being had.

When there were dishes to do I had three chapters of history to read. The beds went unmade while I ground away at algebra. If there was a big cleaning project scheduled Saturday, I had a research paper.

My mother was terribly proud of my academic record. She should have been. She paid dearly for it, but, alas, I have paid ever since. "As the twig is bent . . . " you know, and this twig was mostly bent over books. I never bent much over dishpans or mop buckets or ironing boards. The practical realities never fell into place for me.

I think that accounts for my years of failure with all those little "extracurricula" that are the joy—or despair—of parents.

Take lunch-packing. I got straight "D's." I was always fumbling frantically with soft bread and hard butter while the bus was turning around out front. How many mornings did I chase down the sidewalk screaming, "You forgot your baggie of bologna and your bunch of grapes"—or worse—make a pilgrimage to school with that humiliating brown sack. By the time my third son came along, he was pushing me out of the way and packing his own. I finally capitulated to the school lunch program.

And PTA. Another "D." By the time I got supper off the table and the dishes done, the Harper Valleyites had banged the final gavel. Sometimes I got there for refreshments, but seldom.

Field trips: "F." I never even got asked—probably blackballed by the State Patrol.

Special Projects: "B." Well, this was more my bag. I was so good at it, in fact, that the teachers were always wise. "Did your mom do this?" And my grade went down a letter, along with the kid's.

Communications: "D-." My permission slips, insurance forms, report cards, school picture money, and so on go back to the teacher three days to six weeks late.

Conferences: "F." I would look up from the noon mail at 3:00 and wonder why my kids weren't on the school bus—and then remember we had a 2:00 conference.

Homework: My only "A," but how many times did I get to the bottom of the page and realize that the kid I was helping was in the next room watching TV?

Fifty-cent gifts: "F." I *never* found a 50¢ gift. Once or twice I almost fooled the clerk by putting a 50¢ price tag on a two-bit slingshot but she wouldn't take my money. If I bought a dollar item and tried to pass it off as a fifty-center, it was still labeled "scuzzy" by the kid who had to give it.

Room mother: "D-." By the time I'd come slithering in with my dressbox lid full of cupcakes and a sack full of balloons and drinking straws, the teacher was usually on the verge of suicide and the kids were hanging from the chandeliers.

Car pool: "F." When it was my week to drive, the kindergarten teacher declared a state of emergency. Ours were the only kids in the class who attended both morning and afternoon sessions. Sometimes the janitor brought them home; sometimes the teacher; sometimes they sat with the office girl until she reached a neighbor. Or I would show up late with a truckload of potatoes and they'd have to sit up in back.

After sixteen years I thought I had dealt in my slipshod way with all the little extracurricular minicourses. But this year I'm flunking gym clothes.

My oldest son brought his gym clothes home for laundering two or three times a year whether they needed it or not.

The younger ones think they're Marcus Welby going into surgery. If I get all the clothes clean and dry before 7:00 on Monday morning, I've overlooked the shoes. If I remember the shoes, they're wet inside. If I get the shoes dry, the socks got in with the overalls and turned blue. If I carefully wrap shirt and shorts and socks and shoes and lay them on the piano, gym is canceled that day. If I go out of my way to press and fold them, I am greeted with, "How come my gym clothes aren't white like Dale's?"

You have to make up your mind what you want for these kids. Give them free rein with Thoreau and Latin verbs and they grow up to be idealistic dreamers. If you want to orient them to the real world, buy them wristwatches and order their lives and emphasize driver training. There is little call for scholars anymore since most of the monasteries are winding down.

Little League Losers

The Little Leaguers have hung up their gloves for another season. Ours was the Avis team—No. 2. Almost better, I've decided, to be last than second. Feelings run too high and disappointment too deep.

But I do have something to show for the season, a trophy of sorts. In the course of the many summer evenings when I sat cross-legged in the shadow of first base, I hemmed a linen napkin and tediously embroidered it with a bunch of violets.

This was not, of course, considered good fanlike behavior. Little League fans are expected to holler and shake their fists and bite their nails, to shout little baseball nothings like "Way to go!" or "That's gettin' a piece of it!" Between innings they're supposed to relax into their folding chairs and criticize the umpire or the coach or the opposing team and its coach.

Somehow I can't get with it. I can't seem to overlook the fact that we are all there because some few people—coaches, managers, umpires, scorekeepers, and so on—give their time to work with our kids, and that nagging criticism is "dirty pool." The opposing team always seems to look very much like our team and a poor little pitcher who's given up three hits and four walks is a poor little pitcher no matter whose team he's on.

Parents, and adults in general, are very big people in an eleven-year-old's life. It must feel good to win a ball game for one of them. But it must be devastating to lose for a parent who assumes an intensely personal stake in the contest.

I cheer the good plays, of course. I am delighted when my second baseman does something just right. Surely I want him to win—but not always. Life is not always a victorious game, and where can one better learn to cope with this fact? Most important, I want him to win for himself, not for me.

And so I embroider between pitches and innings. I know the other parents think I'm off my gourd. They have no way of knowing how much I have sewed into that square of linen—so many soft and lovely summer twilights; the gay panorama of the crowd across the field; the noisy enthusiasm of little children who play unconcerned nuisance up and down the sidelines; the flirtation of teenagers with this Little League excuse to "go someplace" and discover each other; a nonchalant pitcher standing on the mound, his face contorted behind a Double Bubble; a centerfielder emerging from a black cap and glasses to snag a fly; a right fielder stamping on his hat when thrown out at home; or triumph emerging from the dust of a steal at second. These, and so much more, all folded away in the violets.

The scoreboard says they lost "the pennant," but I am of another mind. When Orrin climbed into the car following defeat at the play-off, he said: "I don't care what they say. I did my best. That's all I could do."

In my book that constitutes a winning season.

Fairly Frantic

I am asked on occasion how I manage to do all that I do. The *truly* accomplished are quick to tell you "careful planning." My secret is the exact opposite—nonchalance and neglect. It is madness, for example, to make a plan that says, "At 3:30 on the afternoon of Monday, August 19, I will drive to the county fair in the pickup and take 2 kids, 2 cousins, 3 neighbors, 3 lambs, 3 bales hay, 4 bales straw, 3 sleeping bags, 2 pecks potatoes, 3 tents, 1 pumpkin, 2 bookcases, 1 suitcase, 1 backpack, 1 basket melons, and 1 square of plywood mounted with 300 parts from an electric motor. Keep it simple—on Monday I am going to the fair. . . .

At 7:30 Monday the phone jangles you out of bed and it's a little voice from down the road. "Are you going to the fair, Aunt Pat? Kin I go along?"

Why not? All we have are two boys, two lambs. Heck, yes. Anyway you're too sleepy to think it through, and saying yes will get you back to bed sooner. Five minutes later, same scene. Bleary-eyed, you answer. Little girl's brother. "Kin I go to the fair with you, too?"

Well, one more—why not? We can put the bookcases back with the sheep. The varnish has been dry at least a day. "Yeah, come along if you want."

"When ya' goin', Aunt Pat?"

Now you're being crowded. Somebody's trying to schedule you. Keep that end open!

"Oh, sometime after lunch. Don't know for sure." Then back to bed. Five minutes later, phone again. Ignore it. Some kid answers.

"Shawn wants to know what time we're picking him up with his lamb."

"What lamb? What's that all about?"

"Remember? We're taking Shawn's lamb to the fair. His mother took ours to get it circumcised."

"Oh, yeah. Tell him after lunch." You could go back to sleep, but the odds are against it. At breakfast you are confronted with the remembrance that two nieces are visiting and counting heavily on the fair today. If you keep remembering that you're driving a truck and don't start figuring logistics, you can still stay cool.

"You guys get your stuff together." (An ultimatum that translates, "This is your fair, not mine.") Then settle yourself to a morning of household projects.

About 11:15 those neighbor kids who eat lunch early show up with their dollars in their hot little hands, ready to leave for the fair.

"Okay, you guys, everybody outside till after lunch. How's that stuff coming for the fair?" (Play recording at intervals till they get the message.)

Lunch over, neighbor kids crowding the porch, nieces milling about, No. 2 son reading funny papers, Shawn on phone asking, "How soon?" No. 1 son walks through with bookcase. "It's got a couple of rough spots. Gonna give it another coat of varnish."

"You're what! We're supposed to leave in a few minutes."

"Mom, it only takes thirty minutes to dry."

Ten years ago I would have argued with him. At forty-nine I know that all it avails me is an argument. No wood project ever has dry varnish at the fair. "Orrin! Load the lambs."

Hour later, lambs bleating in truck, neighbor kids fighting with nieces, No. 1 son in shower washing hair, No. 2 son reading funnies again, Shawn on phone asking, "How soon?" You work quietly at mending, writing, ironing, ignoring realities.

Half hour more, neighbors and nieces wandered off, lambs still bleating in pickup, Shawn still waiting with sheep somewhere, No. 1 son squabbling with No. 2 son.

"He stinks like those sheep and he won't take a shower."

"I'm gonna take a shower as soon as I finish the funnies."

"Enough of that squabbling. Get that stuff in the truck and let's get going." Then settle back to your projects again.

About 3:00 No. 2 son blows horn. "We're ready!"

Take a quick look around for sleeping bags. That's the only essential. They aren't going to use their toothbrushes or their soap or their towels. They aren't going to change their clothes so's anybody'll notice. Take sleeping bags to truck—just one long wince at the accumulated mass, jump in, clear area enough so you can shift. Pick up Shawn and sheep, who look strangely alike by this time.

Neighbors drop jaws when they see you go by with their kids, whom they were expecting home from the fair about now.

Somebody will see you arrive at the fair looking like a truckful of Okies fleeing the dust bowl, and will remark, "I don't know how you do all you do."

Some people take tranquilizers; others sit tranquilly and let chaos run its course.

After the Fair Was Over . . . ——————————

The house is "contaminated" with county fair fallout—mason jars full of grain (with scant hope of ever seeing the granary again), carnival crud from a glorious night on the midway, dog-eared posters, gaudy labels from FFA exhibits, 4-H books that look as if they'd been run over by a truck, a "bunch of blue ribbons," a satchel of jeans and T-shirts neatly folded but soiled and redolent of sweat.

Out in the garage lies a welter of stuff unloaded late at night from a pickup and forgotten by the unloader: a mud-spattered tent with one pole missing, a sleeping bag sloughing straw, a bucket gray with residue of ground feed, half a bale of hay, a plastic sack proclaiming Lorain County Savings and Trust (containing a wad of grimy underwear), a politician's shopping bag full of pencils, rulers, matchbooks, and decals. The whole business bears the lingering odor of sheep manure.

Ted comes in for lunch and says, "Boy, I hope you've got a good home-cooked meal. I'm sick! All that junk food at the fair. . . ."

"That reminds me, Orrin—a guy called this morning wanting to know when he could come out and demonstrate a burglar alarm system. How many of those dumb offers did you sign me up for?" says Ma.

"Not many. Remember the year you won the sewing machine?"

"Yeah, all I had to do to get it was buy a $200 cabinet to put it in. Don't bother doing me all those big favors! Ted, what are your plans for that 'garbage' on the dining room table—that purple snake and that yellow blob with the googley eyes and——"

"Yeah, and that passion pink pimp pillow," adds Orrin.

"Gonna put it up on the rear deck of Ma's car," says Ted with a smile.

"In a pig's eye, you are!" says Ma.

"Boy, all that stuff takes a bunch of money," says Ted, stabbing a boiled potato.

"You learned that, did you?" says Dad, implying the dawn of enlightenment.

"Yeah, and I loved every minute of it," says Ted.

Ah yes, there is nothing so pathetic as last week's enthusiasms. Ma will paw through the mass of fallout between phone calls from water softener and carpet salesmen. She'll nag and holler a lot and the junk will be assimilated with the footballs and school books and next week's obsessions.

I have a feeling, however, that a purple snake in sunglasses may slither around here a long time evoking a shudder for county fair '76.

Alas for Creative Boredom

Winter closes in and there is a lamentable gravitation toward the television set. I find myself doing a great deal of griping on the subject. I even cut out a bit of wisdom I have read somewhere and glue it to the instrument panel: "Life is not a spectator sport."

"What did children used to do, Mom, before there was television?" Orrin asks. I suppose he's expecting me to say that we worked a lot more or read the Bible every day or wrote long letters to great aunts. Truthfully, there isn't a lot of difference between what children do now and what we did, but we did a lot more of it. The cards and games that languish in their cupboards got a lot more use in our day. There was almost no time during the Christmas holidays when there wasn't a Monopoly game spread all over the living room. The Tinker Toy and erector sets were in nearly constant use.

In general we did a great amount of "messing around," which is to say that we kept the house in upheaval. There couldn't be anything much messier than a model airplane in assemblage, and there were usually three of them in process at any given time. If you bought one of those "big jobs" for the monumental cost of $2.50, it was likely to be strewn about for months—yea, years!

Little girls spent a lot of time designing wardrobes for paper dolls and carefully folding both dolls and clothing into the pages of magazines for storage. And folding! There was the doorstop craze when we folded in half all the pages of the Sears catalogue and made of it a huge, round doorstop.

We messed around in the kitchen more than today's kids do. Nearly everybody could whip up a batch of fudge, testing it through the water-in-the-cup process till the kitchen was one big chocolate puddle. We concocted our own snack foods, popping a lot of corn and brewing our own root beer, bottling and capping it by hand. Often it sat around the cellar, fermented, and blew the caps off. We pulled a lot of taffy, small buttery wads stretched into sticky gray strands.

Little girls still embroidered samplers and tea towels or wove woolen squares to make doll blankets. We worked with a crochet hook at one of those spool knitting affairs with the four nails wound with string and a dirty length of knitted rope hanging below. Sometimes it made its way into pot holders. More often it made its way to the back of a sewing drawer, mothers wondering years later what to do with this odd bit of nothing.

Spools gave rise to spool tanks made with a button, a rubber band, and a match stick. Making and racing them was a popular pastime. One of my brothers had a corner of the living room devoted to a shortwave radio set at which he tinkered for several years. And we turned out a lot of crude wooden projects in the cellar—notebook covers shaped like the state of Ohio, castles, water wheels, and one ill-fated rowboat that sank on its maiden voyage.

My sister spent a lot of time at the piano and we sang all the popular songs of the day over her shoulder—"Old Buttermilk Sky," "South of the Border," "The White Cliffs of Dover," and a hundred more. Up at the Croyle house was a player piano and all our spare time for months we spent pumping and singing. I wonder that Mrs. Croyle didn't take an ax to that thing.

There were, of course, the same sports in their seasons, but without the enticement of TV we played at them more—roller skating, ice skating, coasting, basketball, football, and baseball.

We lived life to the hilt in our old house and many outdoor sports were moved indoors—marbles, darts, hide 'n' seek, roller skating. Today's lovelier homes inhibit the free-for-all.

We did do some radio listening; there was an hour of kid programming after school and there were Amos 'n' Andy and Fibber McGee, but listening to a radio was never the endless obsession that TV seems to be.

We did a lot of reading sprawled sideways or upside down in overstuffed chairs—book after book after book, building world upon world in the imagination.

We undoubtedly sat around being bored a lot. Maybe parents called it "dreaming time," but we'd have named it boredom if we had known the word. It takes very little of that to persuade a child to get up and get moving and find something to do.

There was something of yearning in our boredom, a hungering for something beyond the here and now. Alas for "creative boredom." It went out a generation ago with "Howdy Doody."

Nancy Drew Dream

My dreams of having a car of my own go back to the never-never land of Nancy Drew and her mystery stories. Nancy was a self-appointed teenage detective who buzzed around some mythical American county in a neat little "roadster." She changed her own tires and put on her own tire chains and, I suppose, could easily have done a valve job if the case had warranted. And it didn't seem to me that she ever got her hands dirty, rumpled a pleat of her gabardine skirt, or displaced a hair of her pretty blonde head.

At the time I was being tantalized by that fantasy, we drove around in an old black panel truck which we affectionately called "the hearse." It was used principally for hauling produce to market but doubled as the family car. Small wonder I was captivated by Nancy Drew.

When I outgrew her, I moved on to Andy Hardy. Andy, teenage idol of the silver screen, was the "rich kid" son of a lovable old judge living in small-town America back in the forties. We all envied Andy his convertible as he tooled around to soda fountains and football games and beach parties. None of us will ever forget that marvelous moment when he first pushed the button and the top went up. Wow!

That convertible, preferably red, was our consuming passion. After the war we would each have one.

When I got my "red convertible" thirty years later, it was a five-year-old blue Volkswagen.

The first year I had it my oldest son put ten thousand miles on it shuttling between a college campus, a weekend job, and a girl friend. The only time it was referred to as mine was in pronouncements like, "Your car needs new tires," "Your car is burning oil," or "I just had an accident with your car." When it was totaled the second time, I threw in the sponge. I hadn't the heart to go over to the garage and gaze upon my shattered dream.

There is now another car registered in my name. Like the first it bears little resemblance to Nancy Drew's wonder car. It is Stop Sign yellow and referred to by the kids as the rolling cheese carton.

It has been more or less appropriated by No. 2 son, and is used principally for transporting motorcycle parts and F.F.A. projects. I have the feeling that everywhere but in my presence it is referred to as "Ted's car." It is ridden in chiefly by big boys. The seats are pushed way back, the headrests way up. The rearview mirror is adjusted to spot a "Bear" I would never see. The radio is tuned to acid rock, and the under-seat area resembles a refuse can at Burger Chef. Occasionally I find a pillow on the console between the bucket seats.

Nancy Drew must now be pushing sixty. I understand she's still solving mysteries and apprehending crooks. Considering the broadened scope of everyone's activity today, I suppose she flies the world in her own Lear Jet or bombs around the nation in an Aston Martin. I'm sure it's no trick for her. In the first place she never married, but more important, she never had any kids.

On Different Wave Lengths

When my sixteen-year-old says, "It's so boring! All that old Romantic poetry, Longfellow, Thoreau, Emerson," he stabs me through the heart.

We are not the first mother and son who are tuned to different wave lengths. It's more the rule than the exception; many a boy follows in his father's footsteps, but not too many traipse after their mother's, especially if Mother is an English teacher.

Nor is it the first time I've been tongue-tied in defense of literature before sixteen-year-old pragmatists. If I pour out the first defense that comes, "You'll be happier for having read it," he'll only give me a fish-eye glance and an "Are you kidding?"—so I say nothing and let the moment pass.

A love of literature is tied to intellectualism and a love of ideas. An intellectual is inclined to feel that everyone else's experience of life pales by comparison. I think I know what flows through Ted's mind in the endless hours of being. His thing is motorcycling. He's reliving every centimeter of last Sunday's motocross or every mile of woodland trail he followed last month in Tennessee. He could describe the course of a fire trail on the south side of a hill in Mississippi with all the precision of Lichine identifying a vintage by its vine and slope along the Mosel.

Nor need I suppose that this life of the mind will dim for him. I have listened to old motorcyclists ride again the trails of twenty years ago astride the saddles of cycles long since gone to glory, as baseball enthusiasts will replay the Series of '75.

The study of literature contributes to happiness, I said, but each defines happiness in his own way; different strokes for different folks. For Ted, happiness is a trail and a well-tuned engine or the memory of either. As Emerson wrote:

> Life is too short to waste
> In . . .
> Quarrel or reprimand;
> It will soon be dark;
> Up! mind thine own aim, and
> God speed the mark!

I'm sure Ted would "buy" that, if he took the trouble to read it. So I'm not going to quarrel with him about "old Romantic poetry" as opposed to happiness as he finds it.

The vicarious perceptions of literature help me to know what is in Ted's mind, but he'll probably never know what is in mine. On the other hand, I will probably never understand the poetry of a rutted trail on the south slope of a hill in Mississippi. Emerson also said, "For everything you have missed, you have gained something else; and for everything you gain, you lose something else."

HOUSEHOLDING

Keeping house is in truth a holding action with me; I've never been one for ironing the underwear or dusting the plants. Yet I am part of the ageless fraternity of white sauce, Windex, and worn blue jeans. The farther afield life takes me, the more compelling my obeisance to the household routines. Nothing makes a farm wife feel more needed than mending overalls at midnight.

Patchwork of Spring

The ants have returned to my cupboards and the balls and bats and gloves are falling off the refrigerator. There are track pants in the laundry pile and mud tracks all over the place.

The backyard is blossoming with little neighbor girls. Leslie and Kelly climb the golden chain tree and sit there as though painted on a Victorian canvas. Karen and Tammy play hide 'n' seek with Dennis around the oil house.

I have seen the first robin, the first convertible full of teenagers, the first barefoot boy, the first flock of shorn sheep, the first kid with rod 'n' reel. I have enjoyed my first ice cream cone, heard the first peepers in the night, drunk my first sassafras tea, felt the first warm rain, received my first wildflowers (bloodroot from Orrin), and had my first flush of spring fever. I don't need the weatherman to tell me it's spring!

I sit at my sewing machine attaching a ruffle to a patchwork skirt and my mind is a "patchwork" of all the springs I've experienced. In a strange, indelible way I remember the dawn of my awareness of spring. The front door was open to a first warm day. A twittering of birds, a humming of peepers, a scent of flowers impressed me. It was a spring day as commonplace as my description of it, but it lingers in my memory and keeps surfacing. In the isolated way of a child, I was sure that only I felt it. I wanted so much to explain. I had no idea that what I felt was an innate response to the creative force that infects everyone "in Just-Spring when the world is mud-luscious . . . puddle-wonderful," as e. e. cummings puts it.

I remember the springs of hopscotch and jump rope . . . "Mabel, Mabel, set the table . . . I had a little brother, his name was Sonny Jim . . . Down in the meadow where the green grass grows, there sat Patsy as sweet as a rose. . . ."

The springs of roller skates, when the precious possession was a skate key hung by a dirty white string around the neck, and what I longed for more than anything else was a mile of sidewalk. The springs of Easter finery and corsages. The springs of track meets and junior proms, of bashful boys, and decorating committees, and organdy formals. Commencement spring of being a very big wheel. Then college springs in the city, and being homesick for the country, springs of sorority rushing, songfests, sun bathing, and final exams.

Like a throbbing nerve I remember the spring of the broken heart, every sentimental song and sorority dance, every painfully ongoing romance around me, every agonizing letter that made it all worse.

And then the spring of the heart's mending, of falling in love again; not wildly, ecstatically, but guardedly, tenuously this time. Finally a spring of fulfillment, of being pregnant like the world around me, followed by a happy spring of hanging baby blankets and diapers beneath blossoming pear trees. There were foolish springs of being too concerned with housekeeping and refurbishing succeeded by satisfying springs of taking my young children to the fields with me to fit ground and plant potatoes.

There were many springs then of watching them discover the world, a grand recapitulation of all my childhood. As I sew it all into the patchwork, I am interrupted by a light knock at the back door. Kelly stands there asking for a cookie, her pretty three-year-old face filled with wonder, bursting with a secret she wants to explain but can't. She doesn't need to—I know all about it.

Through a Green Shade

"Look at that funny house!" said Orrin the other day as we drove past a new home that had sprung up on a pastured side road.

"Looks like a nice house. What's so funny about it?"

"Why, it doesn't have a single tree anywhere near it!" he exclaimed, dismissing it as a place where any rational being would consider living.

I have lived half my life in the tops of trees and Orrin inherits the wonder of that. At our house at Penton Orchards there were five upstairs windows and each of them had a head or two lying before it at night (draft or no draft). Mine looked out into the top of the linden tree and hence I became friendly with trees early.

When I married I settled down at night among the tops of the three maples that tower above this house. In winter I used to move the bed into a warmer corner of the room where the trees were not visible, but no more. I have learned to love the lean empty boughs, the twigs against the sunset, the dawn, the night sky. The grace of the naked branches is every bit as intriguing to me as the half leaf of spring or the full canopy of summer.

I especially enjoy the full moon shining coldly through the boughs, knowing that I must surrender the sight to the leaf cover for another six months.

Now comes the pleasure of early dawns through the flowerlike patterns of the opening leaves. In another warm week the foliage will be chartreuse and featherlike, then fuller and greener. The birds will move in with their nesting. Shortly before five in the morning as if on some secret signal they start to twitter, waking me momentarily; I nestle back into my pillow and doze again as morning gathers through the leaves.

Snuggling into the warmth of a wool comforter and a down pillow, while the lightning flashes and the great limbs sway, must borrow on the security of a home that has passed. It was my mother who taught me to love a storm. In summer I like to leave the window up a bit and get the feel of the fresh breeze ahead of the rain. The deep shade of hot afternoons—how cool and appealing it is when I come in tired from the fields and flop down by my window.

It has become the vogue to shut oneself away from all that with an air conditioner, but not this little tree worshipper. I'll sweat out the few hot ones for the pleasure of the others.

Then the fall—the radiance of sun through gold leaves, the pleasure of watching the sky reappear as the leaves thin. One early November night a great wind comes and takes the last of them. Dawn reveals the damage of the night; beneath the tree a wet brown blanket of shining leaves. Mine once more, the naked boughs of winter against the cold cloudy sky.

Imposible Pie

Impossible Pie

I just filed a recipe for something called "impossible pie" given to me by a nice little lady in central Illinois, filed it right between my mom's childhood recipe for vinegar pie and a scrumptious hors d'oeuvre called "onion pie" which I picked up out in Nebraska. I have here a recipe for popped wheat that I bummed from someone in Kansas and a formula for "big strong punch" which I got without asking from a swinger up in New York State who was unquestionably the life of the party.

The irony is that I spend a great deal of time and breath exhorting women to rise above their mundane preoccupation with patterns and recipes, to aspire to loftier involvements. In bald fact I am afflicted with those very same diseases. I have an especially troublesome "infection" of recipes as, I conclude, do nearly all women no matter how awesome their accomplishments.

I can sit alongside a perfect stranger in a bus station and ten minutes later be scribbling a recipe for her Great Aunt Minnie's sauerkraut salad on the margin of a bus schedule. I don't even know if *this* lady can cook, let alone her Aunt Minnie! And I don't like sauerkraut! But that's the insidious nature of this "disease."

There's something captivating in the notion that this might be the magic elixir which will finally distinguish me as the Julia Child of Bank Street, or elicit at long last a "Gee, Mom! you sure can cook!" It must be admitted, however, that no woman in her right mind expects the latter reaction with recipes like vinegar pie or sauerkraut salad!

The funny thing about my recipe collection is that I've almost never tasted any of this stuff. I just hear women talking about it with such a sense of sure success that I'm convinced, and first thing I know I'm jotting ingredients on a paper tablecloth. I confess I get turned on by names (Shipwreck Casserole, Never-Fail Fudge, Forgotten Stew), and by two-page test-kitchen color spreads. Nor can I resist the relentless recipe-sharers (a Mexican clerk in an Oklahoma supermarket saw me buying chili powder and insisted on giving me her mother's recipe for Chili Sauce scrawled on a piece of corrugated carton).

This female mania for sharing recipes is a phenomenon for which men have no equivalent. They may share ideas on the way to tune an engine, fish a trout stream, or stave off World War III, but there is no subject which cuts across national, social, cultural, and economic lines as infallibly with men as do recipes with women.

Take Indira Gandhi and set her down alongside Liza Minnelli and in ten minutes they'd be talking over a recipe for curried pizza. Think of the warmth that might be injected into diplomacy if men could get into recipes. Cyrus Vance might have gone to Anwar Sadat and said, "See here, Anwar. Menahem Begin refuses to surrender the West Bank, but he asked me to bring you his grandmother's recipe for gefilte fish just to demonstrate his hunger for peace." Imagine the psychological effect of Jane Fonda's carrying Mao Tse Tung's Chinese borscht recipe to Leonid Brezhnev.

Almost as common as the practice of collecting recipes is the urge to write a cookbook. There's hardly a woman around who doesn't feel that given a publisher and a little push she could do it. It's possible to find cookbooks on any specialty from cooking in a biplane to cooking for an orgy. (To the latter collection I could contribute "big strong punch.")

And what a wonderfully personal thing a collection of recipes becomes. One of the saddest effects a woman leaves behind when she dies is her vanilla-stained, dog-eared, yellowed and tattered collection of recipes. It goes back farther than any item in her wardrobe and has origins in remote and surprising places, usually known only to her. No one can make head nor tail of it. Each woman's filing system is a well kept secret, not because she's jealous of her recipes but simply because she hasn't gotten around to that "cookbook" yet. It might be better if the recipe collection went into the grave with the woman; it should at least merit a ceremonial cremation signifying that this was something that lived only so long as its curator.

In the case of my own battered, breaded, grease-spattered mass of torn pages, scribbled sheets, parts of cereal boxes, tattered notebooks, and crumbling ring binders, I'm sure my family would agree that burning the whole mess would be poetic justice.

The Jewels of June ——————————————————

Well, the can-cover crisis seems to have passed, and I'm jolly well back in the jelly business. Eleven extravagant pints there on the counter, two and a half batches of raspberry and currant. Cost me twenty-one cents a pint, which isn't bad. Of course I didn't pay for the raspberries or the currants. Picking seven and a half quarts of raspberries and currants in Martha Taft's rambling backyard patch consumed about three hours. Throw in seven bucks for fruit and the cost goes up to eighty-five cents a pint, just about what you pay for the middle-of-the-line product at the Stop 'N' Shop or the Piggly Wiggly.

Jellymaking involves a fierce amount of "messing around": cooking and straining, tying up a bag (with time out to run down the road and borrow Christine Niggle's jelly bag, my own having been sacrificed in the year's interim to straining grease to make soap), then cutting down the bag, squeezing, emptying, washing it (yuck!), and so on. What does Ma Smucker pay her jolly jam and jelly juicers, do you suppose—$3 an hour? Add $13.50 for four and a half hours' labor and you bring the cost per pint to $2.07!

It's far better, I've found, to avoid calculations that impress a housewife with how pitifully little her time is worth; 7½ hours labor=11 jars jelly! But other wisdom is mine after twenty-five years of this monkey business. There is the pride that comes with the fact of those eleven jars, the morning sun shining through the ruby red of them; the pleasure of the eating enhanced fourfold by the labor; the memory of the smell that filled the kitchen during the boiling and the skimming, the glub-glub of the thick hot syrup as it's ladled into the jars, and the licking of the spoon. Then the smoking of the hot wax, and the solidifying that seals the job.

Even more enjoyable was the escape of picking berries in the tranquillity of an old friend's garden, and the friendly exchange that went with it. There was the discovery of the serrations in a raspberry leaf and the opalescent quality of a currant. And the neighborliness of Christine Niggle . . . Shucks, I wouldn't sell you a jar of that jelly for five bucks!

Give you one? Well, maybe. That's a luxury only I could afford.

All Manner of Gifts

Every day or two I clip my calendulas, arrange them in the perfect golden arrangements calendulas facilitate, and think about Ruth

Walker sitting cross-legged in her grass pulling weeds, trimming, transplanting, doing the things conscientious gardeners do—for the calendulas were Ruth's gift to me. If I ever break a leg or develop mononucleosis or get sent to prison, I'm going to write "thank you again" notes to the donors of gifts that continue to delight me after years of accommodation to my life and household.

A perfect gift—like my calendulas—invokes the giver, and some things do this in unexpected ways. One of my prized wedding gifts— a huge rose-colored punch bowl, came from Armina Ludwig, a farmer's wife, a cousin of my mother-in-law. I still remember the pleasure she evinced when she brought it awkwardly wrapped in a misfitting box. "I saw it and I liked it!" It was too extravagant for her own spartan tastes, but for Paul and me she wanted it. I accepted the mandate to enjoy it for all three of us. Late at night when the party is over and Paul has gone to bed, I cautiously wash our punch bowl and return it to its place on the top shelf, as Armina keeps me company through the quiet hours.

At the other end of the practicality scale is the step stool we received from one of my school pupils and her parents. It's the sort of thing a bride doesn't splurge on (she just stands on chairs). But how I bless those people each time I pull it from the closet. And an ironing board! When you return from a honeymoon dead broke to face the reality of stocking a kitchen cupboard, it has to be reassuring to know that somebody had concern for the other practical realities—like an ironing board behind the bedroom door.

One of my all-time favorite gifts was from my brother Ted. It weighed about ten pounds, and came in a box about six inches square. It revealed itself to be a thick disc of smooth solid steel. I tried to act pleased . . . "But what is it?"

"Why it's a nutcracker—obviously." He had watched me trying to crack nuts against the back of a flat iron, went back to his machine shop and turned out a "nutcracker." Every home, I am now convinced, needs a portable anvil. Woe be unto him who is caught "porting" mine from the kitchen.

Another memorable gift involved a committee of conspirators. It took Paul and all five of my brothers to carry it in—the old dinner bell from the barn loft, repaired, repainted red, reincarnated as my "Merry Christmas bell."

The most unusual gift of self I've had to date was a "sophisticated country waltz" written for me by a musical friend. And to somebody who doesn't know a G clef from a G string, that's impressive! I can hum it and sing it, and even pick it out on the "pie anno," my "Blue Denim Waltz."

Another gift I prize, and one of my only "valuables," is a string of pearls sent me by a reclusive maiden aunt I never had the chance to know. They arrived on my wedding day with a note that spoke poignantly of hollow dreams and hopes for vicarious fulfillment.

My mother-in-law gave of herself in her talented stitchery. She was a couple of pairs of tatted sheets ahead when she died. "Fancy work" doesn't come as naturally to me, and I'm always a couple of gifts behind. I find myself delivering wedding presents ten months overdue. If anyone had done that to me she would have had to bring along a gift for the baby.

Paul and I do sew gifts these days (yes, he can sew too) for grooms and brides we only half know and may never know well (children of our friends). We may never know either how they react to these gifts as they come to live with them.

Long ago when our childhood was much occupied with standing in waiting lines, the guy on the end would give the next one a poke, saying: "Pass it on." If somewhere, sometime, a long-faded bride feels an answering pleasure from some gift of mine, perhaps it will compensate Armina Ludwig for that "thank you again" note I never did get written.

All's Well That Ends

The smell of peaches pervades the kitchen. A basket of tomatoes turns dangerously ripe upon the porch. The nights are filled with the music of tree toads. The corn has long since dented and the ears sag on the stalks. Maple branches turn prematurely yellow.

Foxtail waves from the fencerows; goldenrod and purple asters are coming on strong. Starlings bicker over the blackening elderberries.

Bathing suits and beach towels fade upon the line, masks and fins and snorkel tubes collect dust beneath unmade beds. A rain-swollen baseball chewed by a puppy lies forgotten beneath the magnolia.

The pickup just went down the road with the last of my bean pickers, a raucous and motley crew of kids between ten and sixteen, dripping wet from a final clothes-and-all dip in the pond. Their pockets were stuffed with wrinkled bills and a few pilfered rubber bands to enliven a homeward trip that scarcely needed enlivening.

Every weekday all summer they came with their brown bags and their rowdiness, their individual drive and pleasantry. Separately I enjoyed each; as a group of twenty, thirty, or forty they were insufferable.

These final days are note-holding at the end of the summer song. The heat and the sweat, the barn and the pond, the endless rows and the farm itself will fade from the consciousness of my little bean pickers to become part of a hazy summer that was.

Forgotten shirts and jackets, pop cans, gum wrappers litter the barns and the yard. The precarious grass beneath the maples has succumbed to their trampling. The picnic table sags and the lawn furniture, like their foreman, looks defeated.

I sit here with a near-empty cigar box of payroll money in my lap, the welcome quiet humming in my ears. From across the river floats the music of a marching band at band camp, and my mind shifts to fall gear.

Somewhere nearby a cicada launches his call, mounting in pitch and intensity to a high, sustained trill. I take my mood from the top of the trill. Hallelujah! Summer's over.

Letters filled with idealistic hopes come from school administrators, provoking thoughts of freshly painted walls ripe for stale graffiti. Football players dream of heroic interceptions, cheerleaders practice routines in tragicomic seriousness. First-graders fondle shiny new lunch pails and kindergarteners sparkle above their new shoes. College freshmen shop for luggage. Last year's roommates write about curtains for this year's dorm room. Junior girls decide to forego their stuffed animals this year, and senior boys return to campus early to rendezvous with girl friends.

Orrin has made his shopping list: "gym shoes, tablets, football." As clearly as anything it echoes "summer's over." The blue jeans on my sewing machine said so two weeks ago. He put them there in two piles, one to shorten, one to lengthen.

A week ago he quietly tore out hems or pinned them up as the case dictated. Yesterday in resignation he opened the sewing machine and went about hemming them.

Ted has looked over his pile of hand-me-downs and rejected them all as too baggy, too tight, or just plain "scuzzy," a judgment rendering useless all loud arguments about privations of your own youth. He'll settle for one or two pairs of pants so long as they're "cool" and brand new, and just like those of his friends (who are also protesting their big brothers' pants).

I am no more ready for fall than I was for summer or spring before it. An end table is piled with the leavings of May lockers—notebooks, lab reports, term papers, tests. My dining room table is spread with the cuttings of a sleeveless summer dress; my closets bulge with clothes wrinkled and soiled from winter.

But the weight of circumstances moves me. I carry the empty money box into the house, sweep up an armload of winter dry cleaning, and go off with my nagging schoolboys to check off that shopping list, mentally adding "jar lids" to deal with those ripe tomatoes.

By Bread Alone

I'll never take any prizes at the county fair for cooking and that suits me fine. The important judgments about such things are made in the kitchen back home by a ruthless panel of judges called family.

To be terribly truthful mine don't give me too many blue ribbons—apple pie, fried chicken maybe, blueberry muffins—they're a hard bunch to please. But in one department I'm a consistent winner and that triumph overshadows all other domestic defeats. I am a bread baker.

I discovered long ago that if a woman bakes bread she can get away with almost anything, including absence. My husband has come in to find the counters splendid with loaves of bread and automatically asked, "Where you going?"

Yes, there's a mystique about homemade bread that's tied in with security and good health and mother. My foremost advice to any bride would be to cultivate a bread-making talent. It's certainly the simplest route to liberation.

While I am not oblivious to the mystique, I am nonetheless a willing victim of it. On those days deep in winter when the farm is a quiet island off the mainland of the world, nothing satisfies the homing instincts like kneading and setting a batch of bread to rise in early afternoon.

By 3:30 my small kitchen is warm with the effort and the house is filled with the aroma of hot bread. Three loaves I always bake—one for the freezer, one for a neighbor, and one for the troop who file in the back door.

They lop it off in big uneven hunks, spread it with butter, and proceed happily to drop crumbs all over the place.

It's not a great thank offering for the blessings of a winter day, but it's what one woman has learned best about promoting domestic tranquillity.

Chrome on the Range

"I suppose when I get married," said Dane one day, "I'll have to buy my wife a cruddy old stove like this so she can bake good bread like yours."

It was the nicest thing anybody could say about a tired old stove (or a tired old housewife).

"Never mind," I assured him. "I'll save you this one." This one bakes good bread, to be sure, but generations of mice have long since carried away the oven insulation. And it throws off as much heat as a space heater. The oven door has sagged since the time twenty years ago when Dane sat on it. The grease buildup makes it a first-class fire hazard. There are chips and scratches and charred, stained burner knobs that signify a heap o' cooking. But the overriding consideration is that a new kitchen is taking shape in a formerly unused wing of the house and it wouldn't do to move into that showplace with this "cruddy old stove."

The stove was the only thing we bought when we went into housekeeping and the purchase was a simple process. We could choose gas or electric; we wanted gas. There were two gas models, standard and deluxe; it took us fifteen seconds to agree on the ninety-dollar standard model, sans chrome and clock and automatic something-or-other. Our only complaint through the years has been that the oven door wasn't made for sitting upon.

So I'm shopping for a stove . . . that is, a "range." (What, pray tell, happened to "stove"?) And how things have changed: Do I want gas or electric? Freestanding or countertop? Will I go with a built-in oven or do I want a drop-in? One oven or two? High oven or low . . . or both? Do I want to go microwave? Do I want the self-cleaning feature or not? A grill? A griddle? A clock, a timer, a hood, an automatic burner, an oven setter? A wok pocket, or a charcoal pit? Perhaps the rotisserie option? Do I want a smooth top or a standard? What about a warming shelf? Do I want the thing in Lichen Green or Golden Gourd, Apricot Brandy, or African Orange?

I am so confused I can't sleep nights. I've invested five shopping trips in this folly and visited eight appliance stores. All I wanted in the beginning was a stove, a shiny new stove which promised to bake decent bread. I no longer know what I want. I think maybe I'll have them cut a larger hole in the counter and move in that "cruddy old" one. The Franklin stove finally came into its own; why not my Magic Chef?

What haunts me is the thought of a Korean woman squatting before a tiny oil pot set into a circlet of stones on the floor. Who am I that I deserve this sort of choice, a choice that was unavailable to the richest, most powerful queens or empresses in history? And, of course, this is merely a stove. The story is the same with nearly every item we buy.

People mutter in near desperation, "What will we do if food prices continue to rise, if fuel shortages persist, if labor and material costs mount and mount and mount?"

What will we do indeed? We might conceivably return to a simpler, saner, more basic economy. There's something satisfying and soothing about the thought of preparing a pot of rice over a tiny fire built in a circlet of stones.

Old Wine and New Wineskins

My husband surprised me with a new set of pots and pans; I think he was hurt that I did not register enthusiasm, and even I am dismayed at my reaction. The truth is, I guess, that these homely vessels and I have come too far together to part without a sigh.

I often think of the thin battered aluminum kettle in which my mother-in-law cooked her potatoes and of the peculiar pleasure she took in it. Every morning after breakfast with slavish regularity she peeled her potatoes and set them aside in that kettle in anticipation of a prompt dinner.

We never discussed that kettle, of course; it was just an attitude one sensed in the way she washed and dried it and placed it in a precise spot on the shelf. In fact she treated every one of her kitchen utensils—her kuchen tins, her slaw cutter, her cabbage pan, her huge pressure cooker—as unique and valuable. Her reverence for those pans impressed her young daughter-in-law as ridiculous.

Delicate china plates and silver spoons I saved to remember her, but that battered aluminum kettle, the essential symbol of her discipline and devotion to the lares and penates, I callously assigned to the Goodwill with the flotsam and jetsam of her life.

My own set of pans with shiny copper bottoms was far finer than hers, but in the long run shamefully treated. The bakelite handles have charred, and the steel proved not as stainless as touted. The relentless years of boiling over or burning dry, or being battered around the backyard by the dog, have taken their toll. My priorities have changed in twenty-five years, and shining copper bottoms are not among them.

"Get rid of them. Had them long enough," Paul says of my lackluster collection. He eyes the bright new ones, subconsciously supposing that new pans will elicit renewed devotion to a gleaming kitchen and prompt, regular meals. Alas, his optimism is misplaced.

All my maiden's dreams faded over those cooking pots in the long years of struggling to master housewifery. I peeled a lot of self-pity into them and poured a lot of self-satisfaction out. I tackled many things bravely and failed. I ventured many things timidly and succeeded gloriously. My dreams faded, but a firm joyous reality replaced them, and we shared it all, those cooking pots and I.

Paul's mother would understand. . . .

Winsome Walnut

Some of my favorite things really do come in brown paper packages tied up in string! This time it's a candy box full of black walnut meats from a nice lady down in Missouri. How long do you suppose it took her to gather, shuck, crack, and painstakingly pick out this priceless boxful?

"Black walnut!"—the words themselves have the ring of quality, like "sterling silver," "hand-carved," "virgin wool," "bone china," "genuine leather," "pure gold," "copper plumbing," and a select few other terms used to distinguish what is rarest and best in our catalogue of material treasures. I always thought that quality was a matter of conditioning, but when I finally made a cake of those black walnuts, the full impact hit me. With walnut, quality is intrinsic.

Paul had often made reverent allusion to black walnut cake but I dismissed it as one of those flavors enhanced by their removal in time. However, when I cut the cake as an afterthought at a family feast, the reaction was unanimous—"Blue Ribbon!" The second day I split the meager remnants between Paul and the fertilizer salesman who happened by at lunchtime.

"That takes me back forty years," said Ken with that same wistfulness in his voice that I'd been ignoring so long from Paul. And then they launched into a discussion of the virtues of black walnut, past and present.

Part of the reverence accorded black walnut derives from the effort involved in utilizing it. Our river banks are rich in black walnut. The steepness of the hill and the crowding of the other trees cause them to slough all the shaded lower limbs. The result is a knot-free butt log as long as twenty-five feet at maturity.

But the lumberjack who hoists those logs up that hillside works like a son-of-a-gun. The sawyer and the carpenter who work with the lumber bid fair to lose their religion for the difficulty of cutting, nailing, or finishing such hard wood.

Paul's pride is a wealth of native walnut cabinetry and paneling he helped install in this his great-grandfather's home. Watching him caress a rosy brown board with its finely flecked grain makes me realize how basic to his value system is this lovely wood.

But few people have such a rich treasure of the stuff as Paul does, so very little walnut is utilized in the solid state. Most of it is shipped abroad, veneered (with cheaper labor) and returned to America, where, inflated in value, decreased in quality, it still stands out as the crème de la crème among the plywood, the particle board, the knotty pine, and the polyvinyl paneling.

Nor do black walnut meats come cheap. The nuts must first be separated from a gooshy green shuck which stains like the very devil. The nuts must then be harbored from chipmunks, squirrels, and mice for a period of drying. Many a faint-hearted soul has come this far in the process. A persistent few progress to the cracking of that very tough nut, and many even scuttle the project at that stage.

As rare as the nut meat itself is the heroic individual who finally emerges with it. Do you wonder that I value this splendid new friend down in Missouri who, after all that, performed the pesky task of wrapping and mailing a "brown paper package tied up in a string"?

Through the Wringer

I like to think of myself as having developed through the years a touch of class and a measure of independence; but there is really no way a housewife can be either classy or independent when her well runs dry as mine has been doing with a confounding regularity. The water table in our part of Ohio is lower than it has been in many years. There's just nothing as chic about explaining to twenty-five Christmas dinner guests that "Uhh-hh, you won't be able to flush the john."

I will take credit for having developed through these years some savoir faire, which involves no more or less than reverting nostalgically (!) to old ways of coping: hauling in a bucket of water, heating it in a teakettle, bathing in a bowl, brushing teeth with a cup of water dipped from the tank of the john, and otherwise employing tactics learned in a household of nine where our one shallow well was sunk in a sand ridge of Lake Erie and the water watch was a way of life.

The family washing, of course, is the big obstacle. I am reduced once more to lugging baskets to town or imposing upon the generosity of my sister Mary, who has clung tenaciously to an old wringer washer, a miserable miscreant propelled principally by profanity. Five minutes with this creature and I have repaired in time to a host of dismal, dank, dark basements where lurked equally sinister and malevolent beasts who tortured me in my vulnerable years as an apprentice laundress.

Wringers take terrible toll of buttons and buckles, grippers, snaps and zippers. And show me the housewife over forty-five who hasn't mashed between rubber rollers a few fingers—her own or those of her too-eager toddlers.

Nobody who hasn't grimly untangled a rag rug dragged back in by its tattered fringe, or unwound from the perimeters a twisted wad of undershirts, bra straps, socks, and apron strings, who hasn't growled and groaned and kicked and cursed, and cried a lot into a sodden Kleenex, and then been ignominiously squirted in the eye by an overall pocket of dirty water from the final wash has the vaguest notion of the value of an unlimited water supply or the miracle of the automatic washer.

On the other hand, there's a certain expediency about a wringer washer. You work at it steadily for several hours and the washing is done. It yields a neat package of satisfaction unfamiliar to the automatic laundress who does laundry in fits and snatches and seldom focuses her brain upon the whole. There's something strangely contemplative about leaning over that tub, with its agitator turning monotonously to and fro, poking with a venerable washing stick, bleached and smooth, at the sorted accumulation of whites and colors, overalls and household furnishings. Pondering the family members and their involvements that created the heap of washing—ball practice, daily chores, teenage dates, motorcycle races, Grandma's visit—one is keenly aware of growth and the passage of time.

My years of wrestling with the wringer washer were certainly years of frustration and tedium and yearning. The frustration and the tedium have vanished with the past and with the realization of much that I yearned for. Strange to recognize in this latter day, in my untimely bout with a wringer washer, that what I miss most is the yearning.

To Build a Fire

When children make pictures of houses nowadays, do they still draw a wisp of smoke above the chimney?

I seldom come up this country road on a winter day without glancing at the old brick chimney above the house for a hint of the temperature within. Coming home to warmth can only be appreciated by one who harbors a chilling memory of finding the furnace out and the house cold. People who live with a coal furnace have *never* taken heat for granted.

There is an understanding among us that the first person up in the morning, the first to come home during the day, or the last to retire at night will tend the fire. It's not a convenient system but it works—haphazardly. Sometimes it's necessary to add a layer of clothing or light the oven to ward off chill; sometimes we must strip to our skivvies and open the windows. The thermostat can be adjusted but the reaction is much delayed and is always accompanied by a trip to the furnace room.

There among the soot and the cobwebs and the piles of wood and coal, poking away at the coals on the grates, I feel akin to the fire builders of antiquity. This is a life-sustaining process and I respect it, but I would not imply that tending a furnace is not often a pain in the neck.

Even the boys know the irksome responsibility of the furnace. Many a Saturday morning is consumed with cutting wood or hauling it to the house and stacking it in the coal bin. They, too, have acquired the fire-building habit and when they are home alone they remember to look after the furnace. Surprisingly enough, they do not complain of the ritual. Perhaps the fire-building instinct is deeper than I realize.

I remember coming home late one Sunday afternoon on a winter day when our son had returned to college. I came with the old apprehension of finding it cold, but there was heat. I went immediately to the furnace room. (With a hot water system heated by coal or wood the house can be warm several hours after the fire dies.) A healthy fire burned in the fire pot, expertly banked and checked, a gift from our absent son.

I think of the old song, "Keep the Home Fires Burning"—few children would find it meaningful in this day. Among the members of a family sharing a coal furnace, a fire is a covenant saying: "We need each other."

AGAINST THE GRAIN

"I suppose you're going to think I'm an eccentric," said my new friend, rattling on about some bizarre matters in which she was intensely involved.

"We think of ourselves as a rather exclusive group," I said with a wink. "Not a bad lot at all." The eccentric has been vindicated in these days of "doing your own thing." Ted probably effects a compromise in terms when he says, "Never mind Ma. She's a little different."

Siding with Sentiment

I always loved the silvery gray siding of Pete Newberry's barn. (We've owned it for twenty-five years but of course that doesn't make it "Paul Leimbach's barn.") I often studied its west face closely at the upper end of the elevator when loading potatoes. There's an integrity about a board that like an octogenarian has weathered the years and the elements and prevailed.

Paul doesn't wax romantic about barn siding. What concerned him was the roof, which was "no damned good." Pete wanted to reroof it once and Paul's grandad, who was no great shakes at repairing anything, talked him out of it, to our everlasting grief. For years it has been little more to us than a haphazard storage for fertilizer and a great arena for sparrows. So by inches we're tearing 'er down.

She has been raped of her beautiful siding, the first thing to go, as the easiest to remove. I suppose that somewhere it'll contribute to some bogus reproduction of America's vanished grandeur. There's something profane and decadent about a cocktail lounge done out in barn siding. A weathered board like a weathered farmer deserves better things.

Now the skeleton of the old hip-roofed barn stands naked against

71

the sky. And lo, it is more beautiful than ever. The huge, proud beams hewed of virgin timber, the ladders mounting to the peak, Mondrian patterns on a blue canvas.

Perhaps it is the form of things that enchants us more than the surface realities. We like slim bodies because they do not obscure the underlying structure. A tree standing barren and leafless has an elemental beauty. The poem with its sparsity of words is the ultimate literary achievement. The simple thing is the most appealing. Less is more.

Apart from the siding I never thought a great deal about Pete Newberry's barn when it stood there in its silver splendor; my thoughts stopped at its surface. Now as I admire its bare "hull" I am prompted to wonder many things. What secrets could it tell beyond the round of morning and evening chores that went on here?

Would it tell of the glorious day in 1920 when all the neighbors came for the barn raising? "I tell you, that was quite a barn in its day," says Louise Kneisel. "We sat on the front porch and watched the men raise those big timbers. It was just amazing with what ease they did it. I remember that we made ham sandwiches and there was a keg of beer."

Would it speak of the pride it gave a man to have a barn so fine, of the hopes it instilled for the future? Would it tell of barefoot children playing Tarzan and hide 'n' seek and testing the hired man's tobacco? Would it speak of 4-H calves being groomed for show, of cows who answered to pet names, of the sweating team that moved gratefully into its shade on summer afternoons? Would it tell of a hired girl seduced in the haymow? Would it come forth with the owner of the whiskey bottles?

Would it tell the basic truth, whispered by the neighbors through the years, that this was too extravagant a structure for a struggling farmer in the 1920s and that it contributed sadly to his defeat?

Paul and I walk down the road in the moonlight and gaze up at its bare, beautiful silhouette. Why couldn't we just leave it there as a monument to the rural past? But progress owes more to expediency than sentiment. Paul is concerned with getting it down, building something functional on the site. Paul's not much for monuments. And I guess it's just as well. . . .

I suppose I heard it once too often. "You mean you belong to that motorcycling Penton family and you never rode a motorcycle?" I decided it was time to change all that.

The kids gave me what you might call a crash course in trail riding. It started, like all courses, with basic advice:

"You'll have to wear long pants, Aunt Pat, and shoes and socks." My nephew was passing on the safety rules he'd been taught, but I smiled at the unlikely prospect of Aunt Pat's doing an "endo" on the trail. I changed my shorts and shoes, hoping he wouldn't notice if I went sockless.

Tim loaned me a helmet and buckled it under my chin, much as I used to zip his little jackets or tie his shoes on his frequent visits to End o' Way through the years. Then he showed me the controls from starter switch to foot brake, gave me one long sentence's worth of instructions, and turned his precious trailbike over to me. (My sons wouldn't trust me with theirs—the ones I "own.")

I cranked it a couple of times and nothing happened. Ted came riding alongside me at that moment.

"I think you better turn on the switch, Mom," he said. It started. I twisted the throttle, released the clutch, and was off on the grand adventure, clutching the handlegrips in that zoom-zoom posture, wind pushing my chest, pavement racing past under my feet, one with all the black-jacketed heroes of motorcycle legend—me and Marlon Brando, me and Steve McQueen, me and Evel Knievel.

Delusions of grandeur . . . and I wasn't even out of low gear. I shifted roughly to second, then to third. I was overtaken about then by Tim and Ted. "Are you using the clutch?" one hollered. "Doesn't sound like you are." There was going to be no sloppy riding with these guys.

My ankle was sending little messages to my brain saying, "There's something very hot down here that's hostile to the anklebone."

"Hey!" I shouted, "I want to go back to the house and get some socks." Tim refrained from I-told-you-so's.

An hour later, high work shoes over my ankle burns, I was speeding with quite some confidence around the motocross course, up and down hillocks, over the ruts and roughs, shifting 'er up and down, leaning into the curves, standing on the pegs—a real hotshot!

One more hour and there I was on Peasley Hill descending a shale ridge at 45 degrees between two knee-deep ruts when—Pow! I wiped out.

Tim had overlooked an important part of the gear. One needs a soft shirt to sop up the blood. I clapped my hand over my face to stem the bleeding. The boys came running and plied me with anxious questions.

"I'm fine," I assured them, unfolding myself and ignoring numerous sensory messages, all of which underscored a Leimbach maxim: "Don't tell me about your hero wounds."

"But what did I do to the bike? And I've lost my wedding ring." Someplace along the way I had switched bikes with Tim and was riding my son's. He was going to be furious. Something told me, too, that when I came limping in, dripping blood from a motorcycle accident, I wouldn't really need that wedding ring.

"The bike's OK, Aunt Pat. You just bent the fender a little. Gee, I've never seen anyone like you!" It was an ambiguous compliment, but it soothed my wounded ego.

I finally found my ring, bathed my dirty face in Chance Creek, and idled the cycle home around the roadway, avoiding the tough, steep river valley. As I entered the house, Paul gave me a disgusted glance and said, "What did you do to the cycle?"

Surprisingly, Orrin leaped to my defense. "Nothing. It's fine!" (God bless little boys with foolhardy mothers!)

I dropped Tim off at his home that evening, hoping to avoid my brother John, who is a national legend in motorcycle circles, the dogged survivor of a thousand cuts, bruises, scrapes, and fractures. As luck would have it, there he stood with a lawn mower right next to the driveway.

"What in the hell did you do to your face?" he asked.

"Oh . . . I, ah . . . had a little skirmish on a motorcycle," I said.

"When are you going to grow up?" he said, shaking his head and releasing me into the select fraternity of the initiated.

That was a couple weeks ago and now nothing's the same. . . .

"What happened to your mom?" say the young bucks sitting around the front lawn as I hobble past.

"Aw, she wiped out over on Peasley Hill," my sons say with a tone in their voices I never heard before.

In the grocery I encounter a familiar-looking young girl with a huge burn on her leg. "What in Sam Hill happened to your leg?" I ask.

"Motorcycle exhaust," she says. "What happened to you?"

"Motorcycle" I say, in the smug manner of those whose blood has mingled in secret ritual.

Confessions of a Nongardener

Admitting to a distaste for gardening is like opposing motherhood. It's unnatural! It sends tremors of shock through people with normal responses. When you are a farmer's wife, you're supposed to be Mother Earth; it's so vitalizing—all tied in with a love of the soil, worshiping the sun, being in balance with nature, a yearning in the womb . . . or something.

Well, I do love the soil; I have a great appreciation for rich loam and light sand, for any well-worked piece of ground. I even have a healthy fund of knowledge about plants and gardens and gardening. I dispense brave advice, as befits a farmer's wife.

I love a garden, to walk or sit in or admire from a window. I have a garden, quite a nice one. I work in it sporadically.

I can't complain that things don't grow for me—it's just that I don't enjoy any of it! Somehow, poking around in the soil just doesn't turn me on. I don't enjoy the feel of loose dirt through my fingers. In fact I can hardly bear it. It's like fingernails on blackboards with me.

What kind of farmer's wife is that, anyway? Oh, I like farming; don't misunderstand. I like field work, tractor work. Picking beans by the endless hour is no sweat for me. I like everything about being a farmer's wife except that indelible image of me squatting on my haunches with a trowel breathing life into listless plants, bringing green order to the neat little frame around the picture.

This is not a new phenomenon with me. I recognize now that I've always hated gardening. When all the other kids were teasing for seeds, creating little gardening plots and arguing with brothers and sisters over territorial rights, I lay on a porch swing and read Big Little Books. Eventually, though, I learned, mostly from my mother-in-law. My husband appreciated her garden so much that I felt duty-bound to emulate her, but the resistance was always there.

I can think of three hundred reasons for not going out in the yard to work. It's too cold or too hot, or too wet or too dry. The house is out of order. I have ironing to do. I have an overwhelming urge to clean cupboards or mend overalls or scrub the cellar floor—all those jobs I avoid like the plague in winter.

If I determine to be in the garden by 8:15, I may make it by 4:30, and at 5:00 I'm due back in the kitchen for supper. More likely I won't get out there till 7:30, and the whole show is called by darkness or canceled by mosquitos.

I invented little ways to cope with my problem even before I could identify it. By and large they involve my husband, who can toss off my meager amount of gardening in his incidental walks from the house to the barn. I rush out the door while he's looking for his cap. Then I position myself before a flower bed and say in extreme agitation as he passes, "Have you seen my spade? Somebody has carried it off to the field again."

"Yeah, I think I know where your spade is," he'll say, and feeling very guilty goes off in search of it.

While he's looking for the spade, I assemble my seeds or plants and the hoe. When he hands me my spade I stab at the ground in awkward and feeble manner, and without a word he takes it back in his hands and goes about the spading. Smoothing out the lumps behind him, I interject a question like, "How deep do I plant these seeds?" By now he's really involved, for in truth he loves this sort of thing. In no time flat the work is done.

There are other little ruses, like, "How about giving me a hand with this burdock?" or "What do you suggest I do about this orchard grass?" Yes, I have learned to survive as a nongardening farm wife and retain a modicum of respectability. But that was before 1) the sensitivity movement, 2) the back-to-the-land movement, and 3) the women's movement. In light of these developments I have been forced to an agonizing reappraisal.

Somebody wrote a psychological study of the relationship between people and plants. Plants know how you feel about them! Holy criminies! All those shrubs and trees and flowers and weeds recognizing my resentment! Fills the whole darned yard with hate.

And while all that hatred is contaminating my yard, the whole country is going nuts doing "the green thing"—raising tomatoes in flowerpots and lettuce in bathtubs and cycling out to the country weekends with the garbage and the grass clippings to pamper a little rented plot and grow potatoes under straw. It's driving me bananas! It's getting so I hate party conversations. All people talk about is their compost heaps or their wandering Jew or how to cook a spaghetti squash. I want to crawl off in a corner somewhere to discuss something down-home like *Crime and Punishment*.

Worst of all is acceptance of the fact that if I'm gonna be a liberated woman, I've got to quit copping out on the business end of that spade. I must spread my own manure and pull my own yellow dock, dig my own shrubbery holes, and run my own rototiller.

So I'm gardening more and enjoying it less. I'm gonna learn to love gardening if it kills me.

Old Peppy

Peppy and I never fulfilled one another's needs.

To me she was a nuisance from the beginning—"Take her away; I don't want a dog!" And I said it so resolutely that I convinced myself. I had two tiny children to lavish love upon and I threw only the scraps to the dog. She courted me every day of her life and I rebuffed her as often.

As dogs go she won my respect. She roamed the fields for woodchucks and mice, found water and protein supplement with the cattle in the barn, always looked sleek and healthy. As a watchdog she succeeded in putting up a ferocious front when in reality she was docile as a lamb. My little boys tugged on her black velvet ears and slept against her flanks.

She seemed somehow to know the boundaries of the property and never strayed unless we were out walking, whereupon she followed faithfully.

Still I refused to relinquish my affection to her. A dog was a redundance, a yapping beast to leap upon you with muddy feet when you came home.

Suddenly I realized that Peppy had grown old. Her muzzle grew white and her gait crippled. She hunted less and stopped leaping. Now she limped out to greet us at homecoming. She walked along as we worked in the field but there was no joyous chasing after rabbits or mice as formerly.

The children, absorbed in other interests, ignored her. Paul no longer thought of her as hunter and companion. There was a new young dog to chase sticks and leap up to be petted. She was nothing but a bag of bones. Her coat lost its luster and collected burrs. She limped in the morning to a low sunny spot in the backyard and lay there, moving with the afternoon to a warm spot out front. Finally I yielded my heart to the poor old soul.

For the first time I bought dog food and tried to feed her. The other dogs snatched the table scraps from her and I had to resort to trickery to feed her anything at all. There were growths in her throat and eating was labored.

Often now I sank down on the back steps where she lay, petted her bony old head and hugged her shivering flanks, wanting desperately to protect her from the ravages of age— from loneliness and starvation, and the mistreatment of other dogs.

There was gratitude in her eyes but those joyous puppy responses were gone. Even wagging her tail was an effort. When the cold weather came I made her a bed of blankets in the basement, but she preferred her old haunts behind the shrubbery. It was too late to turn her into a house dog.

Finally it was too much. I was letting her live and suffer as some sort of compensation for the years I ignored her. I asked Paul to please end her suffering.

Peppy is dead but in her dying she brought something to life in me.

Jury Tampering

The observation has been made that juries are inclined to be very free with other people's money. Alas, my own experience as a member of a damage assessment jury persuades me that this is true. Yet before condemning juries it's important to understand the intensely personal forces that indirectly affect the outcome.

Our case was a property suit. We were to determine the value to a store owner of a narrow strip of property condemned by the state for widening a highway. The improved highway had increased the traffic past the place and yet it seemed that business was falling off. The plaintiff contended that the reduction of several parking spaces out front was responsible for the decreased business. He was asking

for damages that sounded adequate for the Louisiana Purchase—
$350,000.

We heard the case over a period of two days. Testimony consisted
of the involved statistics of a number of real estate appraisers, three
or four representing each side of the case. I learned that like Bible
quotes, there's an appraisal statistic to prove almost anything.

At the weary end of the first court day I drove out to look over the
property in question. I watched the parking lot out front for conges-
tion during this rush hour of the day. Parking was more than
adequate. It appeared that the cause of the reported business reduction might well be a big new discount store across the street dealing
in the same merchandise.

On the strength of the judge's early estimate that two days would
probably finish the case, I invited friends for dinner Wednesday, the
evening of the third day. Even if it ran two and a half days I could
handle the party. No problem.

The case dragged into a third day and was sent to the jury shortly
before lunch. Up until this point even during the long and too-
frequent court recesses we were forbidden, upon penalty of having
our tongues cut out, to discuss the case.

No one had been duped by the $350,000 figure. Jurors began to pare
it down—$250,000? $150,000? $75,000? What did I think? I thought
about $13,000 and even that seemed generous. They all raised their
eyebrows but somebody suggested $50,000 and then it was 4:00. We
were called back to the courtroom. Did we want to recess till
tomorrow or go on until we reached a decision? My dinner party was
going to be late, but even I didn't want to stretch on to another day.

We went into extra innings. There was a sizable group holding
around $75,000, a handful more at $50,000. A few conservatives were
pushing for $35,000. I held the line at $13,000.

It was 5:30. The judge sent in to ask if we wanted to recess. These
jurors were mostly 7:00 to 3:00'ers or 9:00 to 5:00'ers. There was no
overtime pay. It was time for feet up and a beer. Regimented mothers
were usually hanging up their dish towels by 5:30. They wanted an
end to this. But no, we were getting close and nobody wanted to
dedicate another day of his life.

$35,000? Do I hear $35,000?

Few things in my life are scheduled or regimented. I had the heart
for a long siege. I was sure they would eventually be persuaded of

their folly. But it was 6:00 and my friends were storming the house, gastric juices flowing. I might consider pushing it up to $20,000.

How about $29,000? OK with you? And you? And you? The chairman went around the table. Eleven people nodded their heads.

I had to stop on the way home and pick up a box of spaghetti and a pound of coffee. . . .

"OK," I said, "twenty-nine thousand." It was more than the plaintiffs had paid for the whole property a few years earlier. Nobody cared. It was well past 6:00 and they were missing the weather report. We filed back to the courtroom and reported our suggested settlement.

I scooted home. My friends were in the kitchen drinking wine and cooking dinner. It was a good dinner. It should have been. I think it cost the taxpayers $16,000.

Frills and Furbelows

Like other businessmen, farmers these days have increasing opportunity to meet in seminars and conferences to study and socialize, and their wives are frequently invited along. The program of any conference planned by men for the edification of women may well include a pastime that men assume women enjoy more than any other—a fashion show. Fantastic forum of information, a fashion show. . . .

Does anybody remember "brick red"? Well, you can forget it. This year it's "clay pot." And if you're not wearing "clay pot" you're not with it.

"I hope you're having fun," said our bright and breezy mistress of ceremonies, "'cause that's what it's all about."

If one accepts that premise about life, perhaps what follows makes sense. A little voice inside me whispers, "I could tell you a few things about life, Girlie. There's a little more to it than having fun."

The mistress of ceremonies at a fashion show is referred to as a fashion coordinator, and she speaks with the authority of the Emperor's tailors.

"First we have the very lovely Dottie wearing a Bill Blass original, an elegantly casual costume priced at three hundred dollars."

Holy shamolies! Couldn't I knock 'em dead at Farm Bureau

meeting in that! Three hundred dollars! That's about a hundred and twenty bushels of corn.

"A designer's original always costs a bit more, but it's a status symbol so it's worth it," our coordinator continues.

Well, of course, if fun is what it's all about, what's 120 bushels of corn? "But it's a Bill Blass original, Honey." I'll tell him.

"Just who in the hell is Bill Blass?" I can hear him saying.

"Janet is wearing a Halston sheath in one of the new fun fabrics. Notice the marvelous lines. Modestly priced at one hundred and sixty-five dollars."

Janet has marvelous lines indeed. She'd look good in a feed bag. It's her wooden smile that disturbs me.

"Here's Norma in a costume of leather. This is the toga look you've been reading about in your fashion magazines."

My mind flashes to the magazines stacked up on the kitchen counter: *Farm Journal, Prairie Farmer, Cycle News, Dirt Bike,* and all those other "fashion" magazines.

"The lovely Dotty is back now in a stunning little cocktail dress with a fun belt [fun! fun! fun!] topped with a silver fox cape priced at seven hundred and fifty dollars."

Whoop dee wow! Just the thing to fling around the shoulders on winter mornings when he comes in and says, "Get your coat on. I need you to help me tow the truck." Or I could wear it to the next fashion show and affirm that the lovely Dottie hasn't anything over on me.

There's something else I could have told the Emperor's tailors. Those farmers' wives who sat through all that phoney baloney mentally translating prices into bushels of wheat, pecks of potatoes, pounds of milk, and numbers of hogs weren't really wasting time. They were sitting there figuring out how they were gonna go home and copy that Bill Blass original for $22.75 and, by golly, *that's* what you call fun!

Of Grave Concern

My mother-in-law was a cemetery tender. Every Sunday following church she stopped at her in-laws' grave and left the altar flowers. In life they had had their differences, some of them bitter and deep, she and the elder Leimbachs. (It was ever thus where generations succeed one another on the farm.) But no one could have faulted her for dereliction of duty, before or after their deaths.

No sooner was the headstone set following the funeral than Lucy was there to plant a flowering crab. It would have been fun to have teased her for planting a crab on her mother-in-law's grave, but a sense of humor was not one of her assets. It was a serious botanical choice and everybody knew it.

It seemed curious to me that she set the tree at the side of the headstone, off center of the lot. Only years later did I recognize that it was meant to shade her grave as well.

One day when she was chatting about some improvements she had made to the lot—the addition of some peonies—she commented that she knew exactly what she wanted for her own headstone.

"Well, you'd better rush out and buy it," I said, "and store it in the barn, because I'm warning you here and now that I'm not much at tending cemeteries." My father had been dead for twenty years and I'd never seen his grave.

She might have followed my suggestion—she took a methodical approach to things—but that fall she died. The winter passed, and the spring; then summer, fall, and winter again. The second spring a cousin of Lucy's, a notoriously plain-spoken old gal, stopped by for potatoes.

"I want to tell you something," she said, "and I don't want you to get mad. I went out to the cemetery to put flowers on Lucy's grave, and my God, I couldn't find it! I think you should know folks are talking. . . ."

Lucy got her headstone right soon thereafter. There's no force so potent in a small community as a wagging tongue. It's not the stone she wanted. Alas, she never described it.

Her crab tree flowers in April, and her peonies in May, but I put no cut flowers there to wilt and wither on her grave. She and I had our differences, too, and the most serious one concerned cemetery tending.

My mother-in-law introduced me to flower gardening, and she lives in the irises, daffodils, lilies, poppies, mums I watch from my windows, the ones she helped me transplant from her garden. But she's far too potent a spirit to honor with a geranium.

The Waiting Game

As an avid student of *Time*'s medical page I am aware that the suffering souls who go in quest of relief from an ever broadening sea of syndromes have a dizzying range of specialists and technicians to serve their needs. There is, I observe, but one common denominator wherever the diagnoses or treatments are dispensed: everybody sits in line and waits.

One gets the feeling that some have sat in waiting rooms till mold formed on their earlobes. Perhaps waiting is endemic to any facility which aims to minister to multitudes. It belongs alike to employment agencies, welfare offices, ticket counters, good restaurants, induction centers, customs inspections. A medical clinic is probably the only place where you have to wait even longer than at the grain elevator at harvest.

My experience with the latter has equipped me successfully for waiting. I always carry, in addition to a good book, more hand or head work than I could accomplish in three weeks. The mystifying force which works against my ever accomplishing anything somehow shortens all lines in which I wait. I am usually half an hour late for my appointments, so what probably would have been a forty-five-minute wait is automatically shortened to fifteen, hardly time to find your place in the book.

There are a few things you can do in this waiting game which may not improve your position in line, but will at least make you conspicuously memorable to the staff and popular with the waiting room crowd.

First of all, hack it on your own. This makes you a free agent and you may pursue whatever pastime suits you. The person you take along to hold your hand will be someone so familiar that you will be bored with each other before you leave the parking lot.

Take along your putting irons and one of those living room putting greens and practice in the waiting room.

Bundle your worn socks in an old pillowcase and do your triennial mending, or carry along your odd socks and match them up or braid a rug. If a little old lady offers to help, don't hesitate to accept.

Set up a quilt and involve the gang in a quilting bee. You'll only be learning yourself, and you may find someone who knows more about quilting than you do. Take plenty of needles and don't count out the men!

Get a little penny ante game going in the corner. Anyone called from the game automatically forfeits his stake in the pot.

Set your Blue Cross number, welfare number, social security number to music; take along a guitar and organize a sing-along. This project could easily expand to include other people's numbers.

Take your own portable TV and tune it loudly to a channel different from the one playing in the waiting room.

Take along a bottle of Scotch and conduct a raffle. Last guy called gets the Scotch.

Set up your easel and sketch fellow detainees for three bucks a head, pairs of sisters for five.

Carry along a wicker basket with lid, peeking in from time to time. Wear a turban and carry a flute. This will probably improve your chances of being processed through quickly.

Set up a cotton candy concession.

Dress like an Arab with dark glasses and headdress and let the others wonder which Middle Eastern principality you're prince of.

Engage in loud conversation about your malpractice suit in process in the Supreme Court.

Slip a bottle of Harvey's Bristol Cream to the secretary behind the counter.

Set up a collapsible volleyball net and organize an interclinic tournament.

Take along your fourteen children and pack a picnic lunch to be spread out and eaten in the waiting room. Even without the fourteen children the picnic idea can be followed. A sunlamp and a blanket will help jazz up a gloomy setting.

If more than three hours pass and you are still being ignored, begin very slowly to disrobe until you are sitting there in the altogether. You will probably win the attention of the attendants though you run the risk of being rushed off to psychiatry.

If you are a chronic clinician you will most effectively utilize this time by studying to pass your medical boards.

I shall be interested to learn how any of you make out with these suggestions but, please, no calls from prison or psychiatric wards.

When my adventuring brother Ted called the other night inviting me to make a tractor-trailer haul to Baltimore, I was thrilled at the opportunity to indulge a long-standing fantasy. Wow! Imagine me as a relief driver on a tractor-trailer rig!

My son, who had made this Baltimore run with his uncle many times, got the picture right away and voiced his loud alarm: "Mom, you'll never be able to handle that clutch."

I wondered if he'd forgotten who taught him to drive, but I murmured his apprehensions to Ted.

"Never mind him," he said. "We'll be leaving at ten o'clock tomorrow night," and his faith in me dismissed idle worries for the moment.

The huge empty rig, as long as the average building lot, was parked out front at the appointed hour, and the first pang of fright hit me when I realized the door was so high I couldn't even open it. Ted took out his flashlight. "Here's your first lesson," he said, as he proceeded to demonstrate the workings of the $300 hydraulic seat. "With this lever you raise or lower it, with this one you move it forward or back, and then if you want it to float . . ."

Gott in Himmel! I expected to drive this thing, and I couldn't even grasp the workings of the seat! But it was too late to chicken out. I was all the relief he had for the twenty-hour haul.

"It's . . . uh . . . pretty wide, isn't it," I said as I gave a mighty leap and hoisted my five feet, two inches aboard, realizing in panic that my VW would fit lengthwise in the front of the cab.

"Naw," said Ted. "It's the same standard width as your farm truck. You're sitting on the outer limits is all." Then he proceeded to the transmission and I could feel the perspiration starting on the back of my neck. ". . . four speeds, high and low range, best to think of it as eight separate gears. You double clutch and rev the engine in between; and then there's the two-speed rear axle that works off this red button here. Pull it back if you need more power, release the accelerator quickly, then hit 'er again. Then when you're rolling along at seventy or eighty you push 'er forward, let up on the clutch . . ." but I had stopped listening.

"This rig'll pull three hundred and twenty-five horses at twenty-two hundred rpm's and pass anything on the road when she's empty," he bragged.

A hard knot was forming in the pit of my stomach, but I had pledged myself to this foolhardiness, and all those 325 horses couldn't drag me backward at this point.

"I'll take it to the first plaza," said Ted, "and then you can drive to Breezewood while I get some sleep."

I swallowed and strapped myself tightly to the right-hand seat. Those miles to the plaza seemed like hours to the gallows. Oh, to get the agony of starting behind me.

Then finally, there I was in control. I depressed the accelerator and let out the clutch and we lurched forward.

"Think I'd better try the brakes," I said as the rig screeched to a halt and everything not tied down plunged ahead.

"Man, you've gotta watch those brakes," said Ted. "You can stand this whole thing on its nose with the braking power." (I think he was beginning to have second thoughts.) "This lever here is a separate brake for the trailer, but you needn't worry about that unless you have a blowout."

Sufficient unto the hour is the evil thereof; I didn't intend to worry about blowouts. Ted climbed up behind me onto the wide, comfortable sleeping compartment. I ground off into the night trying desperately to coordinate hands and feet and head. Amazing that it all worked! Dane had been right; the clutch was a "son-of-a-gun," but wrong, because I was operating it.

The chief problem seemed to be keeping a steady foot on the throttle, and I questioned Ted. "Well, the best way is to put 'er all the way to the floor and keep 'er there," he said. "Uh . . . yeah. Well, I'll see what I can do," I said, edging out around the first lowly auto far below. So small and insignificant, like a flea on the highway. I passed another, and another, giving myself a quarter of a mile to pull back in line, feeling the power and the possibility. When I passed my first semi, Ted seemed satisfied that I was firmly in charge and lay back to sleep.

I worried my way to the Ohio line, afraid I'd pile up on those brakes at the tollbooths. But I eased it through the gate without taking either booth with me. I grasped my ticket with false bravado, and on into Pennsylvania. Wonderful cloak of night clothing me in anonymity and courage. Hour after hour, up hills and down, high axle and low, rev 'er up and slow 'er down, around curves, over bridges, through tunnels, around cars and other trucks—all happily unaware.

Finally—Breezewood! I pulled through a tollgate and into a gas station. Ted awoke. It was 4:00 in the morning.

"Well, how'd ya do?" he asked.

"Well, we're here," I said with deep relief. "You'd have been proud of me. I passed a couple a' trucks going downhill at about eighty. It was either that or put on the brakes. . . ."

Infiltrating the World of Ginger Apple Blush ————————

As an accidental attendant at a cosmetics demonstration I feel like a CIA agent infiltrating the Politburo. Cosmetically I never got beyond Max Factor's Pan-Cake makeup, and that I abandoned in the fifties along with acne and adolescence. Persuading women that there is something repugnant about a shiny nose is a rip-off to rival the purchase of Manhattan Island. But think on these weighty matters: Have you ever considered that you might be suffering from protruding brow bone? Let me hasten to assure you that it isn't fatal and that Estée Lauder, Germaine Monteil, Yves St. Laurent, and many another cosmetic giant has devised an antidote. You can dab on a bit of magic product called Browbeater to de-emphasize, or highlight—I'm not sure which—the condition. Actually, protruding brow bones strike me as being somewhat erotic. One would do well to subdue them with very thick eyebrows or very long bangs.

If that is not your problem, perhaps you are stigmatized by small eyes. Have no fear, there is a product—some sort of shadow liner— to open up and enhance those piggy eyes. (If you cannot afford $4.95 for the liner, a copy of *Hustler* magazine at $2 is guaranteed to enlarge small eyes.)

Perhaps your problem is not physiognomic but cosmetic. Does your lipstick bleed? No problem. There is a hard cosmetic pencil with which to line it and stem the bleeding.

Do your eyes feel dry and tense? What you need is a "toner" just beneath the eyes. Pat that on with your ring finger, your weakest finger, note. Always use your weakest finger in dabbing on this stuff.

? ? ? Don't ask me. Tender tissue, I guess. If you've ever been belted across the face with a cow's tail you may marvel at such delicacy.

"There are three places where a woman's face ages first. Can you tell me? . . ."

"The supermarket, the auto repair, and the loan office," I shot back.

"The corners of the eyes, the corners of the mouth, and the throat," she corrected. "These require special attention. We recommend an imported special protein formula to nourish the skin morning, night, and under makeup. Asian Activating Cream. Four ounces for eighteen dollars."

Holy Toledo! That's about what a dairyman nets for two hundred pounds of milk! One would do well to settle for a can of udder balm—five bucks would buy you a ten-year supply.

"Soap" and "wash" are dirty words in the cosmetic vocabulary. One "cleanses" the skin with a special hormone-enriched product. Then there's a rinse and a toner and an astringent and a moisturizer, then a base and a blusher and a concealing cream and a few area products like eye shadows and eyeliners, and the lipstick and the lipstick liner, and then to top it off iridescent powder and a highlighter and a lipstick polisher, would you believe!

And then, of course, "no woman is dressed until she has a fragrance," our cosmetic coordinator assures us. Doodle-e-Dew is what we call a 'good-time fragrance.' It drives men wild. The rule for a fragrance is to apply it any place that moves. And if you're a belly dancer . . ."

Would anybody believe that mature women, sound of mind and serious of purpose, sit and listen to that kind of prattle and permit themselves to be influenced by it?

Helena Rubenstein, who made herself a multimillionaire in the cosmetics industry, was not intoxicated by her own potions. "I am a worker," she said. "I have no time for it." And to her pragmatic comment I say, "Right on!"

Reflecting to my husband on my afternoon as an infiltrator in the powder puff world of "Ginger Apple Blush," I posed that nagging question.

"Why do you suppose they pat that stuff on with the weakest finger?"

"Simple enough," says my farmer. "They've got to save the strong one for the cash register."

Thanksgiving "Turkey"

Any woman who still scoffs at liberation will do well to reflect upon her Thanksgiving "holiday." If her day was typical, she rolled out of bed early to sew up the bird and get him in the oven. Or perhaps she was up until 2:00 A.M. ironing a tablecloth, shining the silver, unearthing platters and pickle trays and stuffing an especially big bird, and only got up several times in the early morning hours to baste him.

Did she then plop herself down to gaze leisurely upon the Thanksgiving Day parade? She did not. She went to work rolling piecrust, peeling potatoes, putting leaves in the table, arranging a centerpiece, cutting up a squash and proceeding otherwise with the makings of a feast.

At 12:00 or 2:00 or 6:00, depending on the schedule at her house, the relatives gathered. The kids came home with the grandchildren or with boyfriends, girl friends, roommates. Maybe the womenfolk brought a contribution to the feast, the foodstuff that got *them* up early to peel or mix or simmer slowly. But finally the board was spread by the women and the men were called.

At the inception of this glorious feast day, I envision patriots in pewter buckles and Pilgrim hats out stalking the wild turkey and the deer. It is perhaps fitting then that Thanksgiving remains a day of big game hunting. Yes, now they pass the day twisting a TV dial looking for the big games and then sprawl about the living room watching the gladiators. So from the big games the men are called to the table to lay waste the feast.

This is by no means a relaxing moment. The culminating minutes of any meal are hectic ones for the hostess. She has probably been hassled about being late with her offering by children and husband alike. Somebody brought an in-law not included in the count and they're one place short. Nobody remembered to light the candles, the salt shakers won't shake, the gravy ladle is missing. But there is a deep satisfaction at that point in seeing her beloved ones gathered around this labor of love (a satisfaction bordering on blindness . . .?).

In a half hour her feast is reduced to carcass and garbage and spots on the tablecloth. There may be a brief interval before the "dessert offering" is separately staged, but it will be crowded with a frantic scraping of plates and rinsing of forks. When the flaming pudding is only an ember, does she retire to the living room and put her feet up to read the paper or share in the triumphs of the Buffalo Bills? Ha. She repairs once more to the kitchen, where she grapples with gravy and tussles with cold turnips and emerges from the dirty dish detail just in time to hear some kid remark, "I'm hungry. What is there to eat?" or to fill turkey sandwich orders sent in by the big game hunters.

Of course, if you spent Monday, Tuesday, and Wednesday of Thanksgiving week buffing your nails, having your hair done, and going to ceramics class while the man of the house put in heroically productive hours, then perhaps you owe him this peace offering. (That kind of woman probably eats out on Thanksgiving.)

Most women's days are at least as productive as their husbands' and they are just as deserving of a holiday.

Any way you carve it, Thanksgiving is a male chauvinistic triumph.

Cheap Chic

Skiing is by nature of its inaccessibility and flair a sport for the well-heeled, or at least the uncommitted. If you are not yet overburdened with mortgages, tuition bills, orthodonture, replacing the appliances, or the more basic demands of feeding and clothing a pack of kids, if you are a rock star or an unwed secretary on the make, you may well afford a $200 jumpsuit of glistening silver; you could be justified in exchanging last year's red leather gloves for $20 orange ones that match your $90 orange parka. Really sleek stretch pants range from $70 to $125, but you may look fashionably camp in $18 Levis, freeing more of your substance to buy an extra pair of powder skis ($200) with the latest and safest in release bindings ($125), into which you clamp your individually molded fiberglass ski boots, priced between $70 and $250!

A red bandanna ($2.95 in a ski shop) around the neck of a blue chambray shirt complements the look of nonchalance, but you'll probably top the costume with a $50 sweater and a $50 goosedown vest. You'll need also a $15 pair of goggles, a $20 hat, and socks at $5 or so. If it gets really cold you add an extra layer known as warmups, which can run from $40 to $140.

No one costume is satisfactory for all ski conditions, there are variations on every weather theme from spring sun to winter blizzards. The ante moves up accordingly. For some unfathomable reason, ordinary outdoor garb that you hang in the kitchen closet or the cellarway isn't considered suitable for ski wear. Skiers are a fickle and fashion-conscious bunch. When wide-pant legs came into vogue, all the narrow-ankled models disappeared like snow in summer. The things are so indestructible that I can imagine the needy of the world unfashionably clad in them for generations to come.

There's a similar fluctuation in the fashion of every item connected with the sport—boots, skis, poles, parkas, shirts, goggles, socks—you name it. And the hunger after new acquisitions is fed during those long waits in the tow lines, during which there is little else to do than shuffle along scrutinizing fashions.

Needless to say, a peon who hopes to survive in this chic milieu without plummeting into bankruptcy must latch onto his values and cling tenaciously. And so it is that I have finally made it! The warmest, most comfortable, most comforting garment I own is the red quilted underwear jacket I wear to the barn, the field, the coal bin, the cellar, or wherever farm business takes me. (At our house it is referred to as Mom's security blanket.) It dates back to the early sixties, and, having been routinely snagged on barbed wire, baling wire, nails, screws, and rusty bolts, it is of necessity covered with patches. For some curious reason, patches seem to have come into their own these days. So there I was bombing the slopes of Snowbird on a pre-plowing holiday (which is the only time vegetable farmers holiday) garbed in the regalia of the moment.

"Oooo!" said one little snow bunny. "You're all patches! Isn't that cute!"

I interpreted the looks in the lift lines as tokens of admiration, but for those with a tendency to scorn, I had sewn in script across the bottom rear patch Thoreau's cryptic observation on the subject of fashion: "Beware of all enterprises that require new clothes."

There really isn't much of my life I'd like to surrender to being somebody else, but when I "grow up" I'd like to be Anne Thompson.

Anne lives on the rugged North Sea coast of England in the shadow of Hadrian's Wall in a three-hundred-year-old cottage built of stones two feet thick. I'm sure that life in that cottage is austere, for Anne lives on a widow's pension of thirteen pounds a week. Out of that thirteen pounds she manages to save eight for her one great indulgence, travel.

I encountered her one September up along the New York State Thruway. She stood beside the road—short, plump, and grandmotherly—displaying a Union Jack on the side of her single piece of luggage. She was grateful for my lift and acknowledged that seldom had she been given a ride by a woman.

No, she hadn't had any lunch and was delighted with the home-made bread and butter Orrin and I had to offer. Said she was a vegetarian so didn't eat a lot of what other people eat.

Anne Thompson was en route to New York City and home, following her third trip through the United States. She had seen a great deal more of the USA than I have and had made hundreds of friends here. She has a love for Americans in their openness and generosity that her reticent English friends were at a loss to understand. Said she'd never had any unfortunate advances from men. "I just tell 'em I'm not that kind of girl."

She admitted that she was sixty and, in her single touch of vanity, said, "Twon't matter, for ye don't know anybody I know."

Anne had been all over the world in her travels—Australia, New Zealand, the Far East, South America, Africa, Hawaii, Bali, Russia, Yugoslavia—you name it, she had been there. Europe she knew like the back of her hand.

Most of her traveling had been done by bicycle; perhaps her age had caused her to resort to hitchhiking this time. How does one afford a room every night, when one is on a widow's mite? You stay at Salvation Army hostels. "Not very fancy" she said, "but clean and adequate."

Her misfortunes on the byways of the world had been few. Only once had she been robbed, in Bogota, Colombia; and then strangers had aided her in getting back to Northumberland. More than the seven or eight hundred dollars the thieves had stolen did she value the two British passports they had taken. They contained an irreplaceable collection of border crossing stamps, and she had been offered as much as three hundred dollars apiece for them.

We talked so fast and furiously of her extraordinary experiences as we traveled the Mohawk Valley that the hours and the miles flew past. I failed to noitce my gas gauge had dropped into "reserve," and suddenly the Volkswagen sputtered to a stop. Then it was my turn to hitchhike while she and Orrin passed the time looking through her collection of souvenirs, most prized among which was an Indian arrowhead.

The very first driver along was the head of the department of highways for the state of New York. "I always bring people good luck" said Anne as he filled our tank from an auxiliary can. As I revved the engine and took off, I smiled. It didn't occur to her that without her conversation I might have remembered the gas earlier.

We said good-bye at the Salvation Army home in Albany. I wondered how far she'd have to walk next morning through this dismal slum area before somebody would again befriend her. What courage it takes to be a vagabond.

She wrote me the following year from a hospital in England. She had been struck by a car on a street in Italy, been flown home by the embassy, and was temporarily out of commission. But she had high hopes of coming someday to End o' Way.

One day last summer when I was stranded along the Ohio Turnpike and sat knitting on the grass waiting for my son to rescue me, I watched the traffic come and go at the exits. I appraised the rich variety of humanity moving in and out and was seized with an urge to drop everything and take to the road like the young hitchhikers lingering there.

I would once have said to myself, it's too late. You have to do those things when you're young. But Anne Thompson has changed all that. Yes, "when I grow up," I tell Orrin, "I think I'll be an Anne Thompson." I hope that when my ride puts me down outside that stone cottage in Northumberland, there'll still be a little old lady dwelling quietly there with a host of rich memories.

COUNTRY SCENE

There is little in the profuse and varied portrayal of America today that translates the small community fact. A map of the country drawn from an "intellectual's eye view" appearing on a New Yorker cover shows nothing but the Hudson between the Big Apple and the Rockies. But intimate communities still exist by the thousands across our land in tiny towns and rural areas; and they are a stable and viable force. Traditions are strong there, but so are stimulating outside influences.

Watering the Roots _____

If you haven't noticed that it's family reunion time then you're probably more than a generation or two removed from the farm, or you don't have roots in the Middle West. The family reunion is an institution fostered and cherished in rural America, and through changing lifestyles, it does persist. Just as predictably as the cicadas arrive, so does the appointed Sunday in July or August, and the clan gathers to water its roots. Everything about a reunion is, in fact, predictable.

If one has children beyond the age of ten, there will be an inevitable difference of opinion about the day's activity. My sons, for example, think a motorcycle race is a good reason for not going to a family reunion. Their father does not. Obviously it's his family that's "reuning." There follows a noisy and inane squabble about the relative importance of our two families.

Children are usually bewildered by the strangely familiar assemblage at a reunion. Once when we were encouraging a thumb-sucking four-year-old to "go off and play with [his] cousins," he remarked, "Those aren't cousins; they're girls!"

They always get more of "How you've grown!" or "Are you Paul's boy?" than they want to hear; and their self-images are blurred by being mistaken for their brothers and sisters.

These family conclaves give aunts and grandparents great opportunity for comparing cousins and seeing atavistic resemblances: "Those are the Heinzerling eyes!" or, "They've both got Great-grampa Henry's nose." (Is it any wonder that a motorcycle race has an edge on a reunion!)

When you're secure enough in your choice to bring a boyfriend or a girl friend to these family affairs, the misery diminishes; and if that swain is smitten enough to endure, you may judge that he's "hooked." But when you return with your first-born, equipped with high chair and walker and small pans for heating baby food, then you really belong.

Some long-suffering female is usually the prime mover behind the family reunion. She keeps addresses and sends out cards and will probably be the family historian.

The act of "breaking bread" together is basic to the family reunion, and you can make book on the menu at these affairs. They are very long on fried chicken, potato and macaroni salad, and baked beans. There is always some fad recipe that will appear in triplicate with minor variations. The same people often bring the same things year after year. The Leimbachs always take a kettle of corn on the cob and a basket of melons. Bernita and Jim bring a freezer of homemade ice cream. The children look forward to Nellie's tray of Rice Krispie squares, but the person who really wins their hearts is Cousin Bill who comes with a trunkload of pop cooled in a big washtub.

The family reunion is the annual news forum, and so "visiting" is its principal preoccupation. "Where is George living now? . . . How many children does Dan have? . . . How old is Mary? . . . Is Judy going on to school?"

We evaluate one another's achievements; we find out what we've done. Conversation glides smoothly over the surface of life lived, too seldom dipping beneath it. Our common ancestry is no help to us in revealing our common humanity.

What the great-aunts consider to be eyebrow-raisers—divorces, illegitimate pregnancies, drinking problems, "meaningful relationships"—will be discreetly avoided, unless, of course, all parties remotely concerned are absent. You won't hear anyone claiming the guilt in phrases like, "It's the old Leimbach lust coming out."

In late afternoon when the flies are settling on the leftover pie, surface conversation has been exhausted, the ball game outside is deteriorating, and the children have begun to discover they have more in common than last names, the party breaks up. There is a gathering up of picnic baskets and high chairs and ball gloves, and a saying of farewells with promises never kept to "get together more often."

During the drive home we rehash the whole day, pooling the news from separate conversations, straightening out puzzling relationships. Our teenager wants to know how closely we're related to those "cool" girls from New London. Another is full of questions about Uncle Nelson's wooden leg. The third one brags about how much pop he drank, and then comments brightly, "Gosh, I never knew I was related to Marty" (a friend made through other channels). "How come we don't ever go to see them?"

There's no one good reason. Life and geography just don't allow us to "keep" all the people we'd like to keep. And that's probably why we persist with family reunions despite their shortcomings, trying to hold onto the thread of relationships once very important, trying to pass on to our children a sense of having derived from somewhere—a sense of tradition, and of a heritage meriting honor and support.

Requiem for a Red Tree

The red tree fell last week, as unobtrusively as you can fall when you are a red tree. It was rather as though it heaved a final sigh and released the spirit.

For truly this was a tree with spirit. My friends the Lyles of Amherst held title to the red tree, an Italian elm grafted fatefully to the breed of American elms that succumbed to Dutch elm disease. It grew in their yard for many years, casting a friendly shade and spreading its arms uniformly to the neighborhood. When it died, it stood so lifelike above the decaying roots that the Lyles were reluctant to remove it.

So they painted it red, and it became the wider possession of all who delight in celebration. At Christmastime a partridge perched in its top. At Easter a nest of large papier-mâché eggs nested in its solitary crotch. At Halloween a black witch poised there with her broomstick, and on the Fourth of July it was bedecked with flags.

Most of the year it simply stood there, bare and bright, a sudden reminder to the passerby that humor is an essential part of life, that life is joy, that death can be overcome, and that resurrection is a reality.

We will all miss the red tree. The Lyles have plans, of course, to transform and preserve the relics. Perhaps it should be cut into morsels to be distributed to those of us who rejoiced in it.

Like the image that remains in the mind when a candle is extinguished, the red tree will glow in our hearts. But there is an empty space against the gray house up on Park Avenue. The spirit of fun and celebration is loose in the universe and searching, I suspect, for a new host to inhabit.

Country Store: Where the Action Is

We got a right smart new store over to Brownhelm Center (Brownhelm, unincorporated, population 150, give or take): "Cutcher's Brownhelm Store," polebarn rustic.

It's not exactly the classic model of an old country general store. You can't buy your winter galoshes there or your bib overalls. There's no pot-bellied stove or cracker-barrel philosopher. Bill Cutcher, proprietor and general manager, is about as close as you're gonna come, and he isn't into philosophy yet, though he has the bemused nature for it. If he sits by those gas pumps long enough . . .

The people who run "the store" at a country crossroads have a unique function foisted upon them: they are ministers without benefit of cloth to a whole community, for "the store" is the social crossroads. Sooner or later everybody passes through for a loaf of bread, a pair of work gloves, a can of pop, the Sunday paper, a sack of potatoes (Leimbach's), or enough gas to nurse them home to the farm pump. It's still the place to go when it's "too wet to plow, too cold to paint, too hot to think."

All the news of the countryside funnels through. A "where'd you hear that?" over lunch will more often than not bring "over at the store" in reply. If somebody dies you can leave a dollar for flowers at the store. Coming events are prominently heralded there with cluttered hand-done posters.

You can stop by the store during a blizzard and find out which roads are impassable.

On summer evenings the 4-H'ers meet around the picnic table in the side lot; the Little Leaguers swarm in on pickup trucks to celebrate a victory; young bucks hang around to admire one another's souped-up "bombs," or to ogle a carload of girls who went five miles out of their way to happen by there.

An endless succession of young kids have their first jobs down at the store pumping gas or punching a cash register. It's a good contact point for a better job. But there'll never be another they'll look back upon with such nostalgia, because "the store" is "where it's at" in a country community in any generation.

R.F.D. ———————————————————————

I always regarded that silver box under the pear tree at the end of the driveway as something of a marvel. You could put a letter in there and in two days it was in somebody else's box halfway across the country. And from it you could take a letter somebody had written out in Kanakakee and now here in your hand it lay. My child's mind didn't encompass all the stamping and sorting, conveying, cancelling, and bundling, trucking, transporting in between. It was a simple kind of three-cent miracle: now it's here, now it's there.

Even today's much increased rates seem cheap for a miracle, especially when I consider all those people and processes from box to box. The fact that I can get up in the morning and fly out to Kanakakee for a late breakfast doesn't alter the miracle. And though some grousing somebody is always pointing out that in some Utopian country you can, or could, post a letter in the A.M. and have it delivered in the P.M., that really doesn't concern me. I'm satisfied with minor miracles.

Nor does my experience tell me of letters sent me that did not arrive. (There are many I could wish had never come. Alas, they came just the same.)

My experience of the postal department is dominated by the dedication of my mailman and my maillady through the years, who chased my steers and signed for my C.O.D.'s, retrieved letters that I mailed accidentally, sold me stamps and made up my shortages out of pocket. Some even stopped around after working hours to deliver something I wasn't home to sign for earlier, and buy a sack of potatoes.

Can you call it "free" at current prices? I suspect that like many things Americans have enjoyed too cheaply, too long—like food and fuel—postal service is going to cost us more. As far as I'm concerned, I get a lot more than I pay for.

On the 15th of April a letter appears in my box from somebody in South Dakota saying, "When you come to the stop sign in Redfield at Highway 281, take a left turn and proceed across the tracks and you will see a National Guard Armory. This is where I will be." And on the 1st of June I walk into that National Guard Armory in Redfield, S. D., 1,200 miles from home, and a fellow walks up and says, "I'm the guy who wrote you." How can that be anything but a miracle?

From This Day Forward

Paul rushed us through the dressing ritual so we wouldn't get stuck in the steaming balcony of the tiny church. We lucked out with the last pew on the bride's side next to an open window. From here we have a cool view of Harold Bauman's silo and an excellent perspective on the wedding guests.

My sons look relatively splendid here beside and between us. That is to say that their faces are clean and their hair is combed and they have shoes, however unpolished, on their feet. Teddy was determined to wear his blue jeans but Mother put her foot down.

"Then I'm not going!" he said.

"If you see anybody at that wedding in jeans I'll pay you two bucks," I said. So he had to come on the certainty of winning two bucks. (He lost.)

A pretty young friend of the bride sings a love song from "Romeo and Juliet" and there's time to sit and reflect. My first-born comments sardonically that he and his "bride" are going to have something entirely different in a wedding.

"More power to you," I whisper, reserving my suspicions that the illusory bride will arrive at her wedding day with a lifetime of traditional notions and that his shindig will probably differ little from the one in progress. But I'm really pulling for Dane in his assault on tradition.

Country weddings these days have a great deal more pizazz than they once had, despite the view of the silo and the omnipresent babes in arms. That is doubtless due to the fact that most of them are masterminded by photographers and florists, whose prosperity depends on polished productions.

My sister's wedding, which suffered the privations of the war years and probably cost twenty dollars, was the first in my memory. We had a "lawn reception" and believe me, we didn't have that kind of a lawn! We made a special effort to hack the tails off the plantain, moved the produce out of the roadside market stand to make way for the homemade almond cake, and decorated everything liberally with blue crepe paper. It aimed to be a "dry wedding," but my brother Ted sneaked in a case of beer which he iced in a washtub in the cider mill across the driveway. It all seemed to me ultra-chic. (Teddy could have worn his blue jeans.)

Six years later, when my mother became resigned to the fact that I was to marry, she announced that she had fifty dollars to spend on a wedding. It seemed extravagant but I managed to squander it all. I spent twenty dollars on dress material and blew the rest on flowers and a reception. Having been a bridesmaid seven times, it was a simple matter to borrow bridesmaids' dresses. My brother-in-law shot a few random slides that we get out and look at on cold winter nights. They serve us well as an unglamorous view of an unglamorous occasion.

There is more of the traditional in the wedding in process. Lavender bows on the candelabra foretell lavender bridesmaids. The men enter at the front wearing longer hair than the bride's father would approve. The organist plays the march from *Lohengrin* and the girls come, coifed and scented and lovely, beholding a lavender world through contact lenses.

Next the ring bearer, freshly combed and kissed and aimed at the altar. The bride's niece follows in carbon copy lavender. She breaks the measured stride of the others, walking slowly at first, then more and more quickly as she approaches the security of her mother, the matron of honor, who awards her a "well done" smile. (I cheer for flower girls because they refuse to be programmed.)

The organist pulls out all the stops and takes *Lohengrin* from the top; the bride's mother stands, and here comes the bride, poised and pretty and very much in command. The black tuxedo does not camouflage her father, the farmer. He wears the badge of his occupation—white forehead above deeply tanned cheeks.

He delivers his precious daughter to the space reserved for her beside a quaking groom. And the minister takes charge as the firm, symbolic voice of this loving but rigid community, who never have and never will take marriage lightly.

No three-hour ceremony could do justice to the months of preparation and anticipation. In short minutes it's over. Linda Born is Linda Brown. Wayne gave her a "w" for her name and got in exchange a whole township full of relatives.

A Bushel and a Peck

There is a breed of farmer's wife who stands before an altar (in the off season) with a strong wind-burned youth, dreaming of bliss with a rural view, only to find when the white orchid wilts that what she has married is a roadside market.

While other brides experiment tearfully with poulet marengo and creme brulée, our heroine struggles with the subtle differences between the Hale and the Red Haven peach, and tries to learn which apples are good for eating AND cooking, which for baking and eating, which for eating, cooking, or baking alone, and which will do for all three.

Sympathetic customers worry through each pregnancy with her, cautioning against lifting a peck of potatoes, heedless of the fact that when they aren't around she has to lift them by the bushel.

Later, an infant securely draped on one hip, she masters many a task with one hand, weighing string beans, billowing paper bags, stripping sweet corn husks, and making change.

While a two-year-old screams from his potty chair she watches in dismay as three more cars drive in. While her potatoes boil dry in the kitchen she smiles politely and fidgets, as a compulsive talker drones. She is tempted to tack a notice alongside the "Eggs, 3 dz. for $2.00": "Counseling Extra, and by Appointment Only." There is little that a ten-year veteran of the roadside market doesn't know about human nature after watching so many thoughtless women finger through quarts of peaches, tear back the husks of the corn, punch the end of the melons, and listening to them quibble over pennies. One thing of which she is certain is that men make better customers than women.

The roadside market wife becomes familiar with the "nostalgic flavors" of a hundred forgotten varieties of produce. After futilely explaining 300 times that the Beefsteak tomato has really been improved, and is seldom raised commercially, she is willing to concede, integrity to the contrary, that "Yes," this is a Beefsteak tomato and "No," there'll probably never be another variety as good. (The customer is always right!)

On her first anniversary her solicitous husband makes her a gift of a bell-ringing device triggered from a hose in front of the stand, and the poor frazzled creature is even grateful.

If the business prospers beyond the expensive expansions of added display area, walk-in coolers, hydra-cooled vegetable tables, and a sure-enough cash register, further thought may be given to convenience. She'll get a table out back where she can share her hectic meals with the flies and the passers-by. She'll be treated to a telephone out by the road which improves the business and compounds the problems.

Maybe she'll even get a kitchen at the stand so the long talkers can wander in and watch her transfer the burned potatoes to a fresh pan. Because she is the one who operates the place she will be thoughtfully consulted about all major changes and ultimately observe that most of her counsel has been ignored.

The Sundays she was brought up to cherish now haunt her dreams. Relatives and friends sit about on upturned crates and make small talk, or are pressed into service as makeshift clerks, while she dashes off in a pickup to replenish the produce.

The dreams of children running barefoot through a meadow are displaced by the reality of dirty kids hauling toy truckloads of slag across an acre of parking lot, in peril of life and limb.

And as she daily hurries from house to roadside to corn patch out back, she formulates the words that would deliver her from this nightmare. It's an ad that she thinks of sending to a small town newspaper somewhere in Appalachia:

"Situation wanted: will exchange thriving roadside market business for small shack with front porch and rocking chair, turnip patch, pig, and few chickens. Paved access neither necessary nor desirable."

A Best Friend at Last

If you live on a farm you have your pick of fine city dogs. Urbanites are pushovers for cute little puppies, but when a full-blown dog is anchored to the garage they have second thoughts. And so I came by this two-year-old beauty, a "yellow" Labrador who answers to the name of Heidi.

It was love at first sight. I saw her racing frantically about that small yard, and my mind's eye flashed her against a background of meadow and woodland, legs deep in grass, tail wagging, nose high and alert—calendar picture for dog lovers. And so it now is. She leads a dog's life, unfettered and free.

In the early morning from the upstairs window I see her amble into the woods on the river bank for a prebreakfast tidbit. Later I call at the back door and she comes bringing her dish, leaping and eager. She is Paul's supportive companion as she follows the plow down a furrow, patiently trotting, stopping now to sniff and to paw briskly for a field mouse. On days when we work at potato planting she hangs about the machinery, disappearing to the pond or the river for the swimming she loves, then returning to be certain we are there.

Coming home after nightfall I am welcomed by this frolicking beast who comes to the car, licks my hand, and escorts me to the kitchen in the darkness.

"See my new dog!" I say eagerly to people, like a little girl with new shoes; and by the nature of their response I sort them out, the dog lovers from the rest, those who share that warm flood of feeling for a cool nose, velvet ears, soft pleading eyes, quivering body, pink slobbering tongue.

There's no faking it; you feel it or you don't. Dog love is a new thing for me, and I have been among the ranks of the unresponsive enough years to know their pretenses. But like any lover caught up in the delirium of wanting and being wanted, I have to pity outsiders who look on and feel nothing. "I am the poorer for anything I don't enjoy," a wise old friend once said to me.

Waiting for Paul this afternoon by the barn well, I sink down beside this taffy-colored creature lying among golden dandelions. I babble the silly nothings to her that one whispers to a lover. She licks my face. Life has indeed acquired a new dimension.

Whelp Does Not Imply Help ⎯⎯⎯⎯⎯⎯⎯⎯⎯⎯

Once before we had pups around here; it was a totally unremarkable business. The female dog, the runt of somebody's litter, came to us by default. When she ran off and committed an indiscretion with the neighbor's German shepherd, nobody thought much about it. She appeared one morning with ten pups. Cute ones, I suppose. I wanted to guard my heart so I never went to the barn to see. Paul disposed of them and I never wanted to know how or where.

Later Peppy was spayed for what I remember as an exorbitant sum. There were no more puppies for Peppy who, I came to understand, was a Labrador Retriever. It didn't mean a thing to me.

But ah, what conditioning accomplishes in the snobbery department. It's fifteen years later and Peppy's successor is purebred and "registered." Somebody paid a lot of hard cash for her, then gave her to us with an envelope full of registration papers, pedigrees and health certificates. This time our "bitch" is "whelping." (The vocabulary comes with the papers.) And believe me, it's not nearly as simple as just having pups.

The complications begin with the mating. You don't just settle for the neighbor's mutt even though he may have a more impressive pedigree than your own dog. You must, of course, find a paramount stud of the same breed. I got on the phone and discussed the business with the owners of several studs. They talked of the weight of their dogs, the size of their heads, their field trial records, the champions in their lineage, and fees and shots and hip dysplaysia and a lot of other things that nearly put me in shock. I felt like a Chinese marriage broker. I limply hung up the phone and decided that dog breeding was not my bag.

Paul, in his no-nonsense way, located a handsome black Labrador up around the corner, quietly carried Heidi off every afternoon for a week, and the deed was accomplished. During those two months of incubation, people worried me with accounts of difficult dog births, of strangulations and rejections and smothering. Reason told me that a dog was capable of delivering a litter of pups; but could a registered bitch bred to a pedigreed stud for a handsome fee whelp unassisted? I had grave reservations.

The first five pups were born almost before we noticed. Heidi carefully carried them to a nest of old newspapers she had located in an outbuilding. When we found her we oh'ed and ah'ed and gawked, and I fretted. (Mistake No. 1.) Heidi crawled off to an inaccessible spot, leaving the first five cold and alone. Paul went to plow assuring me things would be fine.

About then a potato customer showed up and I mentioned my dog concerns. He turned out to be a Pekingese breeder and offered his assistance and advice. I listened to him. (Mistake No. 2.) He was aghast at the less than sterile setting of the kettle house. There were flies on these pups! Where was my "whelping pen"? They were getting cold. Better get a heating pad and a blanket. When were they born? Her first litter? Thought so. She's rejecting them. If they don't nurse within three more hours, they'll die. Better get the bitch out of that place and into this clean box with the other five or her milk won't come in.

Heidi had her own ideas. She growled at me, but she snarled at the Pekingese breeder. He took the hint and left. In desperation I decided Heidi was a better source of heat than a heating pad. Maybe she'd smother one in the process of giving birth to the others, but that would be better than losing all five. I carefully lifted them one at a time and laid them beside her. As I deposited the last one I picked up her dog dish to move it out of her way. (Mistake No. 3.) She snapped at my hand and crunched down on my little finger.

I dashed up to the field where Paul was plowing and frantically inquired if we should call a vet.

"No," he said in amusement, "I don't think we should call a vet. Dogs were having pups long before you went into the breeding business. Now just leave her alone."

We had nine lovely black pups. Heidi delivered, cleaned, fed, and accepted them all with a tender instinct for propagation that no dog breeder or kennel club or pedigree or complex vocabulary could negate. The moral of the story is, I suppose, the Lord helps those who whelp themselves.

Dog-Gone

Once again I am come to heartache—the lost-dog syndrome. Inexplicably, another of Heidi's puppies has disappeared from the pen. We have reconstructed the details of everyone's last encounter, but to no avail. He's gone. We have searched the farm, phoned the neighbors across the river, driven slowly and hopelessly up and down the back roads, walked the fields squinting into the horizon, called in our no-hope voices. Nothing. We made the sad trip to the dog pound, peered with eager promise at excited pets with equivalent hopes.

All through the day I watch from every window for the happy flag of an upright black tail. In all the trees and bushes and fencerows I see outlines of puppies, as you perceive the figures hidden in drawings for children. Every black thing that moves contains the black velvet promise of puppy fur.

The bright sun touches the day with beauty. Greens are greener, golds golder, reds more brilliant in the contrast. Light and shadow play through the clouds and through the thinning foliage. People come and go on pleasant autumn errands.

It should be the happy end of a successful harvest week. But through the day runs the sad obsessive shadow of a fat black puppy, lost, hungry, and bewildered somewhere.

For this aching heart there could have been only one satisfying picture, that black puppy taking shape against the autumn color. Alas, I never saw it. And the grief leaks out slowly, like a toothache that will not be numbed with resignation.

Chairman of the Board

In a moment of sheer bravado and libertarian zeal this winter I accepted a nomination to serve on the church board of trustees (the last bastion of male domination in most churches). The congregation was dumbfounded; but while they stammered around for arguments, I got elected. Then those lousy male chauvinists elected me chairman!

Since then it's been nothing but trouble. Every time my phone rings I tremble. No wonder men die young. Inevitably it's some angry church member or another trustee saying, "Hey, Patty . . ." and going on to catalogue a peck of problems.

First it was the church sign: the glass was broken. Feature an apprentice glazier working on a four-foot glass door in a February gale. Me. Then we had a small blizzard and somebody pointed out that the roof was leaking.

"Let's ignore it and hope it goes away," I said. It did. It wasn't as simple with the ailing furnace. "Thermostat don't shut off," says the old custodian. "Fire pot's bad. Need a new furnace." I take the short course on heat engineering.

"Hey, that light in the downstairs closet don't light. Keeps blowing a fuse. Better get somebody in here to look at it," says the old custodian. It's not the light, or the fuse, it turns out. It's the sump pump. I do two weeks of research on sump pumps, and then one of the other trustees brings in a Brand X he got wholesale from his brother-in-law.

Then there was the matter of purchasing a stepladder to clean the chandeliers. I go with my little rule and measure and order out a ten-foot stepladder.

"Too short," say the men after church one morning.

"'Tis not. All you have to do is set it up on the pews," say I, climbing to the top step and removing a globe to demonstrate. Guess who cleans the chandeliers.

"We gotta renew our oil lease," says the old custodian.

"Gee. I didn't even know we had a well," I said.

"No, I mean the fuel oil lease. We could save a lot of money." So now I have to go out and tilt with the oil merchants.

"That grass is getting pretty high," says the old custodian, "Better get somebody in here to mow it."

About that time the parsonage neighbor calls and wants to know if he can fence our little woodlot and pasture some sheep.

"How about including the parsonage yard," I suggest.

Next thing I know, the mother of the boy I have commandeered to mow lawns calls and wants to know what to do about gas.

"Unless you're into siphoning, you better buy it," I said.

That's the way February, March, and April went. Then in May we decided to refurbish the parsonage. And the problems really compounded. Do we go with paneling or dry wall? A well-placed crowbar in the heart of the plaster and we're with dry wall. Then we're into insulation, and into wiring, and there's a break in the soil pipe and we're into plumbing. I get a work party going on a Saturday and they take a three-hour lunch!

I'm establishing liaisons with all the electricians and plumbers and dry-wall contractors in the area. I'm on a first-name basis with all the hardware and lumberyard clerks. I'm learning all about eight-penny nails and shims and male and female plugs.

The only church member I haven't heard from is the treasurer. I've signed more invoices than there are spiders in the parsonage cellar. When she calls with the financial report I'm gonna file for bankruptcy and slit my throat.

"Where's Mom?" ask my kids.

108

"Where else? She's up at the parsonage scraping the calcium crud out of the bowels of the toilet with an old table knife," says my husband from his place at the kitchen sink.

Ah yes, send your daughter to a good liberal women's college, and these are the heights to which she will ascend.

How do the men feel about the female trustee? They're delighted. They go off to work every morning and Pat Leimbach stays home to troubleshoot. I've struck a great blow for women's rights. I'm sure they recognize it was long overdue. Me? I'm getting ulcers and an unlisted telephone. And next year when my term is up I'm going out and get a job as a maintenance superintendent at $20,000 per.

The Ladies of Monday Afternoon ─────────────────

My mother was neither a joiner nor a descendant of the staid old families of the village, so it was remarkable that she was invited to join the Study Club and equally remarkable that she accepted. Her important credential, I presume, was a rare college degree, and even though she had a pack of little kids and worked hard for a living, that degree carried a lot of weight.

The Study Club met on the first Monday of the month to discuss erudite subjects in a great deal more depth than I was ever persuaded anybody wanted to hear. (My interest in those days was mostly boys.) Mama spent the better part of one winter amassing material on the subject of Colonial Williamsburg, a pursuit I considered to be deadly dull, though I never said so. In my student years when I was writing a major paper on Robert Frost, I was tapped to do a program for her club. (Also done in a great deal more depth, I assure you, than anyone wanted to hear.)

They were a big-bosomed and stately bunch of ladies, gracious and genteel, every one. If scandal ever touched their lives, mention of it was discreetly avoided. Poised treacherously on the point of degradation on a back road or tempted by strong drink in some den of iniquity, the pious faces of the ladies of Monday afternoon always passed before me. They were a more formidable deterrent to sin than all the Heavenly Host. The Lord was a forgiving Father; I wasn't so sure about Mama's Study Club.

Their civic raisons d'être were two scholarship awards made to senior students in the fields of history and English. And who could have blamed them if the secret desire of every mother's heart was that her little George or Irma would one year merit the prize? I seem to remember my mother's scoffing at the "niggardliness" of the amount (that's the word she would have used) which they contributed from their meager dues. It was probably the year I got the award.

But they had certain prohibitions in the Study Club, and one of them was against earning money after the crass manner of bazaars and bake sales, box lunches and cake walks. I think they saw it as profane and undignified. The other prohibition was against food. A cup of tea was about all the indulgence they allowed themselves on club afternoons. Mama ventured the opinion that some of them were "a teeny bit lazy," or worse yet, "getting old and feeble." (In symbolic protest she and a ladyfriend who shared her viewpoint usually went out for dinner on first Mondays.) Once a year the group consented to partake of nourishment together, and that was the meeting my mother liked to host.

Dear, dear ladies. Their husbands dropped them off at 1:00 and picked them up at 4:00. They went home to their circumscribed routines. They read their *Atlantic Monthlies* in their Victorian parlors in the yellow glow of their silk-shaded bridge lamps. How I came to love them through the years for their ideals and their dreams.

Where are they now, the gracious ladies of Monday afternoon? Theirs was a society castigated and unmasked by the Sinclair Lewises and the Sherwood Andersons of the first half of the century. They faded slowly, and they changed like all of life. . . .

The women's clubs are with us yet, their ideals less constricting, their goals more ambitious. They are a new breed—freewheeling, freethinking, hardworking. The daughters of Monday afternoons live lives their mothers never dared dream of. They drive themselves cross town or cross continent. They meet nights so they can work afternoons; and if they aren't challenging men in the career world, they're ministering to society in some concrete way. They will tackle anything from building a hospital to changing the Constitution.

They are casual, purposeful, and unpretentious, with a strong sense of their own identity. They indulge their frivolous whims with abandon and freely acknowledge that they have personal problems.

They are more intent on living their dreams than in foisting them on their children. They face honestly the fact that this has always been a man's world, and they are intent on balancing the situation in a more than sneaky, seductive way.

I have to love them as well, for I am one of them.

Museum Piece

It's a setting to gladden the heart of a farm wife, midwinter—a warm kitchen making no demands, a hearthfire, a cup of tea. Outside, snow as far as the eye can see, in drifts and broken patches stretching across the rye to the fringe of the woods along the near side of the river. The opposite bank is a steep shale cliff making of the gorge a moat for my island and its "castle" of peace.

In the momentary seclusion of my tower I meditate upon a chive plant hauled home from the supermarket two weeks ago to garnish the place with green and lighten the mood of winter. Like a hand raised in silence it calms the clutter of this kitchen. Today it surprises me with the eruption of lavender blue blooms at the tips of its tendrils. "Your wild onion's going to seed," said the resident pragmatist this morning.

Alas, an emissary penetrates the peace with news of the world beyond the moat. She has seen a disturbing exhibition at the Oberlin museum. Have I seen it? It's the sort of cultural involvement one should find time for on a winter day; I forsake my retreat in pursuit of the art exhibit. A gallery of modern art is a kick in the head no matter how conditioned one is for the shock. There is always some whimsical oddity, some outrageous absurdity to snap your garter and offend your taste.

A blue and gold banner in the shape of a carpenter's saw floats from the ceiling. An assortment of fifteen or twenty white plastic cubes are in neat and sterile arrangement on the floor of the gallery along with an enormous tangle of wire fencing, four bundles of binder twine, a perpendicular rectangle of pale pink Plexiglas, a suspended wisp of diaphanous fabric, a four-sided gray ladder draped with writhing gray spaghetti, a delicate stairway ascending from nowhere to nowhere, and assorted other conversation starters.

111

The paintings, too, are provocative, though less jarring: a couple of black rectangles with white space between, a total canvas of café au lait, a strawberry pie with the polyethylene appeal of a Howard Johnson's menu, a gay garden of flowered fabrics in collage, a disembodied bathrobe set before with its own sculpture garden of broken marble statuary. . . .

Isolated at the side, the crowning obscenity of the whole exhibit, a baby carriage with an advanced condition of gray cancer, so ugly, so repulsive that one is drawn in evil fascination like a spectator to a hanging. Irregular gray protruberances "grow" from its every surface—a grotesquerie to sicken the soul.

"The blue and gold saw gets my vote," said my only companion in the gallery, a nearly bald fellow in wire rims and a red and black mackinaw.

"Whatever turns you on," I said, happy for a blithe spirit to help dispel the mood of evil emanating from that baby carriage. "What do you think of that tangle of wire over there?" I asked, indicating the fencing.

"Like the bramble bush it resembles, it would be a nice shelter for Brer Rabbit but a pain in the—— if you had to go through it. I suppose everything here can justify its existence in some way," he added thoughtfully.

"What about that abortion over there?" I asked, pointing to the cancerous baby carriage.

"I see dismembered bodies, carnage, excrement, garbage, filth, pornography, pollution—all the evils and the ugliness that beset us—deteriorating societies and their misery and crime." We fell then into animated conversation, bent on discovering what common search had brought us to this happening.

As we talked I gazed around the high-ceilinged gallery at the shapes and the textures and the colors embodied in the variety of art forms. By itself nothing seemed to make much sense, but there was a harmony about the whole that one could feel if not define.

Art imitates life, isn't that the premise? The sordid face of evil is an unfortunate aspect of the whole of life, so "Rosemary's Baby" in that carriage over there belongs to this exhibit. But there is always a compensating loveliness. Maybe it's a chive plant—or a guy in a red and black mackinaw. . . .

The air terminal in Cedar Rapids, Iowa, is not exactly the hub of the universe. Activity there on a normal Sunday is relaxed and sleepy—a grandmother or two hopping down to Moline, a handful of insurance salesmen leaving a weekend conference, a student going back to Chicago.

But when I passed through there one February Sunday, the place was jumping. A mass exodus to "fun city"—Las Vegas—was in progress. Some slick talkin' travel agent had placed a charter brochure with the right spark plug, and everybody was goin'. The few remaining behind as baby sitters had gone down with the kids to see the others off.

The mood was brave and gay, approaching hilarity. Every woman had called some other woman and they had agreed that "we" would wear pants suits. The men were programmed devil-may-carishly into turtlenecks and blazers. Hair was all newly teased and lacquered into place.

Standard baggage appeared to be two enormous suitcases, a carry-on garment bag, and one shoulder bag per celebrant.

"How long you guys staying?" I asked incredulously of one pack mule struggling through the melee toward the baggage check-in.

"Four days," he said. "She thinks she has to take everything she owns." (And he?)

The fun had begun and sitting by, watching, I envied the spirited crew. Oh, not the trip to Las Vegas, especially. I don't suppose it's my kind of place. When the stakes in a poker game hit a buck and a half, I fold. I can't even bear to watch other people lose money. But the experience of having a group adventure to savor ever afterward! The weeks of anticipation (perhaps the best part), sharing the extravagant plan with envious friends, the shopping trips! There'd have to be an outfit or two, a long dress perhaps that would not betray its origin as Cedar Rapids. (Of course she'll wear it next Christmas and apologize for the expense: "I got it for our trip to Las Vegas.")

I pondered the other things in those suitcases: a lounging robe of the sort not geared to scrambling eggs on school mornings, cameras with flash attachments and gobs of film, pictures of grandchildren, wigs, playing cards, a bottle of booze naughtily stashed away, or a little "portable bar," gift of a client of the firm last Christmas.

Ah, the fun they would have or fancy they were having: the Bacchanalian revels—eating and drinking too much and rising to "Bloody Mary mornings"; defying routine and sense by doing odd things at odd hours—staying up all night, swimming early in the morning, eating steak for breakfast.

And the memories, the "inside" jokes and the off-color stories, the box scores of celebrity viewing, the predictable accounts of somebody's winnings, and somebody's losses, amazing tales of thousands won and thousands lost by "the big players" (none of them from Cedar Rapids), memories of flirtations, innocent and not-so-innocent, and harsh words behind closed doors hastily loosed, leisurely repented.

Even as I contemplated their boisterous departure with its show of bravado, I pondered the return, equally noisy but relaxed and untidy, the baggage mass expanded with shopping bags full of over-priced novelties and gifts for kids and grandmas—the dispersal then of a community that would never exist again, but which had in these four days represented in an "alien land" the provincial security of Cedar Rapids and home.

The Country Parson

The Reverend F. Howard Maull is leaving. No minister ever stays long at Brownhelm Church. It's a first-ministry kind of place—small country congregation, low starting salary, modest parsonage. Every three or four years a young man moves on, another moves in.

The standard excuse for leaving a church, and every congregation has heard it, is: "I've achieved what I set out to achieve here," which has always said to me that either the guy lies a lot or had very limited goals in the first place. But Howard Maull isn't mumbling the usual platitudes of separation; and I respect him for that. He's leaving us in despair that the Christian ideal can ever be achieved in our conservative, capitalistic, bourgeois midst. Somebody ought to warn young ministers about Brownhelm Church. In fact, somebody ought to warn young ministers about churches—period.

Perhaps every minister's secret aim in taking a new charge is that the millennium will be achieved during his tenure. Surely it all looks good on the surface. He has been assiduously courted by the pulpit committee and the strengths of the congregation have been pointed up. The smiles are broad and the handshakes firm. The parsonage is clean and freshly redecorated. Everyone seems eager and ambitious; surely miracles could happen here.

But miracles don't happen, at least not perceptibly. The months pass and enthusiasm wanes. A handful of the faithful, hardworking and zealous, float to the top, and the majority sink back into apathy. The minister marries a few, buries a few, baptizes a few, confirms a few, alienates a few, wins a few. He makes his rounds and meets with his committees, and prays his prayers, and preaches his sermons, and nothing seems to change.

A year passes and then two. He realizes the honeymoon is over and he doesn't know when it ended. By now he knows the shortcomings of his congregation—that the serene and smiling faces often mask unhappy, tragic lives; that the shows of bravado conceal weakness and fear; that the open, generous natures have mean and narrow aspects—and disillusionment sets in.

The Reverend F. Howard Maull is not reverent in the classic ministerial tradition. He is, rather, irreverent in the antihypocritical style that epitomizes our era. He came not to make peace in Brownhelm, but to make waves, to stir us out of pious lethargy and create an awareness of injustice and need both in our midst and beyond.

Despite its rural character, Brownhelm Church has a history of liberalism rooted in a century and a half of exposure to seminarians from nearby Oberlin College, who always found our pulpit a green pasture for the latest heresies. It wasn't difficult for us to accept a long-haired liberal; it was, in fact, exciting. There was a great deal of wailing and lamentation and gnashing of teeth when the church members got together. And there was open argument when we met with the parson, which surely beats a lot of mealy-mouthed whispering behind his back.

We seldom agreed with him and were repeatedly shattered by his radical ideas. We granted him the right to be an individual, but reserved the right to be critical of the way in which his lifestyle conflicted with his ideology. He taunted us about our materialistic values and our bigotry, and we were defensive of our hard-won property and privilege. The antagonism and the frustration mounted.

His tenure in Brownhelm climaxed in his reading to the Board of

Deacons, along with his resignation, the text of Amos 5. Amos was a crude, unlearned shepherd who came in his rude garments of skin as a prophet to the Israelites and cried out in rage:

> *I hate, I despise your feasts,*
> *And I take no delight in your solemn assemblies.*
> *Even though you offer me your burnt offerings and cereal*
> *I will not accept them, and the peace offerings*
> *Of your fatted beasts I will not look upon.*
>
>   .   .   .   .   .   .
>
> *. . . . . let justice roll down like waters,*
> *And righteousness like an ever-flowing stream.*

Howard Maul feels that his tenure in Brownhelm has been in vain. But who can measure change or the provocations of it? I remind him of a line from Emerson, "Thou knowest not what argument thy life to thy neighbor's creed hath lent."

1976

The Bicentennial Minutes finally ticked away and we were left with a shroud of sagging bunting and plates of melted ice cream in nostalgic flavors of Minute Man Mint, Valley Forge Fudge, and Yankee Doodle Strudel. Or was there something more? For one who started the year 1976 with a large measure of Bah! Humbug! I must confess I enjoyed the "party." It was moving to realize that a nation that conducts seminars on the Uses of Power and Creative Divorce was the same nation that painted its garbage cans red, white, and blue and created winsome little fireplug people. Celebration, I am convinced, does good things for people.

I shall not soon forget 1976. I have a fine brass replica of the Liberty Bell, another in red and blue leaded glass, a commemorative plate from the nation's capital, and a bulging shelf of eagle and patriot glasses hauled home from Burger King and Burger Chef at Bicentennial bargain rates. It's not the same as having crystal paperweights from the Franklin Mint, but our experience of Shirley Temple pitchers and Mickey Mouse watches should warn us that those glasses may one day go on the block at Parke-Bernet.

More precious, however, is the memory of those glorious Fourth of July tall ships storming Manhattan like the Spanish Armada. To have been born in an era when we could share that as a nation is something to make the spine tingle. But even the local Fourth of July fireworks seemed a greater occasion than usual following six months of lift-off. I had another spine-tingling view in the Bicentennial year. From four miles above northwestern Illinois I looked down on a two-and-a-half-acre flag of flowers, "all that planted by one man," our pilot said. "I'll bet he had a woman helping him," said I to the pilot when I was getting off the plane.

Out in Nebraska I had the pleasure of viewing a needlepoint tapestry made by farm women throughout the state. They staged contests for the best design from each county and involved hundreds of people in creative endeavor—a woolen memoir of sod huts, windmills, and cowboys against the sky.

In like manner people all across the country—schoolchildren, senior citizens, community committees, ethnic groups, church congregations, service clubs—all were challenged to think about our heritage, individually and collectively. State and county fairs had afghans, quilts, and antique displays. Meetings were opened by color guards of Minute Men; people wore Colonial costumes to all manner of festive gatherings; lost Colonial skills were revived and nurtured. I was profoundly touched by one old man at a banquet I attended who had assembled a remarkable collection of all the nation's flags and explained each with a wealth of knowledge and an open sense of pride. He took me back to an unsophisticated time when the Grange Hall, the Legion, the VFW, and even the Town Hall seemed a lot more important than they have since become in our lives—to a time when Memorial Day nearly blew your mind, when people sang "The Star-Spangled Banner" right out loud and off-key.

Perhaps the most significant memento of the Bicentennial left in our community (for who knows how long?) is a huge Colonial flag painted on the outcropping of an abandoned quarry along the Interstate. It appeared there anonymously on a surface long marred by obscene graffiti. In a strange way it seems to symbolize that long year of celebration. For a time, at least, our better impulses surfaced in a patriotic flowering that obscured the ugliness.

BROADER MEADOWS

We shall not cease from exploration
And the end of our exploring
Will be to arrive where we started
And know the place for the first time.
T. S. Eliot, *Four Quartets*, "Little Gidding"

When I sat on the culvert as a little girl and looked down the road wondering if
I would ever go anywhere, I never conceived of giving speeches for farm groups
around the states, or cheering my sons at motorcycle races abroad. I couldn't have
known I would have a foster family in Austria or a Danish sister-in-law, or a
husband in search of bigger and better snows.

The wonder of all this perambulation is that it has only drawn me closer to the
land.

Overview

It's early morning and I am aboard a Convair C5 homeward bound
from a small town in southern Minnesota. It's my first real look at the
Great Plains and it stirs dormant emotions. I knew that agriculture
was the leading American industry but the geographic proportions of
the fact never hit me until this gray dawn as I look down on these
thousands of farms laid out in mile after mile of square plots. One can
easily measure distance by counting the sections.

And in the corner of each section what humanity adds—a house,
barn, silo, garage, a cluster of grain bins and any number of tiny
outbuildings, all as neat and orderly as the model farms we built as
projects in grade school.

No farm was ever so orderly and predictable as it appears from this
height. The burdensome details of farm production are as obscure to
observers at 2000 feet as they are to those who lift its end product

119

from the supermarket shelves. But my intimate involvement with all that production detail, my awareness of life lived in those farmhouses draws me earthward in spirit.

Tiny lighted windows in the barns tell of farmers out milking or feeding the stock. Some have finished the chores and are warming themselves now at breakfast, talking of what is to be done after school. From this height big yellow buses are visible, moving over their routes, lights aglare. I think of the commotion prevailing in each house as that bus approaches.

To get this perspective on American agriculture, you have to take something like the Blue Goose of North Central Airlines running between Kansas City and Minneapolis, the "milk plane of the Great Plains," intimate with silos and grain elevators, putting down at fifteen-minute intervals in places like Fairmont, Minn. (elevation 1,161), Worthington (population 10,000, home of an Armour packing plant and Campbell's Chicken Soup), Mankato (home of the State University).

A few people get off, a few more get on; several cartons of freight are unloaded, several more brought aboard. The stairway folds up and in. On to the next stop. A red sun creeps over the horizon and full day is upon us by the time we reach "the cities," local jargon for Minneapolis and St. Paul.

There I transfer to a jet and the Cleveland flight. We soar above the clouds and the features of the rural landscape are lost to me; but I won't soon forget the impact of that early morning peek down upon my landsmen, the realization that I am part of something so individual, yet so vast.

In Transit

The Country Wife has spent a good part of the winter running around the country giving speeches, telling people (who already know) what it is to be a country wife. And believe me, that's not much like *being* a country wife.

The glamor of air travel is created by the excitement attendant to it—weeks of research and anticipation, the big call to make "my reservation," leisurely packing, the trip to the airport with envying well-wishers, the eager faces when you return. T'ain't the same when you drive yourself there, drop off a car, wrestle with your own bags, emplane and deplane alone, and drive home to a family who are little involved with where you were and what you did, and much engrossed, as they should be, with what they were up to in your absence.

You can't afford the time luxury of building up to a trip and easing back in. It has to be Pow! you're gone; Bang! you're back. At 5:05 I'm over at Miller's delivering a truckload of potatoes; at 5:30 I've exchanged my jeans for a skirt and I'm dashing for the airport clutching a bottle of shampoo, a muddled handbag of what I hope will amount to a change of clothes, a tattered portfolio, my knitting, and the daily mail I didn't have time to read. If I'm lucky, I have a few minutes at the airport to sink down on my knees and "pack." If not I keep clutching till I crash in a Holiday Inn somewhere.

But I thrive on confusion, and this is nothing if it isn't confusing. Most of the pleasure derives from the people one meets. An avid people collector is never lonesome or bored. My prize "item" for the winter was a director of the World Bank, a specialist in Middle East affairs who had been a friend to Nasser. It is to my credit that I needled him to do most of the talking.

Then there was the dear little grandmother carrying an enormously heavy carton of homemade grape jelly to her children in Florida. She scolded me for walking three and a half miles through the terminal sharing the burden, and expressed her thanks and relief with "If you ever get to St. George, Utah, everybody knows Mary Williams. . . . " She thinks I'll forget . . . .

Or the widowed fireman from Pipestone, Minnesota, on a holiday junket to Lake Tahoe to lose a year's savings. "Gee, Pat," he said, when I left him in Rapid City, "You really oughta' come along. We could have a swell time." I assured him that some merry widow would find him and that he would have a blast.

The ones I enjoy especially are the pretty young things I can mother, like Kathy LoPresti of San Francisco, who confessed after a few minutes that airplanes terrify her and melted into puddles of insecurity all over O'Hare Terminal when the planes were two or three hours behind schedule. Or the girl en route to a rendezvous with her fiancé whom I befriended when I observed that she was struggling with daisy loops in her embroidery. She needed me.

But not so much, perhaps, as Clement Izzi, the industrial tape salesman who sat on the plane in Green Bay hand-sewing a smock for his girl friend. I gave him a few pointers and a couple weeks later received by United Parcel a huge box of "silver tape," to my sons' delight (motorcycle racers use kilometers of the stuff).

Sometimes I make friends because I need comforting myself. In such a way I fell into conversation with a reserved and quiet attorney's wife from Saginaw. It turned out we had granola and poetry and *The New Yorker* in common. "I would have sat here in silence," she said, "if you hadn't spoken." And it had been a delightful encounter.

There's a fascination, too, about the conversations you hear, but are not party to. "I did have a job," the girl was telling the fellow across from her in the coffee shop, "until I booked my boss on a plane to Los Angeles when he thought he was going to New York."

Or the young woman going home to confront her father and the "scheming floozie" he had married, who kept telling her seatmate, between nips on a bottle of Thunderbird, "Ain't they gonna be surprised when I walk in this mornin'."

And there's the flirtatious salesman on the midnight flight who strikes up a conversation walking down the ramp and tries to coax you into the bar for a nightcap.

"A farmer's wife! Oh, that's rich!" I think he thought he heard "farmer's daughter."

Unsolicited Testimony

Zola Hanthorne drove me to the airport in McCook, Nebraska, kissed me on the cheek, and packed me off on Frontier Airlines with a quart of homemade mincemeat, a pint of strawberry jam, and a winter "bouquet" of milo wrapped in a plastic breadwrapper. Twenty-four hours earlier we had been strangers. Now it seemed that I was "family" and my departure cause for a lump in the the throat. That's the open and generous way of farm people.

In 1891 Grandpa Hanthorne homesteaded the original quarter section of two thousand acres Zola and Richard and their son Ellis now farm. Sound like a millionaire farmer's spread? Not when you understand dry-land farming and its rotation of wheat, milo (a corn-family grain used for cattle feed), and fallow. The fallow year aims to store sufficient moisture to produce a crop the other year. The "crop" on this farm is around 40 bushels per acre of either wheat or corn. Divide the yield by two (allowing for the fallow year), subtract the sixty thousand dollars that Richard calculates he spends annually to produce a crop, and well—you just better love to farm or you wouldn't bother.

"You wouldn't believe how hard that man works," said Zola. "He was out at six this morning doing chores," and the night I stayed for supper he came in at eight-thirty, a long day for a man of sixty-four.

"Wouldn't you hate to work in an automobile plant?" he said, as we watched the ten o'clock news. "All day at the same dull job, year in and year out. On the farm you work the same job for a couple weeks, and then you do something else." Generous wages or not, he preferred his 14-hour days, though he hadn't had a vacation for four years.

"I was born just a few feet from where you're sitting," he said, "and a few years back I built Mama this new house right around the old one." It was a comfortable yellow brick, modest by Eastern standards, surrounded by a green yard and flowers painfully won from the prairie sands with persistent watering.

Zola clearly loved the place and would never take it for granted. She brought out a yellowed photograph of the old homestead as visible testimony to her gratitude.

"Did she show you her canning?" Richard asked me, then proudly led me to the tidy fruit cellar lined with apricots, peaches, pears, pickles, cherries, tomatoes, beans, corn—all the fruits of Zola's garden. He pointed out the two freezers stocked with their own beef and pork and chicken. His pride in her accomplishments reflected her pride in his.

We sat over breakfast the morning I left and he bragged about Zola's jam. "That's the best jam you'll ever eat," he said, and it was he who insisted I take a jar home. "Did you taste that bacon?" he said, pushing the platter toward me. "We butcher that ourselves."

They shared a reminiscence of their lives—of farming with a team of horses, of the dust bowl days and the Great Depression, when he married the teacher at the local one-room schoolhouse.

They talked of their struggle to educate their children—a teacher, a doctor, and a farmer—and of the satisfaction these three brought to their lives. Richard told of winter blizzards when the steers would be trapped in the canyons and lost. They spoke of this year's drought and of falling farm prices: "Hog market's about as healthy as a leper colony, down to thirty-five cents today—sausage in the store's still a dollar fifty-nine." The underlying tone of the conversation was of security born of diligence and frugality in the face of great odds. This is perhaps the most abundant fruit of the American prairie.

As Nebraska receded into the clouds beneath me, I glanced at the magazine the stewardess had proferred. "Debbie Reynolds Talks About Men, Money, and Sex." I smiled to myself, considering the contrast between what I'd learned from Richard and Zola Hanthorne, this unglamorous little farm couple on the stark and lonely stretches of southwest Nebraska, and what I might learn from the glamorous, articulate, and much-favored Debbie Reynolds. Sad that the people who know what's important and real in life seldom tell their stories.

*M*om's Place

If you have read James Michener's book *Centennial*, you may feel that you've already learned more about the South Platte Valley than you ever really wanted to know. But I think I discovered a bit of color there that Michener overlooked.

Mom's Coffee Shop in Merino, Colorado, stands in the shadow of the grain elevator across the railroad from the fertilizer depot a long stone's throw north of the South Platte.

It's a diner, after the vanishing breed of converted streetcars, newly splashed with white paint. The parking lot is dusty and weed-fringed. The windows are red-sashed and hung with cottage curtains. The only hint of the extraordinary is a total lack of brand advertising—Coca-Cola signs and the like.

If you are not obsessed, as I am, with a recurring vision of a friendly little eatery where the food is like home (before Birdseye and Banquet) and the prices circa 1955, you could easily speed past Mom's place in this nondescript village on Route 6 in anticipation of swinging, sophisticated Denver and the Rockies beyond. All it says is "Mom's Coffee Shop" in amateurish red script on a white board.

It was half-past breakfast and I was reluctant to leave the Colorado farm country where I had been received like a native daughter. I hit the brakes and backed up. A little handwritten notice on the window said, "Step up." I stepped up and into an epicure's delight. The aroma of fresh cinnamon rolls filled the place, and I surrendered my appetite to "Mom."

She's a plump and pleasant sandy-haired widow on the other side of fifty who chatted with me as she ate her breakfast pancakes in the end booth. "With nine kids you learn a lot about cooking," she told me. "But that was about all I knew how to do when my husband died last year. I could have gone into Sterling and worked in a café for a dollar an hour, I guess. This place was shut down and the folks at the factory wanted somebody to open it. So I decided to try it. The kids all helped.

"I didn't know nothing about restaurant meals, so I just said, 'We'll do it like we do at home,' and it seems to be working out."

"Mom" gets up at 5:00 to start the dough for the breakfast rolls and the raised doughnuts which she also bakes. She opens up at 6:00 and serves breakfast for the boys at the elevator or farmers in transit between their scattered fields.

"A lot of the farmers come in midmorning for coffee breaks. Boy! We never done that when we was running the farm. At lunch the folks come over from the Wisdom Plant where they make amusement park equipment, and some of the kids come from school on their lunch hour.

"We have a daily special for a dollar twenty-five," she said. "Cabbage pockets on Monday; 'hobo dinners' on Tuesday; hot beef sandwich on Wednesday; fried chicken on Thursday; barbecued beef on Friday; chicken 'n' noodles on Saturday. We bake everything ourselves—pie and cake and rolls. If I'd a known what a headache the paper work is, though, I'd a never started. One of the girls helps me, and she does real good. We close at six and get out of here by seven-thirty or eight."

I didn't ask Lottie Cline if she was making more now than a dollar an hour, but she has three employees and she's running her own show. I'm sure she's making a lot of people exceedingly content in Merino, Colorado. She certainly "made" my day. For forty-one cents I had coffee, a homemade cinnamon bun, and a slice of life that will nourish me through many a sterile preportioned meal in the neon palaces along America's freeways.

You can have Howard Johnson and Colonel Sanders, Arthur Treacher and Ronald McDonald. I'll take "Mom" Cline any old day of the week—especially Monday. I like the sound of those cabbage pockets.

Where the Beefalo Roam . . .

When you drive northwest from Grand Island, Nebraska, in February, pass through Hazard and Broken Bow and Dunning-on-the-Dismal River you might fear, as ancient mariners did, that you would soon fall off the map. The Sand Hills in winter are not the most inspiring place you'll ever drive through—mile after mile of low grayish grass-covered hills punctuated at long intervals by a windmill, a water trough, a few head of cattle. Houses, trees, and settlements are almost nil. There's a general lack of things to stir the imagination.

My good luck in the experience was in having a "tour guide" who knew the area and loved it with good-natured detachment. Like any enthusiastic guide, Jack Martin expressed regret that I was not seeing the region in its prime season, but he proceeded to translate its April characteristics to February.

"You never saw so many wildflowers of varying colors," he said, "as grow along the roadsides and among these grasses. And when the Yucca blooms it's glorious." He told me of a spring morning after a rain-washed night when he'd traveled this road. "I came to the top of a rise; a buck and doe and several small deer stood against the sky. The cattle were in the valley drinking at a windmill tank. A great blue heron was gliding down into a water hole. I pulled off the road, turned off the engine and just sat there."

He described the natural hazards of the area, showed me where the extreme drought of the past season had allowed the grass to loosen or where cattle had trampled paths along fencerows, destroying the grass cover, and the persistent wind started a condition called a "blow out," creating great troughs, then gulleys and valleys of open sand, ultimately allowing whole hills to shift.

He looked with great concern upon flatter fertile areas where irrigation prompted owners to try to field-crop the land. "That should never be allowed to happen," he said in a tone that retained a memory of dust bowl tragedy. He showed me where fire had destroyed hundreds of acres of laboriously planted national forest. "Throwing out cigarettes in this territory is cause for native rebellion," he said.

Jack Martin knew who lived up every ragged lane disappearing up a draw, and the lore of their lives added to the color. We passed an arrow at a crossroad that said "Uptown Stapleton" and he chuckled. "You oughta' see Uptown Stapleton," he said.

"Is it different from 'Downtown'?" I asked.

"Never been able to tell," he said.

We stopped for lunch at the Cowpoke Café in Thedford ("Uptown or Down?" I asked) where Jack promised me the best steak in the world. We ran into a friend of Jack's who ate with us. "Who are all these strangers in town today?" asked Jack. "They're a bunch of fellows promoting 'beefalo' meat. That's a beef-buffalo sixty-forty percent cross," said the friend. "Just how do you achieve that sixty-forty ratio?" Jack asked in amusement.

Farming in the Sand Hills deals almost exclusively with grass-fed cattle, which leaves a rancher a sad margin of cushion in very lean cattle years. (Farmers through the ages have survived by letting income from one crop "cushion" another. A bad year in hay might be offset by a good year in corn, for example.)

As we ate our steak (not the best in the world) the two men talked. A few cattlemen wandered in for coffee and were introduced. Bit by bit the picture of the rancher took shape in my mind and the "Minimum Requirements for Ranching" somebody had given me once took on credibility:

1. A wide brimmed hat, a pair of tight pants, and a pair of two-hundred-dollar boots.
2. At least two head of livestock, preferably cattle; one male, one female.
3. A new air-conditioned pickup with a gooseneck trailer (for horse) long enough to make a splash parked in front of the café in town.
4. Two "leopard" dogs to ride in the bed of the truck.
5. A forty-dollar horse and a four-hundred-dollar saddle.
6. A gun rack for the rear window of the pickup, big enough for walking stick and rope.
7. A place to keep the cows; a little land too poor for crops.
8. A spool of barbed wire, cedar posts, and a bale of prairie hay to haul around in the truck all the time.
9. Credit at the bank.

I have a faded green spot on the seat of my white slacks, testimony to an idyllic hour passed on a prairie meadow.

I was in South Dakota last September when five or six months of drought had made some areas look like a moonscape and others like a stage set for "Grapes of Wrath." I felt like Dorothy awakening in the Land of Oz returning here last week to a Technicolor wonderland of purple and gold hayfields interspersed with shimmering acres of heading wheat and barley. There must be a few special days in the year when the light yields full sway to shades of color, and I hit those days this first week in June.

The alfalfa and sweet clover along the roadsides crowd right up to the pavement like border plants on a garden path. Birds dart back and forth twittering—swallows and "canaries" and red-winged black-birds. There are butterflies—orange and black monarch and small yellow ones—and bees in profusion and a waving of native prairie grasses the beauty of which I wouldn't attempt to transcribe. It's about 70°, there's a sweet little breeze, and I wouldn't be altogether unhappy to lie down and die. I open the car windows wide and let the perfume of blooming hay blow through, tune the car radio to country western, and have myself a South Dakota "high."

The only "nuisance" plant among the luxuriant greens is mustard, which in its golden June bloom is still a treat to the passerby. I pick a bouquet for a friend I haven't yet met in Aberdeen.

Tiny pocket gophers and ground squirrels sit on their hindquarters on the pavement and gaze impishly about, then scurry away. The furry bodies of dead relatives litter the highway. They remind me of naughty kids intent on playing where their mothers have told them they absolutely must not.

In South Dakota I will be speaking to four electric cooperatives in four little towns. The annual co-op meeting is one of the wingdings of the year in these small farm communities. The firemen throw a barbecue, a little carnival is set up on the vacant lot next to a service station and at the "the-atre" they show cartoons for the kiddies.

On a banner strung between the bank and the hardware store, or on a big cardboard box at the crossroads beneath the water tower, it says, "Rural Electric Co-op Meeting Tonight!" You follow the stream of people to the only place in town big enough to hold them all—the high school. After the meeting and the speech, everybody files out for an intermission. A few go to the tavern downtown. A combo tunes up for a square dance.

The country wife goes back to the Hilltop Hotel. (The "hill" was created when the highway piled up dirt for an overpass above the railroad.) It isn't what you'd call an exciting place to pass a night, but after a day with the bees and the butterflies and the hayfields, the only thing that's important is knowing that I can open the curtains of this small room and the prairie moon will shine in unobscured.

Patchwork Perspective

Some impressive vistas of America are the exclusive possession of the airborne—it isn't fair, but that's the way it is. Even the northeastern Iowa farmer who holds title to this broad acreage of the Mississippi watershed northwest of Dubuque can't appreciate this aspect of its beauty as easily as the computer salesman flying from Milwaukee to Des Moines.

Anyone who flies over the prairies of the Midwest must acknowledge that the American heart beats to the rhythm of the square mile. (How will the square kilometer ever vanquish the square mile?) Here and there, however, the prairie is punctuated with rolling hills where farmers have risen to the challenge of producing crops and preserving their topsoil with the practice of contour farming. And in the patterns they form they defy the square mile. Fitting and planting a field crossways to a slope is an ancient phenomenon. But American farmers, spurred by the crisis of the dust bowl era, advanced it to an art form. There is a precise formula for the width of these contour strips which relates to the steepness of the slope—thus, the visual effect is one of geometric rhythm and beauty.

Strip cropping is a practice that is combined with contouring for minimum erosion. Strips of open-soil crops like corn or sorghum are alternated with strips of forage or hay crops that have extensive root systems to catch and hold the water. In long steep situations, a system of terracing is practiced with permanent grass waterways easing the water down and across hills to lower terraces.

The airplane and aerial photography are indispensable tools of the Agriculture Department's Soil Conservation Service, which has been extremely helpful to farmers in diagnosing and dealing with erosion and other problems. Drainage patterns, field sizes, crops, plant diseases, and plant nutrition can all be determined from the air. But these are agricultural facts best appreciated by the Iowa farmer. The patterns belong to the computer salesman, the Coast-bound executive, the fancy-free vacationer taking in the scene—who will, one hopes, appreciate the genius and skill of the men who bring this patchwork into being. God hath wrought wonders, indeed. But looking down on the contour-tilled panoramas of southeastern Ohio, Kentucky, Tennessee, Pennsylvania, northern Alabama, southwestern Wisconsin or any of many others in the United States, one must be impressed by what man has added.

Last of the Freeloaders

There was an extended period in most of our lives when trips were not planned from Point A to Point B, but rather from Friend A to Friend B to Relative C. It wasn't so much a matter of saving money as it was a choice between going or staying home. There was simply no money for motels, or their tourist court forerunners, tiny cottages built after the simplicity of a kindergarten drawing—door, window, steeply pointed roof. There were also big old moth-eaten, down-at-the-heels hotels in the center of all the towns.

Or for a dollar or two you could stay in some widow lady's musty upstairs bedroom with its high Victorian bed, marble-topped washstand, and sagging easy chair spruced up with antimacassars—a tourist home. You had to sacrifice some privacy to the widow who sat conspicuously around the front parlor and asked a lot of questions; but the tourist home appealed to the provincial sort for whom any trip was a great adventure and who took a homely pleasure in telling the widow all about it.

The tourist courts and the tourist homes and the woe-be-gone hotels have passed. There is money now for the tiled, carpeted, French Provincial luxury of the Holiday or Ramada Inn. If I'm off somewhere to give a speech, somebody else pays the bill with BankAmericard ease, and I don't have to go slinking in as of old to inquire the price and stall with, "Well, we'll see. . . ."

But how soon it all palls, the carbon conformity of the Sheratons and the Hiltons and the Best Westerns. How one longs for the personality of a friend's home and the person of a friend. And so I call them, my friends, saying "Guess who's at the airport?" or "I'm coming right through Millersville at about 9:30."

Last week it was Tom Fitzgerald—handsome and promising young bridegroom of 23 grown suddenly 50 and white-haired standing there in O'Hare at midnight in his Saturday afternoon Little League jacket to retrieve this stray cat from the country.

He drove me home to Wilmette, and in half an hour skimmed the top off the intervening decades, giving me mini-portraits of the six most important people in his life, Mary Alice and the five young Fitzes. We sat up late over a glass of wine, Tom and Mary Alice and I, collecting the lost years, polishing forgotten dreams.

My experience teaches me that old friends become remote friends if you do not inflict yourself upon them. Suppose I had not called the Fitzgeralds saying, "Hey, I'm on my way to Chicago, and I need a bed for the night."

I didn't NEED a bed. Howard Johnson had plenty. The Fitzgeralds would have had more sleep. Tom wouldn't have been late for his morning's appointment, but I never would have had those word portraits that said more about success than all the trappings of affluence. I never would have seen Billy Fitzgerald dawdling over his toast looking like what you'd invent if you invented nine-year-old kids—a pair of blue eyes peering through freckles and a mop of red hair—telling you about his poster for the book fair contest (You kin win $5 worth of books!) and his hunch that the Mets might win the pennant.

There's something about sleeping between company sheets on the twin bed of an absent college girl among the summer camp sand candles, and the Sierra Club posters, about rummaging around in the medicine chest for toothpaste and Band Aids that puts you on terms of intimacy with life you never lived.

Call it freeloading or what-you-will. In my book it's the sacred rite of friendship.

On the Wings of the Morning

The new Galt House is a reconstruction of a famous landmark on

Louisville's cotton wharf. Its cool, dim lobby in panels of red brocade suggests an elegant time when rich planters with gold-headed canes and diamond shirt studs passed through attended by black footmen. From the balconies, the broad quays, and the brick footpaths one can look beyond the concrete freeways to the expanse of Ohio River and conjure a vision of side-wheelers, tobacco auctions, King Cotton, and river commerce.

A farmer's wife fortunate enough to be sent to such a place expenses paid should be expected, I suppose, to wear little white gloves, carry a parasol, and stand demurely about waiting for gentlemen to defer to her femininity.

She is certainly not expected to show up at the front door in a red track suit at six in the morning and go charging off into the predawn darkness, not in this deteriorating riverfront neighborhood, surely!

Adventure and discovery, I have learned, belong to those who embrace the unexpected, so when a lean, lithe, red-haired jogging nut at the Galt House conference challenged me to a sprint across the bridge to Indiana and offered me his spare track suit, I was quick to arrange the rendezvous.

It was a sweet "Loua'v'lle" morning, warmish and damp, slightly breezy. The bridge hung two blocks upriver against the emerging dawn, a giant erector set strung with lights whose reflection shimmered in the water below.

En route to the bridge we peered down through dusty windows into a number of dreary businesses carrying on their struggles for survival in the low-rent districts—an antique shop, a print shop, a used-paper warehouse, an Oriental oddities boutique.

To the early workers, a faceless stream masked behind the headlights of the autos crowding the bridge, we were idiots, red blurs against the gray-riveted girders.

Now high above the riverfront highways and the railroad spurs that serve the docks, we passed over the water itself. The great white eye of a barge approaching from the direction of dawn vacillated to and fro across the surface of the river.

Ahead was the Indiana shore, where the Colgate Palmolive Peet Company identified itself with a thousand light bulbs against the darkness, and for a premium threw in the time—a gigantic red clock. It was 6:30 A.M., Indiana soap-selling time.

We "coasted" finally downhill on the Indiana side, where the bridge approach extended over a scattering of mean housing lots with backyards and fences and ramshackle outbuildings, everything exposed at this height.

We stopped again, looking through the tops of bare trees, into lighted kitchens, pondering the life that proceeded there beneath the bridge amid the traffic's roar.

"Listen!" said my red-haired companion. "Do you hear it . . . the cardinal singing? If I'm ever reincarnated I want to be a cardinal."

I strained to hear, and sure enough, the bright insistent "bir DEE, bir DEE" of the cardinal sounding forth against terrific odds.

"I've always thought that if I were reincarnated I'd like to be a buzzard," I said. "They float so ethereally on the air currents."

They turned then, the "cardinal" and the "buzzard," and flew back slowly to the Kentucky shore, back to the Galt House, back to prim, proper respectability and the day.

The Country Wife at the Shore

When I was a young bookworm boring my way through *Tom Swift* and *The Rover Boys* there was a puzzling discrepancy in finding my heroes off the home turf. Somehow the Bobbsey Twins in the Orient or the Hardy Boys in Madagascar was unsettling. I have the same unsettled feeling about the Country Wife these days as she crisscrosses the New York-Vermont border at 2:00 A.M. searching for a rustic lodge someone assures her is there, or sits (as at the moment) in the white sand of the Gulf of Mexico staring at her feet shod in winter boots. But a lot of people are off these days to places they never dreamed they would see. And some of them are farmers.

I'm down here for one day to speak to soybean farmers of the panhandle about 60 miles inland, but something told me I deserved a look at the Gulf, a plate of shrimp, and an educational drive through the countryside.

On the trip down I pondered the way in which one's feeling about a region is influenced by the literature one has read. The rich alcoholic planter I met in the airport seemed to have stepped from a Faulkner novel.

"Wheya' y'all from, Dahlin'?" he asked, and when I told him, he related his own arrogant beginning at the age of nine supervising "forty mules and forty niggas."

Driving through the little town of Marianna with its antebellum houses, its streets hanging heavy with liveoaks and Spanish moss, its yards abloom in camellias and redbud, I am reminded of the town where Thomas Wolfe grew up.

Along the red country roads the weathered shacks with their tin roofs still tell a story of poverty and inequality. Memories of Erskine Caldwell's poor whites haunt me as I pass through the scrub pine that lies between the tillable land and the Gulf.

I stop for a quarter hour to wander about the graveyard of the Abyssinian Methodist Episcopal Church.

"Here lies Mary Roberson, wife of Calvin. Her joys are past. Her work is done. She sought the light, the victory won." Rubin Sylvester, Minnie Riley, Esau Holden, Harding Hill sleep, fitfully I think, beneath concrete slabs scrawled with their names. George Tanner's epitaph, "P.F.C. Engr. Corps. WWI," tells all there is to tell with pride. A pink plastic crucifix expresses what there is of hope. I stand gazing at a family plot carelessly guarded by a rusty fence, and a yellow butterfly lights upon me. On that note of "victory" I left.

I have brochure visions of a broad royal palmed avenue gracing the coastline from Pensacola to Tampa, so it is with a shock that I confront the reality of the Panama City strip—screaming neon, peeling pastel paint, gimmicky amusement parks, shops full of kitsch, a depressing string of motels, hotels, condominiums, retirement cottages, mobile homes. Behind it all, the blue backdrop that gives it meaning. (Is there a body of water that could justify this parade of horrors?)

My impulse is to fade away to the pine in the bayous and the soothing quiet of the Abyssinian Methodist Church yard. But having come so far I am determined to see the water. I climb down over a scrappy-looking dune littered with broken bottles and milkshake cartons. I nestle against the sand embankment, and now it spreads before me, this miracle of creation, the Gulf of Mexico. Only a plastic breadwrapper blown into the coarse curly grass distracts one from the perfection. This panorama of blue-green sea and blue-gray-white sky, this picture-puzzle challenge of color shades, is this the womb of hurricanes? Far out at the center of the scene the sun through the overcast sends a silver sparkling track toward the shore.

The couple shelling along the beach are a cliché of white hair, tan paunch, ample bosom, and Bermuda shorts. Maybe they're Minnesota farmers. There's a Midwest joke about "C.B.M. crop rotation" (corn, beans, and Miami). By golly, if the Bobbsey Twins could go "abroad," is it inconceivable that a day may come when the country wife and the country husband (ample-bosomed and paunched) could cozy up to a white sand dune, read the commodity reports, and decide that today's the day to call the elevator and tell them to sell the soybeans?

The Meadows of Bohemia

Some mothers cheer from bleachers and grandstands; others lend support in auditoriums and concert halls. My own pilgrimage after my sons' enthusiasms has led me through forests and deserts, over mountains and valleys, along riverbeds, logging roads, fire trails, and country lanes, and out onto an assortment of meadows in both America and Europe—wherever a trailbike will go and a lot of places, I think, where nobody should go.

For seven years Dane has ridden on the American team in the International Six-Day Trials, and some years Mom tagged along as team mother. It's not exactly like being a den mother, but there are similarities.

We all brought back souvenirs from Czechoslovakia. Dane has a gold medal and a checkered flag. Two of our number returned with Polish soldiers' caps gleaned from a day of camaraderie with the guards at the Polish border. Another brave chap caught in the act of "ripping off" the Czech and the Russian flags from a display of eighteen was stunned to have them given him as a gift.

What I brought home from Czechoslovakia to remember ("Souvenir" as the French would say) are the meadows. There are a number of them up in Bohemia that "belong" to me. They are the meadows where I sat watching for our motorcyclists to pass. (Each rider starts at a given time and is due at appointed places at timed intervals.) For spectators there is time for contemplation of the sort too often lacking in a vacation.

135

The meadow behind the village of Vrklabi was reached by picking stepping-stones across a shallow creek, passing through someone's chicken yard, and climbing the hill. From it one had a long perspective of the village as well as a view of the racers arriving from the "outback" and wending their way down the country lane past the tiny onion-towered shrine and into the beehive of activity that was the service check. I shared that meadow with a hundred enthusiastic schoolchildren who cheered every rider who passed, no matter what his country of origin. A few harried schoolteachers vainly attempted to curb their mounting exuberance.

Impressive too was the long sweep of meadow stretching on either side of the highway near Valterice where one afternoon we saw a half dozen women raking the hay into windrows with long wooden forks. I thought of my neighbor women and myself working together in Ohio fields, recalling Robert Frost's words "Men work together . . . whether they work together or apart."

It was not sheer accident that my meadows were picturesque. I spent the week watching the Six-Day Trials with a professional photographer who sought to capture the character of the country as well as the esprit de corps of the motorcycle racers. The meadow we chose one morning overlooked a wainscoted cottage of brown and gray garnished with a great flourish of yellow flower garden. From my vantage point on the hill I looked down onto a gay clothesline through the branches of a gnarled pear tree and wondered if life within that ancient cottage had altered as little as its exterior in the past hundred years.

The meadow at Vitkovice was a steep one cleared in the midst of great tracts of forest. It stretched downhill to the swift and stony stream that had through the centuries carved this deep valley. Two roads and two streams converged at the base of the meadow, giving rise to a bridge, a guesthouse, and a cluster of small commerce. From the upper edge of the meadow I was able to peer in the upstairs window of an old hay shed and see what one might expect to see in the loft of an old shed—a broken hay rake. I sat there in the afternoon sun writing postcards, wanting so much to send with those cards a sensation of that lovely meadow.

There were other meadowscapes that provided slices of life—the one where the young couple walked with their *kinderwagen,* he pushing the carriage and she trailing behind picking sunflowers; the meadow where I saw an old couple at day's end, pushing a small two-wheeled cart heaped high with hay, she carrying a rake and scythe over her shoulder; the rain-soaked meadows of the sixth day of the race, lined with arrays of colorful umbrellas under which stood people who had walked miles from town to witness the culminating event.

The meadow at Marsov fell from the cool of the pine woods to the walled cemetery on the edge of town. When the racers had passed, I ran down the meadow, passed through the sagging gate, and stood for a few moments studying the ancient churchyard choked with weeds and neglect. A few souls were celebrated in the flowers of well-tended grave plots, but for the most part the demise of religion had cried doom for the cemetery and the adjacent church. It stood barren and cold with broken windows and dusty statues honored by faded plastic flowers.

My favorite meadow was the one in the valley at Jablonec. We took an obscure side road that descended sharply from the highway, a road modest enough to be called a lane but proud enough to warrant a road sign saying "Meksico," and we walked half a mile along a creek. The creek was a delight of shaded glades and mossy glens, and had a strange other-worldliness about it. One might not have been altogether surprised to have encountered a leprechaun, or a shepherd and his wench lounging on a green bank.

The creek meandered to one side of the valley floor to make way for a broad meadow spreading uphill to a farmhouse. The hay had already been cleared from this field and the rustic hay frames stood there empty. I picked flowers in all my meadows—daisies, gentians, cornflowers, buttercups—but in this one I found a delicate stalk of lavender bell-shaped flowers.

I sat cross-legged on the grass stitching "Live while you have life to live" on a blue sampler and somehow life never seemed so simple and rich.

Perhaps the lane led on to Meksico, but for me it ended there. Now I am out in the field every day driving a tractor and wagon alongside the potato harvester. Paul grumbles because I'm not always driving straight and I can't really blame him; how can he know that I'm sitting here "embroidering" a Czechoslovakian souvenir?

In the winter of '56 my brother Bill and I embarked on a once-in-a-lifetime, shoot-your-whole-wad European safari. (Only a couple of farmers would have dreamed of taking a European trip in winter.)

There was a tiny village in Austrian Tyrol where off-season farmers in pointed red stocking caps tided themselves over the winter teaching the local pastime to frugal Germans.

We had it in mind to see "what the skiing monkey-business was all about," as Bill put it, and in preparation we stopped at a shop in Munich and blew twenty-five bucks each on a full complement of equipment—wooden skis of the bear trap variety, leather-laced boots, bamboo poles, and one pair each of long *Unterkleidung* (underwear). Our Ohio farm clothes served us for the rest of the costume. (Twenty-five dollars today might get you the underwear.)

It was a wonderland the likes of which we'd dreamed of while sitting on the register back home reading *National Geographic.* Tiny onion-shaped church towers rose above wooden-balconied chalets. Large wooden sledges drawn by oxen pulled loads of coal and straw and cow beets through the snow-drifted streets. Men in lederhosen pulled smaller wooden sleds laden with milk cans and wine bottles and kindling, beneath picturesque houses decorated with religious paintings. The place swung with the same frenzy as the city of Munich we had just left. We were immediately caught up in the spirit.

Eeny-meeny-miney-moe we chose a pension where we had a room with hot and cold running water, and three meals a day for fifteen dollars weekly. Nobody would believe we were farmers. European *bauers* didn't indulge in such frippery, certainly not in Tyrol!

We enrolled in the ski school; five days of lessons for six dollars. We carried our bear traps out to the foot of the mountain and our *Schilehrer* showed us how to attach them. On the first afternoon following a brief lesson he took us on a chair lift way up the mountain. We looked out on the scene of a lifetime and gave ourselves body, mind, and soul to this idiotic sport. Ah, the schillings, deutsche marks, and dollars that have followed that surrender!

After ski hours we went to the tea dances where everybody clunked around in ski boots. Europe was still bogged down in postwar recovery and the luxury of skiing was more than most could afford without the folly of après-ski garb. Unbeknown to us we had plunged into this gaiety at its height the week before Lent—Fasching season. High up in the mountains we opened the door of a ski shack nearly obscured by drifts to find the place rollicking with laughter and song. The scent of soup and wood smoke and beer drew us in. We warmed our numbed hands with mugs of *Glühwein,* hot spiced wine, and added the word *Gemütlichkeit* to our growing vocabulary.

The village was Kitzbühel. The rest of the world was unmindful of its existence, but when we were there, the rest of the world didn't exist. It was the year of the Winter Olympics in Cortina, Italy. A young Austrian was the hero of the '56 winter games, winning, incredibly, all three "triple crown" ski events: the downhill, the slalom, and the giant slalom. His name was Toni Sailer and he was a Kitzbühel boy. Huge banners were stretched above the narrow streets welcoming Toni home. It was the greatest day in Austria since the war had ended, and it was the day my brother and I arrived.

After Toni Sailer Kitzbühel became the ski capital of Europe. It is no longer a sleepy village, winter or summer. I doubt that the ski instructors any longer farm. They are the wealthy heirs of some of the highest-priced real estate in the world. "Kitz" now has dozens of posh hotels and star-studded ski lines. It boasts some of the world's richest tourists, and its Hahnenhamm race is THE prestigious event of the ski year.

This Ohio farmer will never go there again. If I have the good fortune to get to Austria, I seek a quieter village where the mountains and the prices are less steep, the lift lines shorter, a village with the sort of unspoiled charm Kitzbühel once had.

But when I stand in lift lines anywhere, lean on my old bamboo poles, look down on what must be the only leather-laced boots on this or any other mountain, I think with a sigh of that day in 1956 when Toni Sailer and I came "home" to Kitzbühel.

Gästhaus Schnappsbrenner

A rooster crowed and I awoke to take my bearings. It wasn't the little room with the faded Mother Goose wallpaper where I grew up with the rooster's crow forty years ago. I lay, rather, beneath an eiderdown in Room 12 of Gästhaus Schnappsbrenner, one of the charming "brown gravy" hotels you find, if you're adventurous, on the back roads of Europe.

This was the morning call, but I was out of touch with what time Austrian roosters crow, so I threw back the eiderdown and quietly padded down the long hall and stairway to the kitchen in search of a clock. (Surviving without a wristwatch gives one a sense of one's own temporal rhythms; it also gets one out of bed to prowl around old hotels at ungodly hours of the morning.)

It was 5:30 and only the trout in the fish tank in the hallway were stirring. They cut their nervous figure eights as though eerily aware that any passerby might choose one of their number as that day's specialty of the house—which he might. I returned to my room and watched from my window as morning arrived at a country inn.

Up the lane rode a boy on a bicycle with a bag of the morning *Brötchen;* a fat babushka'd grandmother waddled across to the inn kitchen from a weathered house opposite. In a shed beneath my window the host and his son-in-law set about butchering a buck deer. Somewhere a child woke and cried, to be tended by a fond relative, freeing its mother to start breakfast in the kitchen.

Steep wooded hills rose directly behind the inn. Neat stacks of kindling were piled at intervals along their perimeter to be brought later to the inn for the winter's heat. A winding lane led downhill to the main road stretching on to a succession of tiny villages, each distinguished at this distance by its cathedral spire.

Time to be up and into the sturdy walking shoes, down to the dining room for butter and jam spread on those incomparable rolls, and off to explore those villages.

Gemütlichkeit

There's a distance of more than time and space between an American and an Austrian farmhouse. This house on Brunnbach Strasse in the small town north of Salzburg where we find ourselves today isn't a farmhouse in the true sense of the word—Franz's father goes off each day to work at the leather factory in the village. But his mother keeps a cow and chickens and a great garden, where even in this winter season some greens persist among the naked and rotting stalks of last year's brussels sprouts. And much of the chore routine takes me back a generation to my grandmother's farm in the flat corn country of western Ohio.

These great masonry edifices, so typical of European homes built to last for centuries, are both house and barn. Step through the kitchen door and you're keeping company with the cow. There is a wonderful melange of smells ("wonderful," of course, is relative to your conditioning): hay, cow feed, manure, and firewood in combination with the food smells emanating from the adjacent cold cellar. There apples, potatoes, cabbage, carrots, and onions share the shelves with canned goods and crocks of milk. The woodshed, too, is a part of this barn complex. From here kindling is carried to the stoves in the kitchen and sitting rooms.

The "out" house was never quite out of the barn, but the plumbing that replaced it has never gotten quite "in" to the house. It is still necessary to go out of the kitchen into the barn in search of the flush toilet, and frozen water pipes are a problem. (The older generation of rural Europeans seem to take reluctantly to indoor plumbing. I once visited a bathroom in a rural French home where the bathtub was full of potatoes!)

The kitchen in a European home is not a place to entertain guests; one seems always to be an intruder there. Some sort of estrangement hangs in the air—a sort of apology for not having hired servants to produce the wealth of food treats that appear in the sitting room from behind its closed door.

It must seem doubly strange for a European to visit an American kitchen and be handed a paring knife or a towel and invited to pitch right in. I suppose the difference arises from the fact that Americans never had an aristocracy to which they felt subordinate.

The kitchen is often the only room heated so the family cluster there in leisure time to read or study, to drink their schnapps or play at cards, to do their needlework and chat. But when "important" guests arrive all activity moves to the *Wohnzimmer*.

The winter sun pours into this low-ceilinged white sitting room to encourage a profusion of green plants covering the broad window sills. Beyond the windows a few feet from the house a small swift trout stream rushes through a thicket of white birch. Across a footbridge to a dairy pickup stand beyond, a neighbor woman carries two milk cans.

Franz's mother bustles back and forth from kitchen to sitting room setting the table for tea. Beside the tea served with rum, there's a great cake topped with fruit and a crystal bowl of whipped cream—more whipped cream than our boys have ever seen in one place at one time. They think they've stumbled into heaven, and I am inclined to agree.

Hay Season

The valleys of Austria are a hundred thousand calendar pictures in the waning weeks of summer. Petunias and hanging geraniums spill from windowboxes and balcony railings, an accepted part of every hausfrau's contribution to the national compulsion for beauty. Flowers flourish, too, in every village square, behind every neat little fenced enclosure among the cabbage and kohlrabi that substitutes for an acre of American lawn.

A rocky stream cascades past my window at the Gasthof Steinmühle where once again I am passing a week in attendance at an international motorcycle event in which my son participates. The road bends here at the foot of the hill and crosses the brook.

Every morning as we wind our way down the mountain to pursue the race we pass a buxom blonde milkmaid driving her herd to pasture in the meadow along the stream. Ambling along with her, prodding the brown Swiss cattle with a stout stick, is a crusted old man of the mountains. He wears a Tyrolean hat and corduroy knickers, and has a puckish face straight from a marionette show.

The sight of angular cattle along a creek evokes a Wisconsin pasture, but the sound of cowbells floating down from the hillsides above us in the night air carries us back to Heidi and Peter and the Grandfather on the Alm.

Perhaps it is this sense of changelessness that is most intriguing about Austria. The final hay cutting is in process and just as they have done for hundreds of years, the peasants go out with their scythes early and late and slash away expertly at the grass, stopping now and then to upend the tool and stroke it with a whetstone. True, there are mowing machines, but frugality dictates that you glean every square foot of fencerow and roadside. For these and for the nearly perpendicular meadows high on the mountains the scythe will continue to be indispensable.

Mechanized hayrakes pulled by tractors have come to Austria—we came upon a young woman and her brother struggling to repair one in a high meadow one afternoon—but the small landowners still depend on the broad wooden rakes wielded mostly by women.

Once cut and raked, the hay is wound around poles in haycocks to dry. Or it is draped over fencelike structures strung in long rows across a field. This work, too, seems to fall to the women; young and old they work in the fields in their skirts and oversmocks, hair caught up beneath a bandanna, amazingly feminine for all their arduous labor.

I stopped one afternoon to converse with two of them working their way methodically across a mown field. We chatted for a few minutes about potatoes, then I climbed the mountain beyond them and sat for a long time feasting my eyes on their splendid domain. How different my life as an American farm wife, perhaps freer and more rewarding in a material sense.

Yet how incredibly lovely these Austrian valleys—to live in them looking up to the mountains, or above them looking down on the neat green order, all of your own construction—well, life indeed has compensatory ways. On that sunny afternoon in September, sitting up there on that hay field, I would almost have been willing to swap, even up.

CENTERING

In the midst of winter I finally learned
that there was within me
an invincible summer.
                                    Albert Camus

It's a long life's journey to the center of the self. There are guides a-plenty to
point the way; it often seems to me that it is in the lives of others that I see
myself most clearly. Yet one makes the trip alone.

Secret Places

At home there was a small grove of trees (which we generously
called a woods) where the sweet williams flourished in spring; there
was a shady corner hidden by willows where the creek cut sharply into
a high, stony embankment; there was a cool place in a grassy ditch
under the walnut trees by the road, and a leafy retreat in the tree-of-
heaven where a limb curved to form a seat; there was the "Eden" of
Mrs. Yeager's rose garden in the rear of the cemetery next door—all
places where it was nice to be for no reason that a child could
explain.

Even the rudest of property has them, these "secret places." They
are not secret to the eye, but to the heart of someone who has
discovered and delights in them. Perhaps it is a high point on a knoll
where one can sit cross-legged in grass; perhaps a corner of a field
where fences meet in a stile; or a swampy low spot where one can
rendezvous with marsh marigolds. Children's books abound with the
delight to be found in such places—*Under the Lilacs* and *The Secret*
Garden among them.

People on city lots have taken me "by chance" to spots in their
backyards, and I have recognized instinctively that these were their

"secret places." No matter what the limitations of the real estate, it has a spot that someone cherishes: I felt a very special kinship with the young girl of *A Tree Grows In Brooklyn* who found a world of private wonder on a fire escape overlooking a solitary tree. As a college student cut adrift from my rural haunts, I sought a retreat near the tennis court where a profusion of spice bushes formed an accidental enclave.

End o' Way farm with its hundred acres of wooded wilderness along the Vermilion River valley has so many "secret places" that I have not even discovered them all. I know a wildflower gorge where a trickling spring makes a sponge of all the ground, where a clergy of jack-in-the-pulpits preach to a half acre of trillium, and a jungle of mayapples shades delicate clusters of pink anemones.

I know a mossy bank on a breezy bluff that calls out for lovers on picnics. I know a hundred trees curving out and upward over the valley void that you can straddle to scout a mile of river, north and south.

I know a sapling tethered by a tangle of grapevines to a precarious mound above the valley. If on a windy day you hug it close with your eyes shut, you are one with the swaying limbs, and you know the joy of the turkey buzzards who soar and float on the air currents. There is a fencerow of small pin oaks, their red leaves opening with the awkward delicacy of baby birds' wings. There is a meadow of fading spring beauties, and a barren hillside star-studded with tiny clumps of bluettes—to name only a few of my "secret places," sequestered corners where one begins to make sense of those puzzling lines learned in senior English long ago: "Beauty is truth, truth beauty— that is all ye know on earth, and all ye need to know."

Vicarious Spring

It wasn't surprising that the line stood out on the page: "You've got maybe four special springs in your life, all the others recall them."[*] I had been confined to a hospital room at that point for four weeks, those four precious weeks of awakening that stretch between May 1

[*] *Are We There Yet*, by Diana Vreuls. New York, Simon and Schuster, 1975; Avon 1976.

and June 1. It was obvious that in its strange way this had been one of "my springs." The significant impression I retain of those four weeks is the generous way in which everyone tried to share with me the spring happening around him.

My farmer came harried and pinkish from long days in the sun, bringing news of the potato planting—how many acres today, which ones were "up," how the stand was, where the nut grass was creeping in . . . (I often wonder what couples find to discuss when they grow no crops.)

Evelyn French sent me a bluebird's feather, told how she wired the mailbox shut so as not to disturb them in their nest building. "Just have to put the mail in the paper box a few weeks. Nothing comes anyway as important as bluebirds."

I had my spray of apple blossoms to invoke an orchard. Paul brought me first tulips in an ironstone pitcher, then flowering crab, then huge sprays of dogwood. A neighbor brought in a brief effusive flowering of lilacs for my pewter jug. On one of my tranquilized and foggy days somebody brought an ivy geranium. I never did learn who. Then came long sprays of blue iris to be clipped off and watched in renewal each day. There was a very special rose in a bud vase from Orrin's school honor banquet.

Somebody found a lovely card with a plump and wary baby bird on a flowering branch. I perched him by a window. A yellow pansy came potted in an oatmeal-colored mustard pot.

A dairyman's wife sent me a photo of her new calves. "We have most of them now," she said. "Few stragglers to go, two sets of twins. Wish you could sit with me at my kitchen table a spell, look toward the fire tower on the horizon, see the horses in the paddock, the ewes in the meadow with their lambs, the oats coming up, the corn field turning into green stripes."

Bird-watching friends "sent" me their bird finds. "I hope these yellow warblers will brighten your day as they have brightened mine. The black-masked yellow-throat is one of several species I first saw along the fringes of your lower pond. The first sight of a living creature never before glimpsed is a prime thrill." Another wrote, "The Baltimore orioles are back to enjoy the japonica bush. Every spring we have a mockingbird for a few weeks. I could hear it but couldn't see it in the tree."

I went vicariously to track meets and baseball games. "At our junior high track invitational I was unable to announce your pole-vaulting son as a winner, but it was a pleasant surprise to see his name on the entry sheet. . . ." I was even treated to a reminiscent encounter with spring fever. "The midweek heat wave at Marion L. Steele High made it difficult to decide whether Caesar did indeed die of stab wounds on Wednesday or merely succumbed to heat stroke. At any rate, Brutus and Cassius are fled like madmen through the gates of Rome and we take up their further adventures Tuesday."

I planted seeds with a sister-in-law: "I put my nasturtium seeds in last evening and after soaking all night the morning glory seeds are swelled and ready to put out. Must get the white cosmos and calendulas planted today." (With some people flower choices are as individual as hair styles.) She went on to share the setting of her planting. "It's apple blossom time here and the white and purple lilacs are coming out by the barn door. The redbud tree is covered with its pretty lace."

I pondered spring as never before; I felt the collective hunger of humanity for spring renewal and happily shared the ebullient response when it came. Oh yes, I had spring there in that fourth-floor hospital room, in small whispers and delicate scents, and big bouquets of love. But then daisies came, and I went home to claim my own meadows.

Re-Creation

It's an hour before dawn and somewhere along a Lorain County highway my brother Bill is running. Long, lonely exhilarating miles, before the responsibilities of the day. Strangely, though, this running too becomes a responsibility of the most compelling nature.

"After a while something takes hold of you and you cannot live with yourself if you do not run. It becomes your greatest responsibility to yourself," says Bill.

It isn't as though Bill were a sedentary office worker who needs five or ten miles of running a day to keep in shape. He's a farmer who seldom puts in less than a fifteen-hour workday.

I don't know what Bill thinks about in that hour before dawn but my experience tells me that one thinks a lot about the struggle. Never are we more aware of our dual nature than when we tackle a feat of endurance. It is the confrontation finally with the original adversary—oneself.

And the thought process is a running battle—the challenge, the effort, the achievement, the new challenge, the renewed effort, the new achievement. And against it, the undercurrent from the Id that tells you your feet are heavy, your mouth is dry, your lungs are tight, your armpits are sweating—you're a damned fool, and what are you doing out here fighting off people's dogs when you could be home in a warm bed?

You let him think he's winning, this ugly Id, but you persist; then you appease him by letting him think you'll stop at the goal agreed upon. But coming down the home stretch you tell yourself that having done so much, a little more is nothing; so you take an extra mile, an extra lap, an extra few feet to show him who's the better self. And that is triumph.

In spirit I run with Bill in the morning, but for the body I am back at my swimming in the afternoon or evening down in the pond in the meadow. And I endure the lonely struggle too; but there is more.

Interspersed with the Ego-Id controversy there is time to notice the varying aspects of the cottonwood tree, the texture of black locust fronds against the blue, the awareness of small life where the water laps the bank—a turtle pulled up on a rock like a rowboat on the shore, the beauty of a wild iris against a sun-bleached log, muskrat holes that call to mind Ratty and Mole of *The Wind in the Willows*.

There are the purely sensual responses—the water against the skin, the warmth of sun on bare shoulder, the changing temperature at different depths, the coarse texture of the grasses growing in the shallows, a wisp of algae brushing the face, and the soft touch of mud that tells you to change direction.

The mind wanders from subject to subject, but it always comes back to the struggle in process—man against himself, to the tantalizing prospect of finally triumphing just a little beyond the challenge, hoisting oneself to the dock and relaxing on or under the towel, depending upon the temperature.

People have made goal-line pronouncements in profusion but they never topped that moron we all know so well who, when asked why he beat his head against the wall, said, "Because it feels so good when you stop."

There's a word for it that becomes altogether meaningful at the point where the effort ceases and the exhilaration takes possession—recreation.

Dear Friend

I don't count that day all bad when I get a printed circular beginning, "Dear Friend: the time has come to remove your name from our mailing list. . . ." Anything which reduces the flood of second- and third-class mail to this address is a boon. (I ordered the proper item last year and my name was sold to about three hundred small catalogue companies.)

The thing that bugs me about that otherwise welcome notice is the "Dear Friend" bit. The last thing I would do to a dear friend is to remove him from my mailing list. But I am prompted to contemplate the sacred word "friend." When my father-in-law died there came a very moving sympathy card that said simply, "He was my friend."

My favorite definition for the word is found with a limited few others in *The Prophet:** "Your friend is your needs answered." The day Pete Newberry collapsed with his heart attack, Marney phoned Paul. As he ran out the door, he called back to me, "Marney's in trouble! She needs me!" It was too late for anyone to help Pete, but Marney had blessed a friendship in a way she never realized.

There are those, I suppose, who feel that their needs can be met through a mail order catalog, but I am not among them. My needs are too great:

I need friends who call me "Patty," who never take me too seriously and who keep me from making that mistake about myself. I need friends who will forgive me for being careless and erratic, and love me in spite of myself; friends who tell me the painful truth, like, "You know, plaid slacks are not the greatest thing for you."

I need friends who say, "You're the spittin' image of your mother," friends who help me know where I come from, where I'm

* *The Prophet*, by Kahlil Gibran, Alfred A. Knopf, Inc., 1923.

going. I need friends from whom I can borrow a picnic table or a strapless bra or a cup of brown sugar.

I need friends who give me of themselves, who share a truth they've discovered, knowing that I will rejoice in their discovery though it's an understanding I'm not ready for; I need friends with whom I can disagree and remain friends.

I need friends who need me—little friends who come round to the back door and say, "Aunt Pat, will you tie my hood?"; and big friends who say, "Would it be too much trouble? . . ." knowing that it won't be.

I need friends with whom I can talk small talk of recipes and bridal showers and hemlines, and friends with whom no talk is necessary. I need friends to challenge me with stimulating ideas brought from other environments, other perspectives; and friends who help me weigh and evaluate my own insights.

I have a host of friends I haven't met yet who touch my life in one way or another. I read people's books or I read of their lives and recognize them as kindred spirits. I have had letters from people who recognized me as friend and said so. Once there was a man from South Carolina who got me as a wrong number on a long-distance call and in great good nature burdened me with his problems. I felt a twinge of regret in knowing he was a friend I would never meet.

"Dear Friend, if you ARE my friend, please don't drop me from your mailing list. I need all the friends I can get."

Elizabeth

I have never met Elizabeth. I don't know if she has blue eyes and an Afro or two heads and split ends. Either way I know she is "beautiful." She is one of the many friends who come to me by RFD, writing in response to *A Thread of Blue Denim*, and I should like to nominate her for Mother of the Year.

She writes with such spontaneity of her two-year-old child. "He is so alive. He points and babbles, babbles and points. How I should like to sit down and have a long conversation with Matthew! . . .

"Everything is a potential nest, the pots and pans cupboard, the empty laundry basket, the space between the dining room table legs. I feel so lucky to spend this time with him! . . .

"Spring is flirting with us. Yesterday was mild and tender. Matt and I played outside all day. It's 10 A.M. and when Matt awakes we'll walk down to the village, visit the library, the knitting store and the park. I do like small towns; they seem so manageable, made for people."

She goes on to talk of an outing to nearby New York City with her husband, of visiting museums, disclosing a range of cultural enjoyments.

"I've been sewing new, bigger trousers for Matt, knitting gifts and reading." She speaks then of favorite books. . . .

"So few works seem to capture or emphasize the sheer, small JOYS of living. So much of them is preempted by 'matters of consequence,' as The Little Prince would say. That's why I like poetry so much. Like a sharp knife it often slices the most delicate parts of awareness into a few lines of print.

"Matt will soon be up. He mustn't miss this sunny morning! A small child is so new, so much a discoverer, that life, because of him, is again fresh and full of promise. . . .

"Enjoy May! Don't feel you must sit inside and write me; stand outside and listen to the seeds shed their coverings. I will listen too."

Obviously Elizabeth is a "poet" with little inclination to be tripped by reality. There is a stab of envy in my heart for her gift of lyricism. There is an ache, too, for the many hours, gone now long ago, that I might have devoted to playing with my own little boys.

But reality was extremely compelling for me during those years. A great deal of my young motherhood was of necessity devoted to "matters of consequence."

I stole what I could from the laundry and the overall patching, the canning and the bean picking, the potato harvesting and the chicken plucking. Elizabeth doesn't have a farm wife's long days of driving truck in a cab crawling with kids and cookie crumbs. She probably never mowed hay or disked a field with a tot hugged tightly in her lap. We didn't play together much, but we certainly worked together. I'm sure she would envy me that! I remember wrapping them gently in my jacket when they nodded and laying them to sleep in a wheat field. We too had our lyrical days.

But the biggest joy for me in Elizabeth's letter is her candid celebration of her life as wife and mother. She is so obviously liberated.

You know what? I think I should like to be Matthew.

Dear Abby

I have a sad little letter here from a potato farmer's wife up in Maine who read something of mine in a national magazine and sensed that I might be a friend. She wrote me first several years ago out of a state of deep depression and I tried to reach her with the pathetic sort of advice you proffer at a distance when you know so little of the person and the circumstances.

After a few sentences to bridge the intervening years she gets down to the heart of the matter: "My house is still dirty and I have got fat, 178 pounds. I will be 50 on October 20. I have not gone back to nursing yet. . . ." she adds a couple of items about household routine and closes.

What I hear her saying is "I am ugly and lazy and I'm getting old and I hate myself. What can I do?" It's a desperate sort of cry. My first impulse is to weep, but I know from the earlier contact that the raw material of her life is basically the same as mine—the farm, the good earth, the potatoes, the children (she has five), an education that offers potential, the church . . . I, too, just had a birthday but I seem to find each year more satisfying. I look out the window and start to scold her across the miles: "Can't you think of anything but food! The sun is shining on the goldest leaves I ever saw. The harvest is nearly at an end; a long winter of contentment lies ahead. And the price of potatoes just jumped another quarter! How can you be so miserable?"

I send her what I hope will be a shot in the arm, a bit of wisdom gleaned from a perfume ad. (Wisdom gleams from strange places.) "Love thyself! The art of living is not just living. It is loving—first yourself, then another, then the world."

I know how little I could love myself if I weighed 178 pounds, and I know how disinclined I would be to get off my duff and clean up the house, or get out of the house and pursue an interrupted nursing career. So I suggest she look up a chapter of Weight Watchers and see if she can't change her eating habits.

And yet I fear it's a hollow hope. Probably all I gave her was the knowledge that somebody cared enough to write a letter, sign a name, affix a stamp. That might sustain her for a day, but discipline to an ordeal like forgoing food or liquor or drugs or cigarettes requires motivation that surely won't come in a letter from a stranger.

I had a letter from another reader this week, the heart of which read: "If only one could make people see what untapped strength and talent and love each of us has within himself!"

What shapes our self-image? The people who love us and the people who refuse to love us; the acceptance and rejection we know, the accomplishments and the attainments—the whole of our lives. We subconsciously strive to fulfill the image that we carry of ourselves.

I suppose I could write and say, "Jesus loves you, despite your 178 pounds." But what she really needs is the love and encouragement of the people around her. I can't accomplish that in one letter.

There are, of course, a lot of people closer to home whose lives I touch daily. . . .

Deaf and Dumbfounded

For three days I suffered an ear infection and my world became a dumb show. I went to church, sat in the third row, and couldn't understand a word. I passed a social day with visiting relatives, but the conversation eluded me. I sat through the cacophony of *Jesus Christ Superstar* and it might as well have been a pantomime.

To be deaf is to experience life as through a curtain of glass. It is to be in, but not of, the world—and to know an isolation far deeper than aloneness.

The hard-of-hearing syndrome is not a new one with me. I have through the years had ear problems that were remedied with resultant improved hearing (otosclerosis corrected by stapedectomy); but I have been handicapped sufficiently to know that it takes fortitude to deal with even a minor hearing problem. You ask people to repeat themselves a few times, and then you grow self-conscious and withdraw. You recognize that you are a drag in group conversations. You find yourself smiling and nodding dumbly to questions or statements. It is a subconscious assault on the psyche, a seeming erosion of the intellect.

People can extend all manner of assistance to the blind and do it inconspicuously, but if one comes to the loud assistance of the hard-of-hearing he is immediately conspicuous. So it is the tendency of even the most thoughtful people to avoid, whether consciously or unconsciously, those with serious hearing problems. Like other minority segments of the population they are accorded a psychological invisibility.

The families of the hard-of-hearing are usually little more tolerant or considerate of the problem than the general public. On the contrary, the afflicted individual is often subtly ridiculed and sometimes shouted at in exasperation. Oddly enough one is made to feel guilty for something that is beyond one's control.

This recent bout with infection, however, plunged me deeper than ever before into the tragedy of hearing loss. All the little atmospheric sounds ceased, sound I was formerly unaware existed.

My own voice seemed strange to me and I had difficulty judging its volume. I could not hear the phone or the car motor, the whistle of the teakettle or the dogs on the porch. I couldn't rely on sound to tell me if my appliances were on or off. There was a picture on the tube but it was soundless. The family laughed and talked, about what I knew not. It was almost as if I were not part of them and I was lonely as never before in my life.

I marveled that a Beethoven could introduce a world of music to this void. I empathized with young Helen Keller in her dark stillness.

Except for a brief correspondence, I have never known a deaf mute, and that is probably symbolic of the tragedy. The deaf must seek the company of those who are similarly afflicted and therefore know sign language.

But that has to be a restricted society, for what do any two deaf people have in common besides their handicap? Not necessarily very much. So by and large, I suspect that they keep their own good company and lead quite solitary lives.

When I blew my nose one morning and felt the release of pressure in the eustachian tube that signaled a return to normal, it was with deep gratitude and new wisdom that I returned to the land of those who hear but too often do not listen.

In Praise of Cottage Cheese _____

Some time after the holiday season of self-indulgence comes a deep awareness of sin and guilt and a determined urge for self-improvement. Every third person you meet seems to think that the finest improvement he can make is to lose a little weight. I know it's a general condition, for right there on the church bulletin I saw it: "Prayer for Going on a Diet."

Obviously the supplicant had struggled through the ordeal: "Beginner of everything," says he, "help me to get started. I am afraid of failing. . . . I am dangerously close to believing that fatness is my nature. . . ." Ah, yes!

I am a chronic loser of weight, and through the years I have made a few observations on the subject (I am also a chronic gainer of weight.) My first observation is that one shouldn't be in too big a hurry to buy thin clothes. Better the old ones should hang on you like rhinoceros skin.

Permanent weight loss is about as rare as a cure for heroin addiction. The reason for this relates directly to my second observation, the most important truth on the subject of diet: If one expects to become thinner and remain thinner he can never again expect to eat as he formerly ate. The sooner one comes to grips with this fact, the sooner he can reorient his life to new satisfactions, or abandon the struggle and get back to the old ones, like eating.

It simply takes less food to sustain 115 pounds than it took to sustain 130, a heck of a lot less. If it is your misfortune to be as short as five feet, two inches, you can easily maintain the lesser weight by inhaling the food aromas in your kitchen.

My third observation about dieting is that, like most forms of sin, it is best conducted secretly. This gives you the immeasurable thrill of putting something over on somebody. It also protects you from jeers and snickers when you fall from grace. It's difficult enough to live with your own awareness of failure without having someone standing by gloating!

If the family happens to notice that you haven't sat down to eat with them in three days, just tell them you couldn't wait and ate at the stove—which is what you always did even before you had sense enough to forgo the second meal with the family.

Observation four is that even the most meager diet needs some satisfactions. If black coffee is not your bag, you cannot hope to limp through hours of obsessive hunger on black coffee. Allow yourself the luxury of a bit of sugar and a shot of milk. And if you must choose vegetables over bread and pastry, let there at least be a bit of butter.

And speaking of satisfactions, I observe that most people choose exactly the wrong times to relax their diets. It is much easier to sit with a lean plate when you are out with friends, though the menu be ever so tempting. Camaraderie and good conversation go far toward soothing the savage hunger. Save the small indulgences for those bleak, lonely hours when you pass through the kitchen so hungry you want to eat your vanilla-scented candle.

Success, if it comes at all, comes in re-direction with regard to food. And the author of my prayer knows that quite well. He says, "Help me, O Lord, between the grapefruit and the celery to do what I must do. . . . May there come a day when I praise you for cottage cheese. . . !"

On a day when you have pushed your grocery cart through the supermarket just before supper, rolled past French fries, potato chips, chip dip, fig newtons, breakfast rolls, pecan pie, 7-layer cake, choco-late bars, and three hundred other species of goodies, and drive home to find yourself craving a package of frozen squash, you may consider that you are over the hump. When you feel one of those terrifying weak spells consuming you at 10:00 P.M. and rush to the kitchen to fall ravenously upon a saucer of cold broccoli, you may begin to think about altering your slacks.

Lift Encounter

You don't learn all there is to know about a person riding a mile uphill on a ski lift, but if you have a lively imagination you could often construct a mini-novel around the framework of what you do learn. Take the young woman I met yesterday—thirtyish, pretty, with long reddish-blond hair, Kansas-born, educated in classical music, a professional cellist, a "born again" Christian, childless and divorced.

"I blew it long ago," she said. "My husband was a darling guy." She didn't elaborate, but from the rest of the rundown it was clear that she had simply chafed under the limitations of an early marriage, her creative potential withering away.

She chucked the marriage, took off in pursuit of herself and a career, listing with the wind. Finding it difficult to make it in classical music, she worked with jazz combos all over the country, learned the electric cello and the bongo drums.

For some years she lived and worked in Mexico, then for three years in England. She had played in many of the European spas and along the line picked up the techniques of massage—"the legitimate kind," she hastened to add.

She spoke of one exciting vacation riding a motorcycle from northern France down to Morocco. It had all been a gala time, and yet . . . one sensed that the search hadn't really led anywhere, except that in a small church congregation in England she had come to the Lord. Now she had come home to this ski resort town, was keeping house for a young family, still searching and hoping for one of her own.

I told her a little about my life, and like so many young people I meet she was awed at meeting someone "privileged to lead a life close to the land." "An honest-to-God farmer's wife! Wow!" It never ceases to surprise me, though I suppose it shouldn't—most farm people of necessity lead segregated lives. They must go where the land is and the masses are not.

"You'll probably think I'm strange," she said, "or it'll give you something amusing to write about—but I've often thought of advertising in some farm magazine or newspaper for a farmer who needs a wife, maybe a divorced guy or a widower with young children. That would be OK. I'm good with kids. Are there such papers where one could advertise?"

I was a little taken aback, having assumed that people who resorted to advertising for mates had chronic acne and halitosis. Maybe it was just a very forthright attitude she was expressing.

"Golly, you've led such an interesting and stimulating life. Do you have any idea what you're talking about?" I asked. "Farm life demands a lot of discipline and drudgery. I've never minded it, but then I was born to it. I knew what I was getting into."

"I know, but I think I'm ready for that," she said. "I'm tired of living alone, belonging nowhere. I yearn to settle down to something stable like a farm."

She was serious and there was something altogether appealing in her candor. She insisted I take her name and address "just in case," and I promised her I'd keep my channels tuned to country bachelors.

What filled my mind in the aftermath of this encounter was the hundreds of farm wives I've known, the doubts and disappointments they've survived, brave and uncomplaining women. I thought of the individual dreams they must have had and of how so many of those dreams had been sacrificed to the realities of mortgage and expanded production or, more unhappily, to droughts or floods and crop reversals.

How often had each of us in dark moments wished we could have abandoned it all and pursued our private dreams. How I wished that each of my farm women might have listened to Jane's story of the pursuit of rainbows and sensed the hunger that still possessed her for what rather naturally accrues to farm women—satisfaction in the land and its miracles, in hard work, in being important to a husband and a community, in providing a stable life and a worthy example for our children—not always the dreams one starts with, but the substance of life in the final analysis.

Here—In a Manger

I acquired this little group of nativity figures by default. They were part of a packet of handmade items sent by Middle Eastern missionaries to help support their regional mission. Everything sold but this cluster of twelve figures which had small appeal in haphazard display at an out-of-season bazaar. At five dollars they were the highest-priced item in the packet. It was my responsibility to dispose of the things; so reluctantly I donated the money, collected the figures carelessly in a brown paper sack, and carried them home, where they worked their way to the back of the closet that serves us as attic.

Like most things acquired too easily they were esteemed too little; I forgot them completely. Christmases came and went and the nativity figures never saw the light of day. Sometimes in April or May I would come across that paper sack and wonder again what in heaven's name it contained. "Oh yes, that nativity scene! Next year I must . . ." but I never did. Last week to my great surprise the figures appeared on the piano, unearthed in season at last by one of the children.

"Gee, those aren't bad carvings," I told myself several times as I hurried past the piano en route to a Christmas that had scant time for manger scenes. Finally Christmas eve, in a last-minute fury of decorating, I lay a few pieces of evergreen around them and set the small advent candles close by. "Lovely little animals," I thought, but still no time to really look.

Tonight Christmas coasts into New Year's and at last there is time for that evening I covet, time to light the tree, and sit alone in the silence pondering the season, its peace, and its potential for holiness. Tonight also I lighted the advent candles and in the half light discovered the miracle of these nativity figures.

Roughly hewn of a rich-toned hard wood by an anonymous Lebanese wood-carver, they tell a story far more real and comprehensible than the nativity story. In the soft candlelight one realizes there is not a careless stroke of a penknife on any of the seven humans or the five animals.

No self-respecting European wood-carver would have accepted less than five dollars for any single figure of the twelve. Only someone deeply devoted to the Christian ideal could have done this, someone to whom perfection was more important than money.

He has only imagined kings, or wisemen, this wood-carver—never seen one. Caspar, Melchior, and Balthasar have stern, unyielding expressions after the manner of a Caesar or a Pilate. Their robes upon inspection are intricately carved, their headgear high and pompous. If they crossed the desert on camels they came through remarkably intact.

Mary and Joseph, too, are a bit unreal. There is a smoothness, a roundness, a purity about them, as though sin would slide right off.

It is the shepherd who captivates me. He is a man acquainted with grief and hard work. He is dressed in skins and looks not unlike his sheep, rough and wooly. The wood-carver knows this round-shouldered shepherd better than he knows any of these others except perhaps the animals. He has walked many miles behind sheep, knows their stocky wide-spread stance, their pathetic little faces.

He knows the bony rump, the thin flanks of an ox who has existed too long on the arid pastures of the Middle East. He knows a humble donkey with his head lowered, his skinny back straight, his ears at attention; he knows the gentle eyes and soft mouth.

But it is when I look at the Christ that my heart goes out to this altogether human and lovable wood-carver. Like all of us he felt compelled to create an unreal Christ. The Christ figure is a larger-than-life grotesquerie stretched out crosslike on a coffin-shaped manger. With these other figures he has taken blocks of wood and breathed into them life of a sort known from experience or from keen attention to vicarious forms. For this Christ figure he has labored at length with a piece of wood, and it emerges as less than a piece of wood.

Would he had left the manger empty that I might look there and see the face of the haughty king, the sainted mother, the holy father, the careworn shepherd, or—my hungering self.

Solitude and Loneliness

Anyone who has ever watched women out to dinner go through the familiar dumb-show routine, signaling one another in wordless whispers, then collecting their pocketbooks and trotting off to the ladies' room in pairs or trios, could make a significant observation about women—they are not conditioned to be solitary creatures.

Mothers probably foster this herd mentality (in the interest of safety) with their early cautions to little girls to avoid being alone. As a child I spent many hours wandering by myself in the orchards and the meadows and the broad lawns of the cemetery next door. But when I made friends in town and recognized that they moved in pairs or groups, I began to think of my solitary ways as peculiar.

Far greater priority was put on being popular with a crowd than on developing the strengths necessary to go it alone. This sort of togetherness becomes such an obsession with girls that they reject many pursuits because they can't find a companion to share them or an audience to appreciate them in action.

The habit stays with us into maturity. We marry with the subconscious understanding that now we need never be alone again, a misconception that often crowds a man to the point of distraction. The nature of a man's life is much more inclined toward independence. He customarily travels alone, goes to restaurants alone, shops alone, and may well pursue his pastimes alone. (He can at least find his way to the men's room alone.)

Then children come along to dominate a woman's life day and night for years on end. If there are empty spaces, her habit of companionship may prompt her to fill them with radio and television people.

The net result of all this crowding is that many a woman never learns what it is to be alone for long stretches without a compelling agenda. She never develops the vital practice of introspection, never learns to enjoy her own company. She conditions herself through the years to think in terms of other people, to subordinate, or at best to accommodate, her desires to those of her family, friends, or business associates. Accommodation is such a habit that she may never discover self-indulgence (or worse, a self to indulge).

Traveling distances alone, especially by car, is something women avoid at all costs. There was a time not too long ago when I wouldn't have dreamed of going more than twenty-five miles without finding someone "to ride along." But my trips have become too frequent and too long. So I travel alone, and I have learned to revel in my own company.

I was admittedly slow in accepting the privilege I had finally attained to do things exactly as I pleased. The day the truth dawned I was driving through eastern Colorado with some hours to spare. I found myself slamming on the brakes, backing up, and indulging whims I would normally have suppressed.

I stopped to read historical markers, prowl through cemeteries, wade in creeks, gather wildflowers along the road, examine interesting lanes, sit on a park bench in the square of a small town—nobody saying "no" or "later" or "next time."

In Denver I tried without success to find a companion for a two-day holiday in the Rockies. With a large measure of apprehension I went alone. Those two days were a glorious extension of that indulgent afternoon. I wandered a high mile into somebody's private pasture, sat on a stump and sketched (another "first" for me). I discovered a flock of big-horned sheep and watched them just as long as I wanted. I climbed a glacial stream and had a picnic.

In the mountain village I prowled about in shops full of kitsch, and on an impulse went to a kid's movie and laughed like a ten-year-old. I slept that night in a mountain chalet lulled by a rapid river.

My memory of that surprising holiday is not of being alone. It is of sharing two incomparable days with a "friend" I had lost in the secret retreats of my girlhood, a friend who has found me again in the solitude of womanhood.

NOSTALGIC ROSE

The nicest part about the "good old days," I am persuaded, is remembering them from the vantage point of the comfortable present. The "good old people" now . . . there's a pervasive reality! The great value of looking perceptively at where we have been, of course, is to gain an understanding of where we are.

Paint it all nostalgic rose.

The Tea Set

"Twenty-one piece tea set of blue lusterware . . . $2.98" was what it said alongside the picture in the Sears, Roebuck Christmas catalogue. We were overwhelmed at such value and set our sights on scaring up the three bucks and some odd cents that must be figured in for tax and postage. It was the biggest gift we'd ever tackled for Mama; up to that point we'd been satisfied with the cross-stitch on burlap or the file-card holders or the black construction-paper silhouettes that Miss Zilch or Miss Drechsler or Mrs. Smith dreamed up to motivate us between Thanksgiving and Christmas.

Bill and I had a little money left from selling bittersweet and John made up the rest from his paper route earnings.

With our sister Mary's help we filled out the form and sent it off with a money order procured from the mailman by putting a "Please blow horn" sign in the mailbox. This had to be accomplished on Saturday, when Mama was gone to market. Then the vigil began. Let's see—two days for the order to get to Chicago, a couple of days to process it, three or four days coming back, and a Sunday in between. At the most it ought to come in nine days.

Every day we got out the catalogue and turned it to the dog-eared page where our treasure was pictured. "What do you think of that, Mama?" asked Bill, with thinly disguised braggadocio. "Wouldn't you just love to have something like that around here?" Our tea set was as well kept a secret as a case of mumps.

As good luck would have it, the package arrived two weeks to the day from when we ordered. Saturday again, and Mama was at market, so we set the box on a chair and dived in with all six fists. Not a very big box for twenty-one pieces! But all the same, big enough to make quite some impression under the tree.

We extracted the pieces, one by one, scattering excelsior all over Mary's clean dining room. She was as excited as we and scarcely scolded us for what at other times would have unleashed a tirade.

First the cream pitcher, then the sugar bowl. "The lid? . . . Oh, here." Then the wondrous teapot—shimmering blue laced with a spray of pinkish-red blossoms. To our chagrin one of the cups was a tissue-paper wad of broken pieces. Oh well, even a twenty-piece tea set was not to be sneezed at. Maybe some adjustment could be made.

We counted them all, wrapping them again in the tissue and laboriously fitting them back in the excelsior, hastening to banish all traces before Mom got home. We wrapped the box in two or three pieces of last year's Christmas paper, closing the stubborn flaps with Christmas seals that came "free" in the mail. We adorned it royally with old ribbon untangled from the wad, and then hid it away in Mary's closet.

Everything else about that Christmas pales before the splendid moment when Mama opened the box from Sears, Roebuck.

I don't really remember how she reacted. I'm sure it was a convincing show. It didn't occur to us (as I'm sure it did to her) to wonder where in our crowded cupboard she was going to put twenty pieces of china "Made in Japan."

We used the tea set from time to time and the pieces disappeared. The cream pitcher went early in the game, then the six plates, the five cups, the saucers. The remnants moved gradually upward in the cupboard.

When we went through Mama's fifty-seven-year accumulation of "things," way up in the rear of the top shelf of the kitchen cupboard we unearthed the lid to a sugar bowl long gone and the blue luster teapot. Its spout was held on precariously with Scotch tape; no tea had poured from it for years. But too precious, obviously, to discard were the fragments of a Christmas memory more cherished than the gift had ever been.

I'm pushing fifty pretty hard and God knows I have dealt with change. I have learned to accept "virgin Orlon." I have come to grips with chestnut tables of Formica; fireplace logs of old newspaper don't faze me. My Civil War house of clapboard has steel siding. The "slate" roof is asbestos.

In my lifetime Elsie Dinsmore has been replaced by Charlie Brown's Lucy; Amos and Andy by Sanford and Son. Freeways roll through what were impregnable hills. I have had the experience of taking a plane in Cleveland and arriving in Chicago earlier than I left. I grew up singing "Penny for a Spool of Thread," and I have lived to pay $1.19 for a plastic spool. I grew up with pantywaists and petticoats and underwear that bagged under cotton stockings, and I have lived to see bare navels in school classrooms.

Ah yes, I have lived with change, full circle in some cases. I'm currently trying to wean the family off the "high price spread" and back onto butter.

Every morning before I swing my feet out from under the electric blanket I pause and caution myself, "Today is the day of future shock. Are you ready?" And every day with a willingness I have gone forth.

But today? I just don't know if I can face a world where I can't even depend on jelly beans! Nobody tampers with candy canes; they're always red-and-white-striped and peppermint. Valentine red-hots are always red and cinnamon. A Hershey bar is a Hershey bar is a Hershey bar though they shrinketh smaller and smaller. . . . Licorice sticks are always black unless, of course, they're "red licorice," in which case they never did taste like licorice—but they don't change. Then why did somebody go monkeying around with jelly beans?

In the well-ordered world of the thirties and forties there was none of this confusion with jelly beans. The black ones were licorice; the red, cinnamon; the white, peppermint; the green, spearmint; the pink were wintergreen; the yellow were usually clove; orange were orange; and purple were awful. Everybody had his favorite color with a little strong competition for the black. My own favorites were the red cinnamon. Nobody ate purple jelly beans until almost summer vacation. If your mother tried to pawn them off on you in your lunch bag you threw them across the study hall at archenemies. For that they were good. Nothing else.

War erupted; empires toppled; the whole world changed; but jelly beans were stable. And then sometime in the fifties sweeping changes were made in jelly beans. Sometimes your mom would buy a bag in which they all tasted like perfume and you could take all of them to school for ammunition in study hall. Some mixed-up market researcher crossed a jelly bean with a bird's egg and came up with a speckled variety, an aberration if there ever was one. You soon learned to watch for the ones labeled "spiced," and they weren't easy to find.

Last night I drove fifteen miles out of my way to buy ten loaves of bread for $1 and a gallon of milk for $1.19 only to find myself squandering $.69 on twelve ounces of "spiced" jelly beans. If I hadn't been caught up in impulse buying I would never have been party to such a rip-off.

Would you believe—blue jelly beans! Who ever heard of blue jelly beans? And no black ones! Sure enough, the blue ones were licorice; the color-flavor system was complete chaos.

The orange were clove; the white were spearmint; the green were lemon . . . but what does it matter? The purple—that was the worst—the purple were cinnamon-flavored!

No, I really don't want to get out of bed this morning—not without a study hall to go to.

Saturday Night Treat

"Revival" seems to be the passion of the era. Committees form and struggle to restore old landmarks. Classical revivals give us our best theater. Fashion is a never-ending cycle of revivals. A good song comes round again with new voice and new orchestration.

There's no revival sweeter to my memory than that of the ice cream parlor. I don't know where the ice cream cone originated, but as far as I'm concerned it was down at Baetz's Dairy on the corner of Tenney Avenue and Church Street.

You went in there and plopped down a buffalo nickel for a double-dipper of one of those mouth-watering flavors scrawled on a chalkboard on the tile wall—vanilla, chocolate, strawberry, whitehouse, orange-pineapple, or maplenut. It was all made out in the back room by Mr. Baetz himself from float-on-the-top country cream.

My favorite flavor was whitehouse, which was only vanilla with big old maraschino cherries mixed in. If you were lucky you got five or six, and if you swapped licks with your brother, sure enough he'd waggle his tongue around so he'd get one of those cherries.

Once in a while I'd get carried away with orange-pineapple and go out wishing I'd stuck to whitehouse. For the thirties, ours was a sophisticated dairy with five or six flavors; a friend from the Midwest tells me that down-state Illinois you got vanilla or chocolate, and if they had chocolate it was a really big deal.

There was then, as now, a great art to eating an ice cream cone and the earlier you mastered it, the better your chances of coaxing your mom in the direction of the ice cream parlor. Ah, the sad sight of a little kid standing outside the dairy bawling his head off, his double-dip splattered all over the sidewalk and melting away to the curb.

Very little kids always needed help from older brothers and sisters to keep the ice cream from dripping down the cone to the hands and ultimately down the arms and off the elbows. Many the nasty quarrel waged in back seats over this auxiliary lickin'. Or some smart-aleck older kid would wolf his double-dip and then use the miniature remains of his cone to horn in on the flavor you were trying to make last. Every kid sooner or later discovered the tempting habit of biting off the bottom of the cone and sucking down the melting ice cream, torso bent at right angles to the plush upholstery.

"Billy's back here makin' a mess!" someone would tattle, and Billy would be admonished. Then everyone else was threatened with the possibility that he was eating the "very last ice cream cone" of his life. When parental backs were turned Billy was quietly pummeled for causing all the trouble.

Life was slower then. You sat in the car parked along the curb on a summer night and licked away, savoring every bit. Or you sauntered down the sidewalk, your head tilted sideways. The racy set soon learned that trying to eat an ice cream cone in a rumble seat speeding along at thirty-five mph was a trick all its own.

Ah yes, many of us survived the Depression on the small luxury of the ice cream cone.

Then came the rise of the frozen custard that oozed from the nozzle and produced a longer dollar for the sweet treat merchant. For more than a decade it seemed only Howard Johnson and his twenty-eight flavors kept the ice cream cone alive. There were a very few other underground spots where the ice cream cone survived on the nostalgic memories of old druggists. Finally in the affluent sixties somebody discovered that people could and would now pay considerable money for a good ice cream cone.

The cynics tell us it's not made with cream and it's flavored with everything from flea powder to shoe polish, but I don't wanta hear about it. I just enjoy going in once again, salivating over flavors from dappled apple to Charlie Brownie, peering into all those big cans, ordering a dip of whitehouse and going out thinking maybe . . . just maybe, I should have chosen orange-pineapple instead.

Memorabilia

My housecleaning always bogs down in that fateful box at the back of the closet labeled "memorabilia." I pull it out biennially, determined to cull a portion . . . . I pore through photographs, dance programs, clippings, greeting cards, faded honors, matchbooks, love letters—I squat down on a heap of suitcases and lose myself in a satisfying reminiscence of what I was, what we were, way back when. . . . Ah me, an old autograph book . . . "To Patsy on her 10th birthday from your sister Mary Alice." It's ugly and coverless, the pages dirty and faded. Now there's something I can eliminate . . . then I make the mistake of turning a page:

"When you get married and live across the lake, send me two pieces of your wedding cake. Your friend, Ray" Whatever happened to Ray?

"When you are old and cannot see, put on your specs and think of me." Well, I've made it that far, I think, pushing my bifocals up on my nose with a grubby finger.

"Roses are red, violets are blue, pecans are nuts and so are you!" Loving flattery from "little brother Billy."

From a seventh-grade teacher, "To Patricia" (only your teachers called you "Patricia"), "I shall remember you always." Eternity was fleeting in her case; she died the following year.

"Pigs like pumpkin, cows like squash, I like you, I DO, by gosh!" With that one I was sunk. The cleaning was forgotten, the coming school bus, plans for supper. . . . I was back in junior high covertly passing this silly book around the study hall, collecting nonsense and wit, stilted bits of wisdom, bad poetry, and sentimental gush.

There were the omnipresent entreaties for remembrance:

"Remember me now, remember me ever, remember the good times we had together."

"Down in the valley on a hard hard rock, three little words, 'Forget me not.' "

"When twilight drops its curtain down and pins it with a star, remember that I am your friend, though we may travel far."

"When you see a monkey climbing up a tree, pull its tail and think of me."

"In the big green meadow, under the sky so blue; remember someone's thinking, someone thinks of you."

"Sailing down the river in my little birch canoe, with memories unfailing, my thoughts return to you."

"Forget me not, for if you do, You'll feel the weight of my big shoe."

Aunts and teachers always found more erudite things to say and wrote much neater: "Give to the world the best you've got and the best will come back to you."

"A wise man can profit from advice, while others must depend upon experience."

"Build today strong and sure, with firm and ample base, then ascending and secure shall tomorrow find its place." (All I can think of is the ample derriere of the teacher who wrote it.)

"Over and over again, no matter which way we turn, we always find in the book of life, some lesson we have to learn." (Eeee Gods!)

There were a few wiseacre kids who dredged from somewhere thoughts profound beyond their years. "Labor for learning before you grow old, For learning is better than silver or gold. Silver and gold will soon pass away, But a good education is with you alway." (Small wonder she now heads an English department!")

"Keep truth and your country sacred, and you can never go wrong."

"Don't be sharp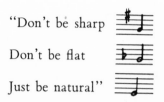

Don't be flat

Just be natural"

And a few hardy guffaws:

"Mule in the barnyard, lazy and sick.
Boy with a pin at the end of a stick.
Kid jabbed the mule; mule gave a lurch.
Funeral Monday, village church."

"I eat my peas with honey
I've done it all my life.
It makes my peas taste funny
But it keeps them on the knife."

Then there were the little giggles pertaining to subjects whispered about in the cloakroom: "Lorain boys are handsome, Elyria boys are sweet, but when it comes to kissin', Amherst's got 'em all beat!"

"When you get married and have twins, don't come to my house for safety pins."

"Two in a hammock attempting to kiss. All of a sudden it went like this—" (and then you signed your name upside down).

"The higher the mountain, the cooler the breeze; The younger the couple, the tighter they squeeze."

"There are tulips in the garden, there are tulips in the park, but the tulips I like best are the 2 lips in the dark."

"Beware of the boy whose eyes are brown, who kisses you once and turns you down. Beware of the boy whose eyes are gray, who kisses you once and turns you away. Beware of the boy whose eyes are blue . . . he's down in the kitchen looking for YOU!" I shut the book quickly, but not before my eye catches that last prophetic verse: "I pity the person who reads this book!" . . . because the closet's not clean, the kids are home, it's suppertime, and I'm about to catch Hail Columbia!

Legacy of St. Valentine

The long shadow of St. Valentine falls on February, giving rise to that most painful of puberty rites, the Sweetheart Dance. This awkward exercise in social graces in my day emanated from the Girls' Athletic Association or some other group of females bent on bypassing the stumbling block of the bashful boy. Awkward kids who weren't even aware that their voices were changing were suddenly torn from childhood and confronted with the perplexities of finding a hand-me-down suit, learning to dance, and buying a corsage.

Information about the color of a girl's dress was usually supplied by her girl friend, who was in most cases the go-between who had arranged the whole thing. At least that was the case with my first and only memorable Sweetheart Dance, the year I was a high school freshman.

As I recall, most of the couples at the Sweetheart Dance had never looked seriously at one another before and never did again. But for that one interminable night they tried to pay a little polite attention to one another.

My date, a myopic and pimply kid named Bill Parker, was a reject of my best friend, Rosemary Wettrick. He had been hanging around her front porch all through the fall and early winter, but when she had a chance to score on her own, she asked the prettiest boy in town, a curly-haired wonder who had moved in from someplace larger and "snazzier." The boys were all wary of him because he hung around only with girls and carried his books hugged to his chest.

Anyway, I was foisted upon Rosemary's heartsick boyfriend, or he was foisted upon me. It was a keen arrangement for Rosemary. He spent the whole evening crying on my shoulder, and she lost neither friend nor faithful steady.

There was only one boy in town I really wanted to go with and my mother had threatened to shoot him if he ever showed up at our house. (My mother was rabid on the subject of "bad blood.") So I was content with the cast-off swain. At least I didn't have to pretend affection.

As I remember it, Rosemary also supplied me with a formal, something she'd worn at a jazzy eighth-grade party in the suburb from which she had recently moved (and where, I judged, they did everything with great finesse and style). I only remember that I didn't begin to fill out the front of it and that under the weight of the enormous corsage—first cousin to a funeral spray—the small puffed sleeve kept slipping from my shoulder, revealing a futile little bra strap.

It was agreed, of course, that I would sleep over at Rosemary's house, so our dates could walk us to the school next door and home. Those were the war years and no other arrangement was even considered.

We spent the morning stringing crepe paper and cutting out hearts to create a "ballroom" (looking very much like a gymnasium strung with crepe paper stapled liberally with hearts).

In the afternoon we had appointments at Mary Edward's Beauty Salon downtown. That part of the ordeal is especially memorable, for it was the first and last hair set of my life. Rosemary's mother loved fussing over girls, a luxury never afforded me before or since. She thought it would be fitting that we have "facials," so some kind of goo was smeared on our faces and we lay around through the long hours of late afternoon giggling at our mud packs.

My mind draws a merciful blank on the subject of the dance itself. It's safe to say that the party didn't live up to the preliminaries.

There was always a gang hanging around Rosemary's house so we piled in there after the dance. As we sat about the living room in our wilting finery, our pert little curls drooping lower and lower, an air of pervasive deflation settled upon us.

In that moment of gloomy anticlimax Rosemary's father had the idea that set this dance off from all others in my memory. He went to the phone, called the bus company, and chartered a city bus to drive us around the county. No one was as delighted with his idea as he was, unless it was his wife, Mary. We all had our private thoughts, I suppose. Life of a sort came back to the party. We laughed and hollered and giggled a lot. It made a great story in Latin class on Monday.

I see them now, that busload of freshmen in their wrinkled suits, their wilting corsages, their pastel organdies—one big gang, all pretense of couples aside—riding through the darkness of Lorain County in that lighted commuter bus like some strange scene from an Ingmar Bergman movie. And Sam Wettrick chortling on the phone to the bus dispatcher, congratulating himself on his stroke of genius.

Sam and Mary Wettrick enjoyed the Sweetheart Dance.

Remember Aaron Slick?

Went out last night to see my nephew star in his high school play, *Flowers for Algernon,* and came home a bit saddened at the passing of the old amateurish class play. It was without question the theater's darkest hour, and only an old cornball like myself could regret its passage.

Last night's play was performed with no great brilliance, but the play was a challenging one, rich in social message; and the cast was convincing, a carryover, I'm sure, from years of watching experts on a TV screen.

Many years ago I was the fledgling drama coach in a country high school, and believe me things were different! The plays were chosen not for message or audience appeal, but for the size and sex of the cast. If there were seven girls and three boys in the class, you sought until you found a play with that balance. Who, after all, would you want to leave out of the class play?

The object of the event was money for the class trip to Washington in the senior year, so siphoning from the profits to pay a royalty was frowned upon. These two conditions left you with an unbelievably limited selection of bad plays.

Typecasting was the rule. The president of the class, who was probably the star of the basketball team, landed the hero's role. The class secretary, a cute little cheerleader who probably dated the class president, was the sweet young heroine. (It wasn't unusual for her to later marry him.)

Performances were incredibly awkward and stiff. The only dramatic models these kids had were the characters in class plays of past years, who were strictly from hunger. Only the class clown in an aging character role was halfway believable, and the audience, of course, thought him fantastic—slated for Broadway or Hollywood.

Staging the class play under limitations of a rural high school auditorium was a grim undertaking. The important emphasis at such a school was basketball, and a stage was a place where you stood to watch a ball game on the gym floor below. You could use the stage any time you liked so long as you didn't interfere with basketball practice or gym class or an academic class meeting on stage for want of a better place.

The curtain—gad, the curtain!—moth-eaten velour in the darker of the school colors, with prominent and convenient slits near the center from too much fingering. Through it you could size up the crowd and make the breathless decision of when to start the show. The curtain was opened in fitful jerks by a bit player from the third act. There was no such thing as a fast curtain or a slow curtain—only a jerky curtain.

Lighting was of the on-and-off variety. Rheostats were something we read about in the production directions but could hardly have defined. Somewhere in the bowels of the school was hidden an ancient spotlight which the director unearthed and foisted upon the physics teacher for repairs. Its performance was fickle at best, and the sophomore pressed into service to operate it never saw his light cues before opening night.

There were no prima donnas in the class play—everybody worked at everything. One of the supporting players brought his dad's pickup truck and all the boys got an afternoon off to haul stuff for the set from a furniture store over in Wakeman.

I always thought that furniture merchant extremely generous, but he was also the local undertaker, and on the strength of that battered davenport and chair he buried a lot of deceased relatives, sooner or later.

Reality was the keynote of the stage set. Pantomime and suggestion had come to American contemporary drama with *Our Town*, but deep in the country a couple of stepladders, a plank, and a few stools did not constitute a stage set; people wanted a window where a window should be and a tree where a tree grew.

Opening night backstage was chaos. There was great anxiety about dressing space. Girls were shy about changing clothes before other girls, let alone at the opposite end of a room where boys were baring their undershirts behind nothing more than a folding screen. Being seen in your underwear was tantamount to scandal.

The play itself, when it finally unfolded, was an endless comedy of errors—misplaced props, forgotten lines, late entrances, and ill-timed sound effects. Acoustics were such that you couldn't hear anything except the prompter past the fourth row.

Every dab of makeup was visible to the back row; no attempt to make sixty out of sixteen fooled any eye. But the audience loved it and suffered with each shy, self-conscious player. The class play was as much of make-believe as most of us were exposed to, and we were anxious to believe. When the simple little love plot unraveled its slapstick misunderstandings and climaxed in that unrehearsed kiss at the end of the third act, we were as caught up in romance as when Nelson Eddy sang to Jeanette MacDonald. The curtain jerked shut on the world's worst—and most appreciated—performance. The cast swaggered forward, the director was called out and given a wonderfully wrapped box which she was expected to exclaim over and open right there, gushing about what a splended group they were and how much fun it had all been.

That was the class play. Today's audiences, saturated as they are with TV professionalism, would hoot and jeer it off the stage. But something in me hankers after that simple, unsophisticated era when *Aaron Slick from Punkin' Crick* was the dramatic high point of the year.

Rickety-Pickety, Clang Ping

I recently bought a new bike for eighty bucks. "So big deal!" say my kids. (They'd each had two or three bikes by the time they were twelve.) But "new" in my case does not imply a replacement for an old one. At the age of forty-eight I've got my first new bike and that's something to write home about!

When I was a kid you could have bought all the bicycles between Amherst and Penfield Junction for eighty bucks, and the guys who owned them would have thrown in their little brothers for good measure. A new bike was something you saved "all your life" for, and few kids made it. You had to have the paper route (there was only one) in order to earn a bicycle.

Billy Van Haun had the first new bike I ever remember, a green job from Sears, Roebuck all decked out with toolbox and luggage rack, taillight and bell. (A "loaded" bicycle was an object of scorn.)

The toolbox on one of those long-ago bikes housed tools the way a glove compartment today houses gloves. It was fitted between the crossbars and contained some sort of battery assembly for the light, which never worked after the first day. The dingaling bell would jiggle loose and hang below the handlebars and a kid who somehow felt the need of signaling somebody had to resort to hollering, "Hey! you dumb cluck! Get outa' the way!" like all the rest of us.

The toolbox on the crossbar went "rickety-rickety," the luggage carrier "pickety-pickety"; the light went "clang" and the bell went "ping." "Rickety-pickety, clang ping" and we always knew when Bill Van Haun was coming up the front lawn and the paper was due to hit the porch.

What few bicycles kids had were passed down from a young uncle or assembled from assorted pieces bought for a buck or two, swapped, or swiped from somewhere. I don't ever remember anyone going to a place as specialized as a bicyle shop, though it was rumored that such a thing existed.

In our immediate society a girl's bike was a sissy sort of thing, and it was pretty generally accepted that anybody riding a girl's bike couldn't possibly be a serious bicycle rider.

Bicycle seats were ampler then, and when new were covered with leather, but as I remember ours, they were usually askew, the leather was torn back, and the excelsior stuffing hung out. Eventually the whole cover disappeared and you sat on the rusty steel. Fenders, if there were any, weren't likely to match; and there was seldom a chain guard. The tires were much patched and a few spokes were bent or missing. As you peddled along and hit a bump, the handlebars would twist downward in their bracket and you found your chin on the crossbar like a French bicycle racer's.

When my brother Johnny was twelve, he sent away to Mead Cycle Company for the first and only new bicycle that our yard ever boasted. It was stripped to bare essentials, which meant fenders and chain guard, and had something called New Departure coaster brakes. The words meant nothing to my little brother and me, but we boasted a lot about them because they were such a point of pride to John. The whole thing—balloon tires, brakes, and all—cost sixteen dollars and we thought it glorious with its chrome fenders and shiny black handlegrips. (Nobody's bike had handlegrips!) We rode it for years in our family, till the fenders were rusted, the handlegrips gone, and the chain guard bent, but in our eyes it was still pure "quality."

My new eighty-dollar girl's bike has three speeds, which in a ten-speed era is pretty chintzy. Does anybody know what to do with ten speeds? In our day a bike had two speeds, fast or slow, depending on how many spokes were left in the front wheel and whether you were going up or down hill. As one faded bicycle champion put it: "The hero of the neighborhood was pretty easy to identify. He had a streak of mud up his back and a hole in his ear where he got poked by the pedal when his pant leg tangled in the chain."

Gentle Flood of Memories

It's a rain to fulfill an Irish blessing, falling "soft upon [our] fields" to end a worrisome drought. In the early morning it started and persists. I heard it from my warm cocoon of blanket, turned on the other ear and slept again. It's a weekend, ironically considered the best time for rain on a vegetable farm.

Paul does today what farmers do on rainy days, goes off to a distant implement dealer's for spare parts, and my sons pursue mechanical hobbies. I do what farmers' wives do on rainy days, and my kitchen fills with the aroma of gingersnaps. As I look from my window at the rain-drenched linden tree I am transported to my mother's kitchen on rainy days of long ago.

A busy, happy place it was, a communal kind of existence. My brothers brought their wives home to live at first, later establishing homes next door or across the road, so my life was enriched by these young women, Alice, Mabel, Gerri, learning homemaking under

Mother's tutelage. My youngish Aunt Maebelle lived in a house-trailer on our farm and often joined us for projects her limited kitchen forbade.

The girls took turns at the ironing board, each pressing what was her responsibility to press, leaving Mama with the towels and table-cloths and pillow slips.

When my sister Mary was home, she spread patterns and material all over the house and sewed up a storm—dresses for Mama, shorts for me, a college wardrobe for herself. There was a lot of standing in the middle of the floor with arms outstretched while Mary fitted and pinned and Alice teased. Somebody worked at the next meal, peeling potatoes, shucking lima beans, making pudding; somebody baked cookies, and anyone not otherwise occupied embroidered in the armchair by the window.

Sister-in-law Mabel contributed the gingersnap recipe; sour cream cookies flavored with a pinch of nutmeg were what Mother made as a matter of course. Toll House cookies were taking the country by storm in my childhood and an instant favorite. Mary baked refrigera-tor cookies for which I always cracked the butternuts. If there was a roll of dough in the "fridge" some kid always knew it and the door was swinging off the hinges. Cookies from the oven were spread to cool on newspapers and what few survived the afternoon were stored in the apple-shaped jar on the refrigerator.

My brothers spent rainy days working on bicycles, motorcycles, tractors, and jalopies in the machine shop down the hill. Like a magnet the fresh cookies drew them, and they crowded in the back door making wet, dirty tracks all over the newspapers spread there. (My mother was a great old-newspaper spreader.) Sometimes they hung around to dunk the cookies in milk, but more often they carried off a fistful, leaving behind the lingering odor of gasoline and grease.

Contributing to the hubbub were folks from the afternoon radio shows—Pepper Young, Ma Perkins, Our Gal Sunday—playing out their breath-holding dramas between singing jingles, organ inter-ludes, and hard-sell soap commercials.

My sisters-in-law canned with my mother on some of these rainy afternoons, their share filling the pints, ours the quarts and two-quart jars. One would peel—tomatoes, pears, peaches, another would fill the jars and somebody else, usually Mama, would work at the salt, the syrup, the sealing. The hope was always that when the pints were opened, the girls would have kitchens of their own.

And so through the damp afternoons the ironing collected in folded piles, the cookies were baked and consumed, the fruit jars moved from sink to stove to cellar. The sewing machine hummed and garments took form. We wiped away the crumbs, and spread a cloth for supper, while the rain fell softly.

Marion L. Steele

Lying here in my seventeen-year-old handwriting is an essay labeled "Eng. 101, Theme No. 1; October 3, 1945: The Truly Great." It's a character study of my high school principal, Marion L. Steele.

How many other college freshmen from my hometown, bewildered and homesick, trying desperately to give legitimacy to the "nowhere" they came from, bled all over their freshman themes with character studies of this beloved lady, the greatest person in their young lives? My indulgent prof gave mine an "A" and wrote at the bottom "sympathetic description." What she should have written was "too many clichés" and "Who's the subject here?"

But perhaps in my naïve way I said the most significant thing there was to say about our Miss Steele: in her encounters with each of us we were always center stage, and what we carried away was the self-confidence she inspired.

We loved her for her spunk and good cheer. "Hi there!" in a hearty voice was always matched with a firm handshake. Her quip "Is that all you can put into a handshake!" dispelled for all time the limp fish grip among her disciples.

She carried herself with dignity, spoke and taught with dignity, conducted her life with dignity. That was what made us devoted students, willing followers.

In an on-the-carpet confrontation with Miss Steele there was only one searing discipline—to be told, "I'm disappointed in you." No one was beyond the devastation of that quiet statement; it accomplished more in the building of character than any detention or suspension (or flogging), and nobody ever joked about it, not even the six-foot blond basketball gods. The challenge to be deserving of Miss Steele's respect was one that everyone rose to.

The morning! How she loved it. Always up and about early and in her office before anyone else arrived, exuding a vitality which inspired positive thinking.

Good health! She radiated it and prized it in others, virtually coaxed it out of them. Perfect attendance was more important to her than perfect grades.

Love and respect for knowledge. Those "literary passages" she insisted we learn—more meaningful now by far than in the days we agonized over them.

"There is something in October sets the gypsy blood astir; I must rise and follow her, when from every hill of flame she calls and calls each vagabond by name."

"Rhodora, if the sages ask Thee why this charm is wasted on the earth and sky, tell them, Dear, that if eyes were made for seeing, then beauty is its own excuse for being."

"Sweet are the uses of adversity, which, like a toad ugly and venomous, wears yet a precious jewel in his head; And this our life exempt from public haunt, finds tongues in trees, books in the running brooks, sermons in stones, and good in everything."

"He who from zone to zone guides through the boundless sky thy certain flight, in the long way that I must tread alone will lead my steps aright." . . . and many many more. Not Carman, Emerson, Shakespeare, or Bryant, but Marion L. Steele, in our frame of reference.

My reflections on Miss Steele are egocentric to the end. Three days before she died she attended a teachers' luncheon where I spoke. It seemed somehow very important to do well for her sake.

Like many another floundering student I had sat across from her desk and heard that crushing "I'm disappointed in you." But on this day she came up afterward, clasped my hand firmly, and said, "Oh, we're proud of you!" and I heard it for those multitudes of students and teachers she counseled, loved, and influenced.

They named a high school for Marion L. Steele, to the pleasure of those who knew her, but a generation passes and her legacy grows less discernible. In the freshness of the morning when a "whining school boy" is urged "unwillingly to school" he little suspects that his life is being influenced by the stately lady whose portrait hangs in the front hall.

Harold Jeffreys

Harold Jeffreys read something I wrote long ago in *Farm Journal* and sent me one or two strong lines of approval. I wrote thanking him for his kindness, expressing disappointment that he had revealed nothing of himself. What a floodgate that unleashed! Thereafter came long, salty, delightful letters of biography. We were kindred spirits, he and I, in love alike with words and books, ideas, people—life.

Harold had been banker, tax consultant, telephone man, advisor, friend, and bon vivant to the farmers of Dixon County, Nebraska, and lived on the outskirts of the tiny village of Martinsburg on the Nebraska, Iowa, South Dakota border, just west of Sioux City.

Reading was the passion of his life, and on the weekly shopping trip to Sioux City he always "went round to harry the virgins at the library," carrying off an armload of books. The points he made in his letters were often reinforced with allusions to things he'd read. (He flattered me unduly by presuming I was as well read.)

"I wonder what will become of all my nice books when I am gone," he wrote early one summer. "They are part of me, and I cannot bear to think of them on the table at the Goodwill for 10¢ a throw."

Like any man of seventy-seven he reminisced a lot. "There are some things I don't like about myself; I had always promised that when I made my first thousand I would go back to France [he was a World War I veteran] see some girls I knew, go back to where I was wounded, but did I? Hell no! In a cowardly and shameful manner I squandered it on a black carpet, furniture, and draperies for my bedroom. How the memories of the trip would have enriched my life now that I am old. I like to think of myself as much TORO, getting my pick of the women and all that, but at heart I am just a miserable poltroon always playing it safe."

He obviously had plenty of memories to enliven his old age.

183

"There is something transcendental in the communication between two really good dancers and let me hasten to add that it involves nothing erotic. It is something like love and something like sentiment, and you can feel electric currents back and forth. Of course I will not deny that a couple of good belts of Canadian Club heighten the mystique." (He told me he "boozed" one day a month on a few bottles of good German beer.)

"I have always been glad I never had any ambition; all I ever wanted was to have a good time." He must have succeeded, for elsewhere he wrote, "Looking back it all seems a blinding glory of warm, moonlit summer nights and dance music and unreasonable laughter and cuddlesome and merry girls with gay, dancing feet."

He enjoyed his memories and the comforts of his old age but he rankled under it. "Things are so relative," he wrote. "I have a cousin in the city who is 95. I am 77 and he calls me 'kid.' If there is such a thing as 'the tragedy of old age' it is that you don't feel old. I don't feel any different than I did when I was twenty."

He told of the day a sweet young thing held the door open for him and his armload of books at the library. "I told her how kind she was, but the incident cast a pall over the rest of my stop and my repartee with the attendants lacked its usual brilliance and side-splitting wit."

He knew himself to be urbane and worldly and a peasant still. Yet he complained. "Why the hell is it that when I am questioned in a doctor's office or some such place the girl always says, 'You are from out of town'? What is there about me that gives me away as being from the provinces?"

In late July he sent me a small packet of his precious books, *A Shropshire Lad, The Rubaiyat, Collected Poems of Keats*—freely scribbled with marginal notes, and I suspected the worst.

In August I was out in Harold Jeffreys' province. I took the little detour off the highway, two miles and twenty-five years up to the "Burg" as he called it. A tiny cluster of houses it is, withering and bleaching in the prairie sun. I found the little hillside Eden on the edge of town where Rosie Jeffreys lives with Pookie the cat, but my friend is gone.

" . . . We get up every morning to resume our private war with Death, but to look her in the face has surprisingly little impact. You would not believe it unless it happened to you. Dying is no great hardship, and if it weren't for leaving Rosie alone I wouldn't give it a second thought. . . . To love and be loved. To feel worthy. To maintain some sort of reasonable moral standard. Isn't that about all there is to being happy?"

He had once written of the death of his best friend, "He was of very humble extraction and some of his clan were not very pure. He was uneducated, but I always thought I was entitled to some degree of good opinion of myself because of Ed's regard and his loyalty and friendship."

Harold Jeffreys was fond of me, and perhaps I am entitled to "some degree of good opinion of myself" because of that regard.

North Ridge Reminiscence

Only a sentimental crowd like the Pentons would hold a wake for an old house; but there we all were out in front being photographed for the last time framed between the spirea bush and the lilac. Infused through the years with a personality reflecting a bit of each of us, the Penton house had stood mute and pathetic for some time now. And in strange obeisance to this derelict of a dwelling, all the family showed up in answer to brother Bill's pronouncement: "She's going down this week."

One by one we straggled through, bemused by our private recollections. "This is the room I built," said Ted to the friend called in to capture the occasion on film. He was pondering the back bedroom where he'd brought his bride forty years ago. "Know any eighteen-year-old today that could make a woodshed into a bedroom? I even plastered it."

When Ted and Mabel moved out, Erik and Alice took over the "newlywed annex," and later Mary and Frank. When my brothers built Mama a new home years later, John and Donna and their brood of seven moved into the old place. They were succeeded by Bill and Gunver and it is their vacating that signals the house's demise.

It's a clapboard house of Civil War vintage and anonymous construction. As far as we're concerned it came into existence in 1918 when our parents arrived the day after their marriage. The ceilings are a little too high, the rooms a little cramped. Nobody ever considered restoration; preservation was about all we managed.

I remember so well the year in the thirties when Mama scraped up a hundred dollars to have someone paint the place and install weights in the upstairs windows. We no longer had to prop them open with shoes and coat hangers. And it was glorious to live in a house with paint!

"Crookedest darned walls I ever papered," grumbled Paul, as he walked through the kitchen on this evening twenty-five years after the fact. He has never forgiven me for conning him into that papering job when we were courting (probably because it solidified the romance). My sister's husband commiserated with him.

"I'll never forget what a horror this dining room was the first time I came here. The table was heaped halfway to the ceiling and it stayed that way for years. It's a wonder you ever persuaded me to marry you," he said to Mary. (Tidy housekeeping was not my mother's long suit.)

"Yes," added Mary, "and your mother was horrified when she found out you were dating a girl who lived in that house where the curtains always flapped from the upstairs windows!"

The bathroom, like the living room, kitchen, bedroom, and stairway, was off the dining room. We never considered the indelicacy of the arrangement, were just grateful for indoor plumbing and the womblike comfort of that little ball and claw bathtub.

"What are we gonna' do with that bathtub?" somebody asked.

"I think we ought to mount it in front of John's house, install a motorcycle trophy, and plant flowers around it," I said, in deference to the family motorcycle business.

Never within my memory was there a functioning knob on the bathroom door. It was secured with a wooden block placed so high that we were in late adolescence before we enjoyed any privacy there.

Erik, reverent collector that he is, went up and dragged crates of stuff from the attic—letters, greeting cards, window shades, old wallpaper, and a mountain of magazines. When does one finally come into the time to reread forty years of *National Geographics*!

Hank's obsession in the demolition process was with locating the jarful of Indianhead pennies he spilled between the wall joists from the attic thirty-five years ago.

"Here's where Pat grew up," said Ted to the photographer, "here in the chimney corner over the register." On winter mornings we all crowded immodestly into that corner to dress. The two upstairs bedrooms were like Arctic barracks. Still hanging in the boys' bedroom upstairs was a naked light bulb with a pull chain. At one time it had five cords attached, one leading to each of the five beds.

Johnny walked around the outside of the house, sized up the sandstone foundation, and decided he'd send somebody over with a bucket loader next week to retrieve those huge foundation stones. "Don't know what I'm gonna do with 'em, but . . . "

"They'd make one heck of a nice pyramid to mount that bathtub on," I suggested.

For my part, I had Paul unscrew the brass knocker from the front door and the roller towel bar from the kitchen cupboard. Those will be sufficient to remind me that once there was a house— uncomfortable, inconvenient, unlovely—but a home nonetheless, overflowing with life and love. Small wonder we met to mourn its passing.

A Wave at the Crossing

The childhood thrill of pulling up to a railroad crossing where the red light flashed was knowing that the engine would in a moment roar through and you would wave to the engineer. His return wave from that high window was more than just a gesture of kindness to a little kid. It was almost a symbol of the brotherhood of man.

Knowing that he and his fellow engineers had waved to every chick and child across the width and breadth of the country made you part of a great American fraternity of friendly souls.

There was great excitement in that moment when a steam engine roared through a crossing and you were close enough to see the huge wheels propelled by the steam-powered drive shafts. You counted the freight cars and tried to read the legends on their sides, the letters that represented dozens of different railway lines—B & O, Burlington, Erie Lackawanna, Norfolk and Western, Union Pacific, Santa Fe—watching then anxiously for the caboose, hoping perhaps to get a farewell wave from the brakeman.

If it was a passenger train, you watched for those lucky people looking out from the coaches, their faces no more than a blur. What a thrill to watch for the dining car, and again for people eating at those white tables, the rich people surely.

If it was night you saw less with the eye and more with the mind. You imagined the scene inside the Pullman cars, the porter making up the berths and people crawling into the luxurious comfort of them.

You only imagined also the places the train had been—the roundhouse, the freight yard, the station stops. You visualized it chugging past factories and tenements, through tunnels under rivers, and then charging full speed through the countryside, over bridges and alongside streams, across the plains to the mountains; then around and around the mountains, higher and higher, zooming into tunnels in rock faces.

In some subconscious way the engineer's wave involved you in the whole adventure of the American railway. Even in the night when you were in your bed and heard the lonely whistle of the locomotive, you were waving in spirit to the engineer.

As time went by it came to have a new significance. A little boy came into my life—my first nephew. Phillip was like the baby brother I'd always teased for, a great delight to a teenage girl. Like other children he was enchanted by trains, but for Phillip they became an abiding passion. Because he was seriously handicapped physically, his life was never crowded with those other excitements that tend to lead us away from our childhood enthusiasms. He was a train buff from the day he could say "Choo choo!"

Phillip read everything he could find about trains, collected stories and pictures and films and tape recordings of trains. He even managed with his clumsy fingers and the help of his Dad and friends to build a small collection of models. And trains more than anything else in life "transported" him beyond his limited physical existence. For him the wave of the engineer was symbolic of so much that brought pleasure to life, and I never "waved to a train" but what I thought of him.

On a day in May 1970, absorbed in thought, I pulled up at a railroad crossing where a light flashed and a diesel horn hooted. Three huge blue and silver engines rumbled through the crossing. From the third of them watched the engineer. Automatically I lifted my hand in greeting, but the young man stared stonily into his void of boredom.

Like an aging fool I sat there humiliated. The blur of computerized containers whizzed past my window. It seemed rudely and abruptly the end of an era. It was the day Phillip died.

IT CAME TO PASS . . .

Future shock is reverberating through the boondocks. It comes in the wake of affluence, increased mobility, expanded communications, and changes in the moral imperative. Existing as we do on the fringe of a megalopolis, the Leimbachs may suffer the waves more intensely than remotely scattered farm families; but none of us is naive enough to presume that the tremors will diminish.

Caveat Emptor!

There was a time when you could send somebody to the "stand" up the road for two bits' worth of onions, and get onions. Nowadays he's likely to come back with a pomegranate, an ironstone pitcher, a wicker basket, a jar of Knott's jelly, and a yard of Trail bologna for $29.95 and forget the onions. In case you haven't noticed, the roadside "stand" has become a rural spread, a cozy little $200,000 emporium where meats and cheeses and wines and rustic bric-a-brac ultimately obliterate the radishes.

The last time I was over at brother Bill's country market everybody was "bent outa' shape" because the microwave oven went on the fritz and burned eight pies and a half dozen strudels. Bill's motivation in putting the pie concession in the market was that the tantalizing smells would transport the clientele. The smell in there that day took me right back to the kitchen of my girlhood, where I was lovingly known as Charcoal Pat.

Forty years ago Mama started this roadside market (now Bill's) with a glut of ten pounds of asparagus. She set it in a pan of water out front with a cup of money and a sign saying, "Make your own change."

"As nearly as I could figure," she said, "I came out money ahead." Things looked so bad around our place that the customers probably took this as a subtle appeal for charity and contributed accordingly.

Roadside markets today are definitely not operated as charitable institutions. We spend a lot of time toting potatoes around to these places and I've made a few observations on the subject.

The allure of "homegrown" was the original come-on. In the face of homegrown pineapples and avocados (to mention just a few of the more obvious anomalies), a realist must recognize that a lot of that stuff made a long trip before it was tucked into those cute little baskets.

Roadside markets seem to succeed on a very freakish trait of human nature, to wit: the more expensive something is, the more desirable it becomes and the more people will buy.

"The quickest way to kill the market on a produce item is to drop the price," says Brother Bill.

And surely the markets which we observe to be the most flourishing are the ones where the prices are the highest. People love country charm, and they'll buy anything if you can create the illusion that it's being grown or fabricated out back by "sure 'nuff country folk." Wrap a hunk of Lever Bros. soap in a square of Taiwanese gingham and somehow it assumes Gatlinburg charm. Pickles forked from an old whiskey barrel are worth twice as much as those in glass from the A & P. Beats me why, but it works.

Regarding the produce proper (assuming that you have been able to elbow your way to the produce counter through the hanging plants) there are, of course, other criteria for success. High-quality produce is probably the most important. That means that the operator must discard leftover and inferior produce, raising the overhead. Variety is another key factor in marketing success. At my brother's market you can buy anything from hard candy to hydrangeas, from Scandinavian wood carvings to Pat Leimbach's book. You can grind your own cashew butter or blend your own coffee beans from a half-dozen hemp sacks.

It helps, too, to have some specialty item for which you're famous. Bill used to run around in a red truck emblazoned "Penton Orchards, Famous for Fresh Sweet Corn." That's a pretty good gimmick if you can find that kind of tree.

One of our customers with a singing talent and real orchards opens his rustic showrooms to groups for meetings. He presents a program of song and refreshments of cider and apples. He does so well with his varied and expanding business that he has to have a cop out front on Sundays to direct traffic!

From what I read on a great big first-grade poster on one of Brother Bill's walls, I judge that he, too, has found a PR gimmick.

"Mr. Penton let us pick our own little pumpkins. We carried the pumpkins to the strawberry patch. Mr. Penton said that the strawberries would sleep for the winter. He said that the strawberries would grow again in spring. He said that the tree would sleep in the winter. Then Mr. Penton treated us to an apple. We got back on the bus and came to school."

. . . And when we grew up we all went out to guess where and bought strawberries and apples and cheese cut from a big wheel by Mr. Penton himself.

A Long Shadow

Now I lay me down to sleep in an heirloom bed in an antique clapboard farmhouse. From the window no light intrudes my neighbors upon me; I feel their sheltering presence through the friendly dark that lies upon the fields between us. I know their names and their ways as they know mine and that secures the night. A sliver of moon, a sprinkling of stars, and the bare black boughs of the maples stand the night watch.

Nine hours and five hundred miles of freeway ago I slept in a Philadelphia brownstone on an artery of the center city. Street lights and auto lights and high rise security lights held back the night. People above, and people below, and the people through the walls behind, people across the way beyond the Victorian shutters and all alone. Three locked doors and the city police force held the wolves at bay. From time to time an emergency vehicle moving at top speed through the street beneath the windows rent the night with wailing and alarm. A phone call in the night and no one there. No one? Or a dangerous anyone? The wary sleeper stands his own night watch.

Who would live this way by choice? Some, oh yes, some who know nothing of the peace of pastures, the freedom of prairies, the shelter of woods and hills, the kinship of country. But not my friend, Laura, of the Philadelphia brownstone. When you come from the Oklahoma-Texas panhandle your roots have to be deep to survive and Laura is a survivor with a deep feeling for the country and its people. As a skilled journalist specializing in Ag economics she serves country people where she can do it best—among Eastern publishers, Washington legislators, and USDA economists.

When Laura moved to the city she pledged to maintain a little land in the country to keep her thumb green and her spirit alive. City streets, offices, pollution, and confusion were tolerable when you could get away weekends to spade and hoe and prune and chop wood. The trunk of her car was full of tools and fertilizer and chain saws and other gear vital to maintaining the country-city equation. The car, of course, was necessary but maintained with great difficulty and expense in garages or open parking lots always at a distance from the brownstone.

Through the years vandalism in the country and street crime in the cities have worn away at her life-style.

When the break-ins at the country "retreat" numbered twenty, she and the friend who shared the expense lost count as well as heart. They sold the country property. For a year or two she gardened the backyard of a friend's home some distance from town, but the car was broken into and her tools and possessions stolen so often that finally she abandoned even that. She replaced so many windows in her car that it seemed simpler to remove everything and leave it unlocked in the lot.

Twice the brownstone apartment building has been broken into. "You add another lock, something they can't saw through," she says "and make the best of it." Last year she was pushed down and robbed while standing in a crowd waiting for a bus.

"I don't like these things, but I have no choice at this point in my life. I like my work; I'm committed to it; and it is here."

We farmers take credit in great self-satisfied hunks for an agricultural technology unequalled in the history of the world. We too often overlook the thousands of dedicated persons in Ag-related industries—like Ag journalism—who labor far from the barnyard, often under abrasive and constricting circumstances, to improve our industry. The majority of these people came from the land. Some left by choice; many left during the long lean decades when it was leave or perish. Our life would be neither so satisfying or secure without them. The very least we owe them is gratitude and a concern for the urban problems with which they struggle.

No man is an island, though in the peaceful dark of a country night, alone with the moon and the stars and bare black branches, it is tempting to pretend so.

Opposed to Improvement

I would like to go on record as being opposed to improvement. I just stopped by the grocery store to pick up my old brand of oven cleaner—a potent, stinking, gooey substance to be smeared around on a messy stove and then removed in a satisfying ablution of restoration. Alas! It has been "improved" beyond recognition or effectiveness.

The cleaner is now lemon-scented and dispensed in a spray can. The price has advanced from 39 cents to 89 cents, a definite improvement—to the manufacturer. You couldn't volatize that thick goo without diluting it three or four times, so it now takes three or four applications to accomplish what I formerly did in one. All that time spent cleaning the stove keeps me off the streets pushing dope and out of alleys snatching purses.

Breakfast cereals I noted long ago have been "improved" with the addition of vitamins, psychedelic colors, pseudo-fruit flavors. In my day it was thought satisfactory if you got your vitamins from cabbage, apples, whole-wheat bread, and the like. I do not like the taste of vitamins, nor do I like the taste of vitamin-"improved" cereal. I still get my vitamins from cabbage and apples and such-like and to heck with Fruit Loops, Count Chocola, etc.

The most ingenious "improvements" by far are accomplished in the packaging field. Everything that can be put in a spray can has been; I'd like to compress hate and send a can of the stuff to the packaging wizards.

Once upon a time you bought a box of stuff: you got out the butcher knife, sawed a convenient-sized opening, and poured out the contents in satisfying affluence. Then the yahoos "improved" the opening process with little "push here" guidelines and nothing's been satisfying since.

If you succeed in "pushing here" without spraining a thumb, the package fails to tear on the dotted line anyway; the opening is still too big or too small. You get all of the product or none. If it fails altogether, you're down in the cellar without the butcher knife. And the vacuum pack! Whoever invented that should be vacuum-packed himself. Emergency rooms must be overflowing with people who have committed hara-kiri trying to open a vacuum package. Vacuum-packed bacon is the worst, probably because you encounter it early in the in the morning when simply coping with the situation is about all you can manage. Many the kid who has missed his bus on account of vacuum-packed bacon.

Whether it's picture hooks or bologna, forget trying to salvage the vacuum pack. Throw it away and find another wrap or container. When you come back to the picture hooks six weeks later and find all the nails missing, you're only going to add foul language to the unpleasantness.

The pour spout is an improvement the world could survive without. Opening milk cartons! Ah, the kitchens that have been bathed in milk in the wake of a fumbling forefinger.

The compound verb has come into its own in a welter of irresistible cures for all the housewife's complaints. Spray and wash, wash and wear, iron and mend, stretch and sew, mop and glow, brown and serve, shake and bake . . . the list is endless.

Floating up from the bottom of all these euphonious "try and err" (rhymes with her) remedies is an old maxim also concocted of compound verbs—(the cost of all these alluring half cures is nothing if not compound). Does nobody remember "scrimp and save"?

The grocery stores where we purchase all these "improved" products are themselves the victims of "improvement." You can dash through and snatch from the shelves forty dollars' worth of groceries as fast as you can say "super-dooper super-market." Then there'll be eight registers, only one of which is in business, and you can stand in line and contemplate progress.

Once we were a nation of intelligent people capable of looking out for our own health and safety. Alas, those responsibilities are now legislated by boards and committees.

They pass laws to "improve" the quality of life and safeguard its existence with "improvements" such as the nonopening medicine bottle. Just awaken in the night severely ill, your eyes bleary, your glasses downstairs on the sink, and try—just try—to match the &$&?—& arrows that enable you to remove the cap. Throw the thing against the wall opposite and nothing will happen. It's plastic.

If it's tachycardia you're having, your blood pressure will have zoomed ten points; if it's nausea, you will already have vomited. If it's a heart attack, you may be lucky and die. But if it's a headache, just learn to suffer. "Improvement" is a way of life, and there are an indeterminate number of headaches ahead.

Blackberry Fracas

My good neighbor Farmer Schmalz has been arrested and hauled into court over a hassle that developed when he tried to evict somebody from his property for picking blackberries. The whole business sounds petty and ridiculous when the bare facts are stated. My younger brothers and I used to make our summer spending money by going off in the darkness before dawn and swiping blackberries from other people's hedgerows. Wild blackberries, like most things wild, have always been fair game for poaching.

But the bare facts in this case—as in most cases—don't tell the story. Farmer Schmalz, like many another farmer, has been plagued in recent years with a swelling stream of trespassers, pilferers, and vandals. Young people with spray cans have painted obscenities on his storage buildings. They have torn down or used for targets his "No trespassing" and "No shooting" signs. They have shot holes in his buildings, sometimes when they were occupied; they have shot out his night lights. The back roads are littered with field corn stolen for "ammunition" in teenage horseplay. Barricades put in place to keep parkers out of his lanes have been moved or burned. Because his property is on relatively deserted roads, there is an open season on dumping. Each year he hauls away truckloads of litter—everything from beer cans to sofas and refrigerators.

The latest plagues he has had to endure are the sophisticated vehicles made to traverse difficult terrain—four-wheel-drive trucks and the even more invincible ATV's (All Terrain Vehicles) that can navigate the rivers as well as the land. Each year irresponsible "kids" run vehicular chases through his planted fields, destroying hundreds of dollars' worth of grain. .

On one occasion Farmer Schmalz was attacked by some boys who were shooting at his equipment. They even tried to drag him by the leg with their moving car. Those boys were apprehended, tried, sentenced, and then released by the courts making no restitution for injury to person or property.

Who can blame a farmer if he is no longer tolerant and good-natured with blackberry pickers? Another of my neighbors across the hollow was arrested several years back for shooting out the car tires of city teenagers who refused to leave his premises. Another farmer of our acquaintance maintains at great cost several wells along his lakefront property. He, too, was arrested for shooting above the heads of vandals caught in the act of destroying his wells.

Our own experience with "wreckreationers," while not so extensive, has been costly to say the least. What perhaps seemed like a harmless prank to a bunch of kids one summer cost us a $4,000 irrigation pump. We have increasing problems with people who dig potatoes in our fields. One can anticipate a time when somebody stealing from a potato field just sprayed with pesticides will institute a suit for insecticide poisoning. (Farmers know when their fields are safe for reentry and when they are not. Intruders are fools who take their lives in their own hands.)

Remember the days of Dick and Jane and kindly Farmer Bob in his straw hat and bib overalls, that bucolic time when the milk of human kindness flowed from a virgin spring? Who could have guessed that Dick and Jane would turn into monsters mounted on Land Rovers, armed with aerosol paint cans, rifles, and pellet guns. Small wonder Farmer Bob no longer points his pitchfork toward heaven.

Grandog, What Big Teeth You Have . . . _____

My cousin, who is an obstetrical nurse at the local hospital, tells me our birth rate is down from 150 babies per month in the sixties to 80 or 85. I suppose it's accurate to say that the baby boom has been reduced to a whimper and replaced by a dog howl. Everywhere we go we find our friends and relatives dogsitting for their married children.

"Would you like to see a picture of our grandog?" asks my good friend Kay Whyte, with tongue in cheek. "They bring him down from Toledo (100 miles) every two weeks to be shampooed, trimmed, manicured, and perfumed by a guy in the old hometown."

"Can't somebody up in Toledo do that for him?" I ask.

"Well, he reacts very favorably to Mr. Crow, so they drive him down in an air-conditioned Monte Carlo to keep his appointment. I think one of the reasons they got rid of the Corvette was that poor Lucky didn't have much of a place to sit in the back." Lucky is a wirehaired terrier whose station in a typically childless family obviously suits his name.

My friends Ralph and Alida number a Collie, a Labrador, and a mutt among their grandogs, and believe me it's a wild household when they all come home for holidays merging their dogs with the German shepherd and the Chow that already live there.

My sister is less than enthusiastic about holidays with her young marrieds. The tree in Karen and Earl's backyard is anchored to a St. Bernard called Brandywine, with whom they share their mobile home and their meager food budget, and Sylvia and Steve have a fluctuating family of Siamese cats.

"Love us, love our dog" seems to be the rule under which young couples operate. Grandogs do not sit home neglected in lonely apartments. Where young couples congregate they pack along their dogs as once we carted our babies. While couples sit around listening to Aero Smith or the Led Zeppelin, their dogs snarl and growl or howl and romp together.

Last Sunday at the family reunion grandogs outnumbered new babies 2 to 1. A Great Dane, a poodle, and a couple of mutts had a barking-sniffing good time.

"Have dog, will travel" is another maxim they live by. A lot of these pampered pets travel in style in carpeted vans with mag wheels, stereos, and their own velvet-lined wicker baskets, but Bob and Vicky and Rusty (the aforementioned collie) make the long trip from southeastern Ohio in the front seat of a small pickup truck.

Many of these pets—cats run a close second to dogs as "family"—are very much a part of the scene before the marriage occurs. There's probably a lot more attention paid to the compatibility to be established with Rover than to the pedigree of the bride or groom's family. Vicky knew well in advance that she was going to have to share Bob and the front seat of that pickup with Rusty. And my niece's husband had carted Sabu, the Siamese cat, back and forth from Iowa two or three times before he ever became its foster parent.

"How effective do you suppose all these dogs are gonna be at looking after these kids when they get into their dotage?" I ask of my friend Kay.

"Boy, I don't know. I surely wouldn't want Lucky looking after me. He hasn't got sense enough to stay in the house when the door's open," she says, smiling.

By and large grandog parents accept these situations with amused resignation. They complain a lot, but I haven't heard of any severe alienation of affection. Where once they collected playpens and high chairs and a few shiny silver dollars to herald their grandchildren, they now set in a supply of Puppy Chow, arrange a litter box, and gift wrap a rubber bone.

Nothing Ventured . . .

At the first lull in the spring rush I slip away to the river bluff to keep an urgent appointment with myself. This year I find to my dismay that my favorite promontory is slipping away.

How many times have I come here through the years to contemplate. It is close enough to the house that I can arrive in two minutes, but so remote that it brings me to another world. A generous hedge of poison ivy discourages the casual stroller from seeking it out. You have to know that beyond the fence and the poison ivy and the scrub cottonwood is a chestnut oak and a grassy bank and a magnificent view of the river and valley.

I have sat here in the night and watched into the dawn, watched the sunset here on summer evenings. I have come here on picnics in early spring and paused here to view the October spectacle of color when we worked the adjacent field at harvest. My "reducing spot" I always called it, where the height and the beauty reduced me to human size.

Now a great crevice opens in the earth behind me, running diagonally along what was in all probability a little game trail.

Perhaps next spring this lush pad of earth will be a mass of topsoil flowing with the spring rains to the river below. The oak tree against which I sit and meditate will have toppled into the void to be washed up as debris on the valley floor.

For me there will be a new edge, raw and barren at first, but the grass will come again and there's a persistence about poison ivy. Someday, perhaps, another oak or sassafras tree, and certainly the cottonwood will regenerate with its whispering leaves.

Once I brought a friend here to this high bluff where we watched the birds flying from tree to tree. I wanted to share with her the freedom and the release that I find here. She is the sort who lives with a constant awareness of cataclysm, and I realized suddenly that she was terrified. She sensed that this crevice would appear and the whole place would sink away.

For her the reward wasn't worth the risk.

The discovery that my "reducing spot" is being reduced saddens me. I am reminded sharply of the impermanence of things. And yet I love to live at the precarious edge of life, not too bound to anything, where the view is clear. There's a motto posted over my sink: "Choose Life!" I know I run the risk of having the earth crumble beneath me, but I'm more than willing to chance it.

Status in the Boonies

A feature in *U.S. News and World Report* on the search for status (in early '77) has left me in a state of ego shock. The first thing that I am shattered to learn is that I don't live in any of the "in" places—New York, Atlanta, Houston, Chicago, or San Francisco. Reading through the list of desirable possessions and pursuits, I am demoralized not so much by my lack of "in" things as by the fact that I never even embraced anything that is now "out."

If you live in New York, the "in" thing to do is sell your cottage at the shore and get a Rolls-Royce, rip up your wall-to-wall carpeting and order Persian rugs, cancel your European trip and buy season tickets for the opera. Only my bathroom telephone (concession to my deafness) would qualify me for any status in the Big Apple.

Now in Houston, custom pickup trucks are very big sitting in front of high-rise condominiums, but where could I go with a battered '68 Chevy with a cracked windshield and not so much as a CB radio or a horse trailer hitch?

I might just merit status in Chicago for my "mixed china and crystal." I have ironstone from the A & P, a Shirley Temple pitcher, and a matched set of ten Kraft cheese glasses. Things that are "out" in Chicago that I never even got into are Indian jewelry, astrology, men's necklaces, and Playboy clubs.

Faded jeans make it in San Francisco, but they have to be imported from France. No dice for the J. C. Penney variety faded in a hay field and patched with the backs of old Levis. The place where I would be most qualified for status seems to be Atlanta. Small farms are the "in" thing there along with cheap original paintings, of which I have several of the third-grade finger-paint variety, and Adidas sneakers. My Adidas are dirty hand-me-downs from a rich relative and they pinch my little toe, but they look very good lying casually around when jogging friends come panting through.

What is passé in Atlanta now is patched elbow tweeds, men's ponytail hairdos, mink coats, and St. Bernards. I think I could sacrifice all those.

Indoor plants are very, very "in" everywhere; the stranger the better. My good old papyrus plant would flip her fronds if she knew!

It seems to me that what is wanting is a list of what's "in" and "out" in the boondocks. *U.S. News and World Report* to the contrary, I know of nothing that gives one more status these days than just living in the boonies. We are slow to discard things in the country, so the list of "outs" is brief, but Saturday night shopping, horse-drawn plows, bib overalls, gingham aprons, horning bees, and applejack are pretty much on the wane. What's "in"?

> Sears, Roebuck charge cards
> Four-wheel drive pickups (with horse trailers out West)
> CB radios
> Daughters studying agriculture
> Combines with air-conditioned cabs
> Snowmobiles
> Weekend golfing
> A Piper Cub
> A second or third farm in Nebraska or Kansas
> Hawaiian junkets

Quilted car coats
Gas-guzzling automobiles
Morning coffee at a corner café
Computerized record-keeping systems
$100,000 mortgage
Wall Street Journal
Private grain storage and dryer
Church attendance

Criminy! Except for the record-keeping system, the *Journal*, the mortgage, and the church, I can't even qualify for status in the boondocks! But eat your heart out, all you backgammon-playing, opera-going, Gucci-garbed status seekers with your customized vans and your pottery wheels and your whirlpool baths! I have my own private gas well.

Things Her Mother Earth Never Taught Her ───────

My peaches are "up," my pickles are "down," my peas and beans and corn are frozen deep and I'm feeling smug way down to the depths of my fruit cellar. Much of the security synonymous with farming emanates from the bright array of red, yellow, and green stuff standing watch on the shelves of the can cupboard.

Down in the boiler room of an LST in the Pacific during World War II, my brother John talked nostalgically of home and of the hundreds of jars of fruits and vegetables Mama canned each year. He couldn't believe that his buddy from New York City had never heard of canning. A generation later there were millions of children both rural and urban who would respond with a blank stare to canning talk.

There is evidence, however, that the Empire City produces a bit of canned stuff besides music and advertising. My young New York editor brought me two jars of jam that she had made herself from apricots hand-picked in Idaho, flown back in a suitcase to the East, thence by briefcase to Ohio. Backyard gardening has had an amazing renaissance in recent years and we at End o' Way have been swamped with people anxious to glean at bargain rates the leavings of our commercial vegetable harvest. Thousands of dusty fruit jars must have been put back into service for the first time in years, but many a station wagon that drives in here in search of beans has boxes of spanking new jars tucked in back with the kids. Women who had been rationalizing away the canning bit on the argument that it wasn't economically feasible are taking a new look at food prices and searching around for angles. (The money saved can, for example, always be squandered on ever more glamorous and "personalized" jars and glasses.)

For young couples who don't know how to tackle a mason jar there's abundant advice available from Mr. Kerr and Mr. Ball, the Agricultural Extension Department, and a spate of cookbooks rushed into print—but the really camp place to get the scoop is the *Mother Earth News*. This publication is a how-to guide to everything for the "alternate life-style" set.

I don't know if *Mother Earth* advocates open-kettle or cold-pack canning, whether she favors two-piece lids over one-piece with jar rubbers, whether she recommends fooling around with pressure cookers or instructs you in the long-boil method; but those are all things old wives haggle about in the canning season and never do agree on completely. Because they address themselves to a group whose priorities lie with purity of food and good nutrition, *Mother Earth* probably prefers honey over refined sugar, frowns on preservatives, and recommends a lot of whole-grain, fiber-rich, trace-mineral retaining methodology. I think I'm too set in my ways to get into all that. I already know more about good nutrition than I put into practice.

My best advice on the canning subject is that a girl marry a man who has been schooled in the canning arts, as my husband was—one who's a hustler with a paring knife and a whiz-bang with a food mill. They come usually from old farmhouses with cool, dark cellars.

Where can a canny little bridal prospect find one? I don't think she should bother to advertise for him in the *Mother Earth News*. The kind of guy I'm talking about would be astounded to recognize that someone has to read a magazine for the sort of commonplace information he acquired with his permanent teeth. But she might place an ad in the classifieds of the *Prairie Farmer* or the *Co-op Country News,* offering to marry the fellow who can properly complete in seven words or less: "Run down cellar and . . ." She should snap up the first one who finishes with: "bring me up a jar of fruit." That's her man.

When the Environmental Protection Agency contacts me for advice on conserving natural resources and improving the quality of life, the first thing I'm going to recommend is that they blow out that "Light the Night" campaign. It's clear to me that the dark-loving night person is an endangered species, and I happen to be one of them. I can't help resenting all the electricity wasted pushing back the peaceful dark.

One of the tenets of Oriental philosophy, the Yin-Yang principle, recognizes the essential of balance for the nurture of the human spirit. One of these sets of balance is darkness and light. I think we are in danger of upsetting the balance in favor of light.

There was a time when you drove out of town into the darkness of the countryside, but rarely any more. Nearly every crossroad has its streetlight and rather than being deterrents to vandals, streetlights are themselves the object of vandalism. Freeways and shopping centers, car lots and fast-food alleys form nonstop neon corridors coast to coast.

There is perhaps more justification for the mercury vapor lights that are a fixture in nearly every farmyard, guarding gas pumps and equipment, but I feel sorry for each family that feels compelled to live with one. I cannot conceive of life with no darkness, of turning off the room lights only to be invaded by a glow from without. Worst of all is the knowledge that we farm people have capitulated like the rest of the nation to mistrust and fear.

A New Jersey friend tells of her delight in the cluster of pinpoint lights that is a prairie town emerging from the darkness. She contrasts this with the uniform pink glow spreading as far as the eye can see along the New York-New Jersey coastline of home. "Amazing and frightening" she says, "to recognize that we are capable of obliterating the night."

Driving home one night through the hill country of southeastern Ohio, I became aware of a strangeness about the territory. Here there were no streetlights at crossroads, no lights in the homes or yards (it was only 10:30), no other cars on the narrow twisting streets.

The farms were small and poor, industry sparse and luxury limited. But the darkness spoke of tranquility, of a people yielding to the temporal rhythms, keenly aware of the distinction between night and day.

One of the special pleasures of summer long ago was lying in the front yard contemplating the galaxies in a darkness alive with sounds of tree toads, frogs, and crickets; or in winter trudging out to the pond in the meadow to skate on a night made bright by snow, falling on the ice and then relaxing there to discover those stars in different attitudes.

Are all children today even aware, I wonder, that one has night vision that sharpens (on all but the cloudiest nights) when one is remote from artificial light; that the night effaces much of the offensive ugliness of day; that seeing things in their night aspects is sometimes to see them for the first time?

How long will it be? Or shall we never again spawn a generation conditioned, and privileged, to live peaceably with darkness?

Mutations

I drove the other evening along one of the little back roads running southward through our county, cutting it neatly into square miles for a distance, dipping down over creeks, shilly-shallying around marshes, correcting here and there a surveyor's muddling, plunging suddenly to cross the river, and then meandering. It's a favorite road of mine, but I don't travel it often. Strung along are a number of farms with modest nineteenth-century houses in varying states of restoration and modernization.

It was a surprise to find that a couple of dozen lovely new homes had taken form on the more scenic and desirable country lots. I sensed a sort of "Aha!" in each family's find. Here was the place for the dream house, the pastoral retreat. Good-bye suburbia.

There was a time when such a discovery thrilled me. I labored under the illusion of a former era that beautiful houses meant beautiful people, people of culture and accomplishment and noble persuasion.

I looked at us country folk and I liked us, but I yearned after a few people of refinement and "class" to "up-culture" us. Besides, these $75,000 houses would look good on our tax base, always a pressing problem in a community with only farm industry.

More and more of those dream homes have appeared through the years, dotted around the community on our most appealing sites with their instant grass, instant shrubbery, instant tennis courts, instant stables, all painted and polished and trimmed for the Christmas photograph. Unfortunately, they have not rendered the great improvements in the community that I naïvely dreamed of.

It shouldn't have been a disappointment to discover that beautiful houses don't always mean beautiful people, that quite ordinary people often build beautiful homes. They have brought about a change, however; our community has ceased to be a farm community. It's only a rural community now, and there's a difference. You know you've been vanquished when meetings are set for 7:00 and Thursday is no longer "church night," when Little League flourishes and PTA dies, when 4-H club projects are weighted heavily to rabbits and guinea pigs and outdoor cookery. Oh, we have class now; we look good! But we ain't no more cultured than we was.

Our kids vandalize our schools; they beat on our mailboxes and shoot out our citified streetlights. They get busted in drug raids and litter our roads with beer cans. Some of the ills we may blame on our urban neighbors, but we spawn a lot of them ourselves.

And those instant people behind their white clump birch and French provincial shutters had their illusions, too. They thought they were buying a sheltered environment peopled with wholesome, hearty, God-loving, sure 'nuff farm folk. Alas, they haven't improved us. They have only diluted us, to a concentration not much larger than the concentration of farmers nationwide (about 4½%).

But I don't give up hope. We have new neighbors on Bank Road, in new houses behind instant junipers and dwarf fruit, and they *are* beautiful people! Their children come up to take summer jobs picking beans and pulling sweet corn, and they try very hard to understand farm disciplines. They are in and out of our houses as if they'd always been here. Adults may hang back and parry, but kids plunge right into friendships. They have involved us all in impromptu gatherings where we perpetuate the tradition of "neighborhood." We wade through drifts to say "Bon Voyage" to someone bound on a Hawaiian Holiday or meet in Mel Niggle's orchard to roast wieners over his brush pile. We're invited to parties with city friends where we enjoy status as resident dispensers of "Ag expertise." (A landscape architect neighbor even has us all trotting off to the annual Home and Garden Show.)

Perhaps the time will come when community-wide, new people and old, we shall merge our illusions and our dreams, intermarry, and improve the strain. Who knows? We may yet produce a hybrid.

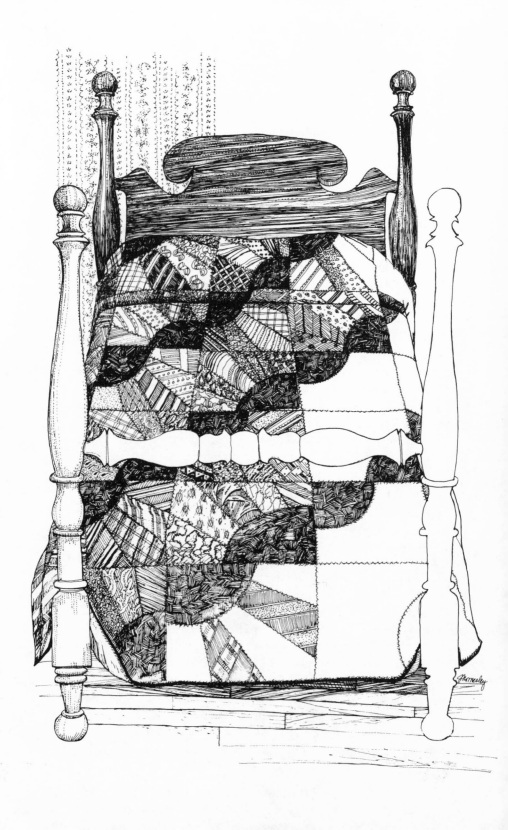

Midstream

A yellowed and water-spattered card that heralded my fiftieth birthday is taped to the casement above the sink. It reads: "Life is like a patchwork quilt. Even if it doesn't have a pattern to it, and even if you don't like every square, when you look at it all together it's a work of art." It is surely in middle age that one recognizes the way the grays and the blacks heighten the effect of the whole.

The wonder of it all is that you find you are able to cope with fortune and misfortune alike. You have discovered that there are strengths and appreciations arising from all your life that will sustain you.

Middle Age Is . . . ————————————————————

Middle age is a state of mind shaped by circumstance and related at least in part to the aging process. There is no concrete definition but there are some signs as clear as the crow's-feet on the outer edges of the eyes:

Middle age is when you get in the car and immediately change the radio station.

Middle age is when you start saying, "Well, I wouldn't mind her tinting her hair if she'd do it the color it used to be."

Middle age is when your age and your hipline begin to approximate one another.

Middle age is when you look at cracks in the plaster, and the crumbling window caulking and say (like Scarlett O'Hara), "I'll think about that tomorrow."

Middle age is when you've forgotten at what age the kids were toilet trained and you've ceased to care.

Middle age is when you check your watch at the party and it's a quarter to twelve instead of quarter to three.

Middle age is when your senior class president is elected a bank director.

Middle age is when you no longer pull out the stove when you're repainting the kitchen, or wax the floor around your area rugs.

Middle age is when the guy your mother wouldn't hear of your marrying comes back to the reunion with his third wife.

Middle age is when you stop screaming at the kids about their bedrooms and quietly shut the door.

Middle age is when you start wishing Dr. Spock would write *The Care and Feeding of Middle-Aged Men*.

Middle age is when words like cholesterol and myocardial infarction start creeping into your vocabulary.

Middle age is when the life insurance policies your folks took out for you are paid-up.

Middle age is when you find out where the action is so you can go someplace else.

But it can't be all bad, when your young adult is lecturing the teenagers in the same tone of voice you used on him ten years ago, and your gray hairs are the first curly ones you've ever had.

"Days of Our Lives"

Because forty-five to fifty-five are the crisis years, we attempt to see our friends weekly, usually at church. Crisis intervention, we call it. Longer intervals get to be more than any of us can stand.

"Well, what's the crisis of the week?" we ask and steel ourselves for the blows. Life is a soap opera without benefit of electric organ. Let me construct a few scenarios:

You are hauled into court by your neighbors, who claim that your kids on their minibikes are harassing them.

Your son who graduated summa cum laude in nuclear physics has joined a commune and is making furniture.

Your husband is in the coronary care unit of the local hospital.

Meanwhile your father-in-law breaks his hip at the rest home and has to be brought in for hip surgery.

Your niece drops out of college. Two *years* ago she dropped out of college! And her parents are just finding out about it. All the time you thought she was the sweetheart of Sigma Chi.

Your widowed father has just married a twenty-three-year-old waitress with three kids.

Your daughter tells you she's having a meaningful relationship with her psychology professor. (A "meaningful relationship" is what used to be known as "shacking up.")

Your brother's job has been "phased out" (this is what used to be known as getting fired). He has three kids in college and his wife has psoriasis.

Your brother-in-law has run off with the wife of a junk dealer from Muskegon. Your sister is forty-eight and pregnant.

Your cousin finds a copy of *Gay Life* underneath her son's mattress.

Your daughter-in-law is an alcoholic and your son brings his two toddlers home to you.

Your nephew brings his roommate to your house for the weekend. She weighs 105 promiscuous pounds.

Your mother, retired and living in Florida, has just collided with a police cruiser on her three-wheeler.

You go back to work on your doctor's advice to tide yourself through the menopausal slump and find that your husband is having an affair with the Avon lady.

Sound like fiction? Some of it is. If I told it as it really is, no one would believe it!

If none of these crises, moral or otherwise, have touched your life, then maybe you're not forty-five yet. Or you live a lot farther out in the country than I do.

Once-upon-a-time when you got together with friends and exchanged confidences you went home defeated. Yours must be the only kid in the world with two left feet and cross-eyes, or yours the only marriage not made in heaven. Of course, you didn't admit it or it might have seemed that you weren't succeeding.

Success in the Crisis Years begins to look more and more like survival. And you recognize finally that you can't make it alone. And so on the Sabbath we make our entreaties and the Lord speaks to us in the care and solace of our friends.

Support Crew

Life as preserved in the intensive care unit of a hospital is a fragile, tenuous, often ugly thing. Even as you pray wordlessly over the helpless bodies suspended in technological limbo, you wonder at the wisdom of synthetic systems which sustain life. And yet there is to be seen in this same chamber of horrors an aspect of life so poignant and affirmative as to seem to justify the sustenance of life at any cost.

For two weeks my brother Ted fought a battle for life in the northwest corner bed of the intensive care ward amid a welter of tubes and bottles and monitored systems. And two by two throughout those weeks those of us who love Ted tiptoed in at four-hour intervals to stand at his side and keep vigil.

The women came—my sister, my nieces, my sisters-in-law—as women have always come to stand by beds of pain, to swallow their tears and speak to their God. This is what one expects of women. But it was the witness of my brothers that moved me most.

Every morning at eight Erik appeared, still in his coveralls from his night shift job as a machinist, having made a forty-mile trip for ten minutes of squeezing Ted's sometime-responsive hand and softly speaking words of encouragement, or not speaking at all. And once or twice a day John came with his robust manner, so accustomed to managing people and forces, confident that by osmosis he could transfer his will for life to this favorite brother.

Henry slipped in on his lunch hour, or between calls on delinquent accounts for the electric company, all tenderness and helpless concern. And farmer Bill brought, with the aura of the out of doors, his tremendous personal strength, laying his hand on his brother's body.

No problem in my life ever seemed insurmountable, because I could take it to my brothers and they would deal with it out of their pioneer talents. My brothers, the dragon slayers, capable and strong.

I have a long memory of the skirmishes among them, the clashes of

212

personality and will. They live by ideologies often at variance, yet they are bound by love and a loyalty fused long ago in the need to cooperate. Together they ran the farm when father died, built homes for each other and for Mother, organized small enterprises, then a national corporation.

The avocation that has absorbed them all their lives (which they built into a successful business) is the endurance racing of motorcycles, a contest of man and machine against terrain and bodily limitation. Each man runs his own race against the clock and must keep his machine in operation. But at appointed places along the trails the support crew appears with gas and grease and tools, cool water and encouragement.

My brothers have been champions of their line, and how many times have they been indispensable crew to one another. I thought of these, and of all their other ties as I watched them in the intensive care unit with Ted. The race was his, but the support crew was there, convinced that he would make it out of the woods.

Going Home

My little mother sits on her suitcase by the front door looking like a refugee awaiting deportation. In her pink babushka and a coat of mine chosen for her shrunken frame, she looks so much like an eighty-five-year projection of myself that I am at once shocked and amused.

"I want to go home, Pat," she says firmly and calmly. "It's been a nice visit but now I want to go home."

"I can't take you home today, Mama."

"Why can't you take me home today? I have things to do. I need to go home!"

"But there's nobody there, Mama."

"My mother is there."

"No, Mama, she's gone. She's been gone for many years."

"But I have work to do and little children to care for," she says with a note of the frantic creeping into her voice. "There are the chickens to tend and I've canning to do and gardening. . . . Oh dear! I *want* to go home! Won't you please take me home?"

And so it goes. . . .

Where *is* home? *When* is home? A remembered yesterday? A forgotten tomorrow?

The seventh age of man has claimed my mother, and like all other ages it has its frustrations and its compensations. The brain has shifted into neutral, and the body idles along. There are placid days of sitting in the sun reading the same newpaper, making the same comments over and over, or nodding and dreaming by the fire. The sensitivities are blunted. The taste loses its discrimination, and the nose does not register the indecencies that affront the culture. And yet—Mama puts me to shame at times with her lovely childlike appreciation of beauty.

"I can't find my headscarf," she says, nearly in tears. "It's such a pretty one, and I like to look at it." In a moment of insight she adds, "There aren't so many pleasures left to me, but looking at pretty things is one of them."

People talk of the indignity of senility. The "indignities," I observe, belong to us who try to cope with senility in a manner of less than acceptance. Oliver Wendell Holmes in a poem called "The Last Leaf" wrote:

> *If I should live to be*
> *The last leaf upon the tree*
> *in the spring,*
> *Let them laugh*
> *As I do now*
> *At the old forsaken bough*
> *Where I cling.*

Why should we lament these aging people for what they are any more than we deplore our children for not being yet what they may become? Each should be cherished for the little flashes of what was or what is to be.

So my mother touches me deepest when she speaks of having "little children to care for." We were her over-riding and most loving concern for more than forty years. If she is suspended sometimes in that purposeful period of her life, she is more to be envied than pitied.

214

"If you can't take me home today, dear, when will you take me home?"

"Tomorrow, Mama. I'll take you home tomorrow."

"All right, dear. I just wanted to know. I can't leave my little children there alone."

"No, Mama, your children are fine. They're not alone."

Orrin comes into the living room at that moment. "Come on, Grandma," he says. "Your tea is ready and I've made you a piece of toast."

"Oh, good!" she says. "I do like toast."

"Let's take off our coat," he says. She obediently removes her coat, drapes it over the suitcase, and follows him to the kitchen.

"Oh, that's the prettiest cup there ever was, I think. I always like that cup. Where did you say it came from?"

"It came from the Caribbean, Mama," I say for the 348th time.

"Oh yes, I remember now. Could I have a bit of jam for my toast?"

She settles herself contentedly with her tea and toast and jam. My mother is home again.

Rites of Passage

During the potato harvest—parts of September and November and all of October—I pass six or seven hours a day sitting rather passively upon a tractor seat, steering with my elbow and pulling a wagon alongside the potato harvester. It's a job I enjoy because it gives me hours to study and admire the autumn metamorphosis.

What I observe in retrospect is the progression in life that broadens our appreciation of the fall process. I used to wait impatiently for the spectacular red of the sugar maples, the sassafras, the sumac, and lament when it passed. Then I went through my "yellow period," doting on the gold of the beech, the cottonwood, the cascade of an ash branch. I came to recognize that the slow turning of the chestnut oak kept a pleasant blend of dark green in the mix. Especially did I appreciate a panorama punctuated with the green of pine and cedar.

In more recent years I have discovered the emergence of the

multihued browns when the reds and the yellows have passed—the burnished copper of the clinging pin oak leaves, the withering, curling sycamore.

I developed a fascination for the falling of the leaves as they terminated their function and were shucked off in surprisingly slow showers in a breeze, or in the angry torrents of a brisk wind. In the stillness of the morning after the first frost I watch the walnut fronds, quietly pirouetting one by one to the ground, lying then beneath the tree in the kind of orderly heap formed by a dress dropped from a girl's shoulders.

Finally the joy of the elemental structure, leafless, stalwart against the onslaught of November. All the trees please me in their phases, but in some I take special joy: the beech, the wild dogwood, the sweet gum with its palette of colors. We are much indebted to Paul's mother for her thoughtful and intelligent planting of trees. She seeded the riverbanks with bushels of walnuts, replaced the chestnuts with disease-resistant varieties, and left a huge yard of ornamentals.

Best of all, the gingkos trees around whose enthusiasm societies could form—the most ancient of trees, "the living fossil." Thirty years old mine are now, and majestic beyond all the others, tall and narrow, with limbs branching off the main trunk as spokes from an axle. Long after the chestnuts, the oaks, the lindens have turned or shed, the gingkos cling to their bright green fan-shaped leaves. And then, little by little as the days pass, a gold blush creeps downward on the leaves until finally, brilliant yellow and magnificent, the tree stands among its bare neighbors. At last, in a glorious flourish on the day following the big freeze, it drops them all and stands naked in a pool of gold.

Many people leave monuments egotistically conceived, opulently executed. There are legacies artistic, scientific, sociological. But there is no memorial that speaks more eloquently, in the language of life itself, than a tree.

Wenzel & Son

Their son is coming home to farm! Already there's a sign down by the road that says, "Kentland Farms, Leland and Brian Wenzel," though the move is still some months in the future. Maybe Leland went out there and painted that sign the day after Brian was born. I don't know, but I do know what it signifies in terms of secret yearning.

You watch a boy grow up, and you want so much for him; or is it for yourself? No, it's for him—you tell yourself. You want him to be happy in his work, in his life. You want him to have substance and ease and experience of the world. You want him to know the admiration of his peers and the wider community.

He'll have to get an education, choose a profession, get away from the farm, prove to himself and the world that he can make it on his own. And you watch it happen, telling yourself you're glad. He'll have it easier than you did, that's for sure. Farming was never an easy life. Long hours, small pay. Big investment, small return. Sacrifice, reversals, insecurity—all this you're telling yourself.

Meanwhile you and your wife are "getting on." There are decisions to be made. Expand and move ahead? Or wind 'er down and ease into manageable retirement? Get rid of the livestock and just keep the cash crops? Or give up the whole thing and get a little place in town where things'll be easier for the wife should something happen to you? These are the questions that shape in the mind during the long hours when you're picking corn or feeding the stock.

Then comes that glorious day when he lets the words fall: "Dad, I think I'd like to come home." And you let the real dream roll out, the one that took shape on the day he was born, the dream that tantalized you the day you painted that sign down by the highway.

"There's a farm for sale down the road . . ." or "There's that tenant house over on the other place . . ." or "Maybe we ought to consider a bigger tractor . . ." or "I've been thinking about replacing the combine . . ." or "What would you think about a farrowing barn?" For every man who finds satisfaction in his life must dream that his son will savor that life, find it good, and choose to emulate it.

So at the Wenzel house there's a sense of something beginning. Marge is over at the other house painting and papering. Next spring there'll be more acreage to plant, so Leland's trying to do more fall plowing. And there are thoughts of longer vacations they'd never dared give in to before.

And still there is the restraint, which comes easily enough after so many years of restraining the dream itself.

"I don't want to hold him down, make him think he has to do things my way," Leland would tell you.

"I don't want her to think she has to be another Marge Wenzel," Marge says of her daughter-in-law. "They will have to live their own lives, and we'll have to accept the fact that their ways are not ours." . . . but oh, how the spirit soars in the echo of those words, "The kids are coming home to farm!"

"As the Twig Is Bent . . ."

I stopped by to drop off my wedding gift, had a peek at the wedding dress and the unfinished trousseau, heard secondhand over a cup of coffee the woes of a bride settling her first apartment, and sensed resignation to loss that pervaded this comfortable, well-ordered home—prelude to Karen's wedding day.

As I left the house, my eye fell on a splendid clump birch in the front yard. A perfect clump birch à la nursery catalogue doesn't just happen; it is effected by a patient, disciplined, loving gardener. This one had created a masterwork.

How much more concern, care, and hope had these "gardeners' invested in their daughter, I thought as I drove up the street. And how similarly had she responded to the "watering, fertilizing, pruning," how perfectly she had "shaped up" in the security of their "yard."

And now to watch her uprooted and transplanted into strange ground! For hours afterward I was mentally sewing a trousseau hem, wanting to help these parents vicariously to administer one last little act of TLC.

We tend our "gardens" in our own ways. My boys and shrubs are very much like my trees—strong and healthy, somewhat shaggy, minimally disciplined. They could be transplanted anywhere and they would grow and flourish, scarcely noticing the change. A sense of hardiness and well-being they would retain, but they would never bring the grace and serenity of that clump birch to an environment.

(Perhaps I understand at last why the Lord never put daughters in the master plan for me.)

Yes, Karen, too, will transplant as any well-tended nursery specimen will whose roots are thick and well-formed. And she will carry with her a healthy sense of the order and the concern with which she was nurtured. I do not fear for the "clump birch."

But there is an urgency, a satisfaction, a fulfillment in consistently tending a plant, or a tree—or a daughter. It is the gardeners who suffer from the transplant. . . .

Blessed Event

It's a girl! Born October 19, brown hair, green eyes, 110 pounds. She's twenty-one, she's beautiful, and she's ours! Her name is Paula.

We got her the easy way—by marriage. We never swaddled her in pink flannel or bandaged her wounded knees. We were not privileged to hear her first words, guide her first steps, brag about her first tooth, weep over her first school day, praise her first star, applaud her first solo. By the same token we were spared many other "firsts"—high heels, eye shadow, cramps, padded bras, dates. We never bought her dollies or pinafores or jumping ropes or paid for piano lessons and dancing class.

She thinks she married our son. But she is our first girl and little recognizes the burden of that fact. In truth she married us all and we will reap the fruits of her womanhood. In exchange we will give her the love and devotion, the accumulated "spoiling" of our twenty-five years of longing after a girlish, womanish, female, feminine dame.

She brings into our house a light step, a lilting laugh, a coy and winsome teasing presence, the fragrance of cologne, the thrill of a bikini, a weathered shoulder bag, a love of cats and horses, shoes kicked carelessly about, a shred of female modesty.

Someone at last to share my gaiety and despair, my enthusiasm and disgust, to break the even-tempered mood of this overwhelmingly male household. Someone to talk with of fashions and recipes, of female complaints and oppression. Someone to notice my haircut, or the herbs in the salad. Someone to respond to gossip with more than a snort. It is women after all who nurture what is feminine in other women, and a woman alone too long with men can almost become "one of the fellas."

Our Paula will be the counselor and confidante to her two young brothers-in-law. Her opinion will be sought and hers will be the small deciding vote on many an issue, honored more for coming from the outside and from the alien sex than for the wisdom of her years or the weight of her experience. (It starts already. "Paula says a brown suit, . . ." and her father-in-law-to-be bought a brown suit.)

She will dominate in status the sisters-in-law who follow her as having the first and best claim. She will illuminate our blind spots, throw at least a bit of light upon our prejudices before she embraces them. Her taste and style will mingle with our own, and as the years pass, predominate and prevail.

She will feed and care for us in our dotage, bathe our wrinkled bodies, comb our silvered hair, and build a soothing bridge for us to a past she never knew.

She will weep at our funerals and inherit our surplus. She will become the guardian of our traditions. She will love our land, cherish our heirlooms, and prize our heritage.

It was a long labor, but we don't begrudge ourselves the wait.

Patricia

All the little girls Franz ever knew were objects of wonderment to him. I think he saw them as life's highest creation. More than anything else in life he wanted a daughter of his own. When his "sweet love" was finally "in bloom," as he put it, no thought was given to a son. She would be a daughter, and she would be called Patricia, and the dream was fulfilled.

The chronicle of Patricia's first two years as written to us by Andrea, Franz's wife, bubbled with wonderment that such a lovable creature should live and share their lives. The goal of their early married years was to bring Andrea and Patricia from Austria to Ohio to visit Paul and me for a long autumn holiday. That had been the season Franz enjoyed most in his year with us (1969–70).

For six joyous weeks we had them. Franz worked with us in the field, and Andrea in the kitchen. Order prevailed as never before at harvest. At day's end there was Gulasche Suppe or Wiener schnitzel or some other Austrian delicacy, and always there was the pleasure of a little girl running around the house, turning somersaults on the floor, singing, teasing, kissing everybody goodnight. It was a rare delight in this household of men. Her parents' eyes shone each time they looked at her. Each evening they carried her to bed, spent a private quarter-hour with her, and she slept without a whimper.

On October 29 it all ended abruptly. Patricia was critically injured in an auto-truck crash at a blind crossing. Two agonizing days she lived in the intensive care unit of the hospital, hooked to all the life-sustaining and monitoring equipment available. Franz and Andrea kept a tragic but strangely beautiful vigil. Andrea wept and Franz solaced her. Franz wept and Andrea whispered comfort in a soft Austrian dialect. Then on All Saints' Day it ended. They asked that I arrange for their immediate return home.

Feeling alien and outside the tight circle that enclosed them, I stood there and mourned the loss of this child, the loss to us of this little Austrian family, so dear to all who knew them, who would surely turn their backs on us, our friends, the farm, and this land which had turned dream into nightmare.

"Franz, if you go today you won't be able to take Patty with you," I said, foreseeing the complexities of shipping a body across national boundaries.

"Oh," said Franz, turning to me incredulous, "we take Patricia with us. She is here with us now. That was only her body. It was a *cute* little body, but only a body."

And then Andrea turned, folded me in her strong, loving arms and said, "Patricia will grow again in my body. She will be born again and we will bring her again to you."

And I became part of a truth little tested in my fortunate life. When love is perfect, as I had seen it to be with this threesome, it endures all things. They returned to Austria, leaving us uplifted in our grief, feeling that we were part of some miracle. Andrea's letters were full of their love for each other and tender mention of the omnipresent spirit of Patricia.

A year passed, and in the ancient cradle of Andrea's family in a chalet in Upper Austria a new little girl appeared to make her father's eyes shine. Iris Patricia was born the following August, a "perfect baby who always smiles and never cries," by her parents' reports.

When you take someone into your home and your heart as we did Franzi long ago, you little know how deeply into life the act may lead you. As Paul and I sat in the hospital through those terrible hours of Patricia's waning life, I recognized that it was a conscious choice to love that had brought us to this precipice. I asked myself if, given a vision clear through to the tragic end, we would have risked so much. Even at the depths, the answer was an awesome "Yes."

The Girls of '49

The Flora Stone Mather College girls of '49 are chic and successful and pretty well-heeled, from appearances. (Of course, if your kids are in jail, you're forty pounds overweight, and you're on the sauce, I don't suppose you bother checking in with the silver anniversary committee.)

The crowd that convened on campus to raise the specter and invoke the spirit of the hotshot class of '49 was, by and large, the same crowd of hotshots who created the original myth (that we were hotshots). The only difference was that now we could bear to recognize that we really had never been all that hot.

I heard a couple of "the girls" tell of coming to "the big city" (Cleveland) on the bus from Akron, walking up Euclid Avenue with their laundry cases, staring at the tall buildings, and thinking with a thrill that now it was all going to happen. Four years later they took the bus, the laundry cases, and their sheepskins back, with the recognition that if it was gonna happen at all it was going to happen in Akron.

As for myself, I always labored under the onus of being one of only two farmer's daughters in the class. Few farmers in those days had either the inclination or the funds to send their daughters to private institutions of learning. (A couple of us made it nervously on the finances of the Alumni Association.) The night of our 25th anniversary party I discovered there had been two more. I was the only one who returned to the farm.

The husbands of this gang of lovelies are probably more brow-beaten than most, for ours was a women's college and we were never allowed to forget it. Our dean was a female chauvinist of the first order. And however much we may have chafed under the exclusivity of our female society, for four years we were steeped in the artificiality of being the number-one sex. Considering that conditioning, our divorce rate is amazingly low.

We were the rear guard of the Depression generation, entering college the month after the "big war" ended. Things had improved so much in our lifetime that we were oblivious to any need for further change. Social protest was the furthest thing from our minds. We did make our little tin-horn protests, of course.

We thought, for example, that it would be nice if the University Library could be reconverted to the private club it had formerly been and used as a student union. We pressured for merger into university life with less emphasis on our unique status as a women's college. We wanted to participate in such frivolities as cheerleading, wanted to be permitted to imbibe on campus, to have less restrictive hours, to fraternize more freely with men, to do away with compulsory chapel. We thought the whole physical plant needed razing, that shining new facilities should arise against the backdrop of Severance Hall, the Cleveland Art Museum, and the University Hospitals.

Alas! By the 25th it had all been accomplished, and our deepest regrets stemmed from the changes. The stately old library is now the student union, and the cry of the student body is of its inadequacy. The women's college has vanished into the body of the expanding university.

"Irrelevant" activities like cheerleading are scorned today as "Mickey Mouse." You can drink beer wherever you see fit. Keeping "hours" of any sort is a relic of former times, and men are as much in and out of the dorm here as they are on all campuses these days. We wandered about nostalgically in search of the quaint and charming old buildings among the new, mourning the loss of the quaint and charming old ways. . . .

No, the girls of '49 were not happy with the changes they themselves had advocated. They suffered future shock. They came back to alum day with their class gift of $1949 (their assets exceed their generosity) and dedicated it to the preservation of—would you believe—the chapel!

We were commissioned into the world by our female chauvinist dean as "women of responsibility." By and large we have assumed it, as women. But when we came back for the 25th, we were "the girls." When we gathered around the piano and sang the clever songs we composed long ago, there was "one shining moment" there when we were twenty-one again and hotshots, and nobody in her right mind would have charged us with any responsibility!

Letter to a College Freshman

The clamor after college degrees for degrees' sake that held sway through the sixties has subsided. There were certainly a slew of kids packing off to the universities with portable TV sets and stereos who should have spared their parents the expense. I only hope we don't slide too far in the other direction, that some of our potentially fine students don't cop out on the misunderstanding that nobody really values a college degree anymore. I have definite thoughts on the subject that I found myself pounding out to a favorite freshman:

Dear Frosh,

Think of you often in this Eastern College adventure. What a credit to be accepted at a fine school! But I have no doubt that there's a bit of a struggle involved. I remember my own first year painfully well. I was so insecure so far from home. (Fifty miles was a considerable distance back in the forties, and you didn't think of calling home unless you had appendicitis.) What is it that makes home take on such a golden glow when you leave it?

But the struggle. Gee, it seemed like hard work! There wasn't any question about doing it. My mom was back home pinning her hopes on me, and what else could I do? What I see clearly now is that after those four agonizing years of tough courses and final exams, nothing ever seemed impossible again. It was like climbing a mountain and being able to run all the way down the other side. What I got from those years above all was a pride in myself that nothing displaces.

I go around delivering pumpkins or potatoes at the back doors of supermarkets, and I know the people in the produce departments are thinking, "Boy! What a poor sap that is!" All the while I'm chuckling and thinking of the secret I have, that I sat for long hours in libraries and lonely dorm rooms through four interminable years and finally was awarded a coveted swatch of parchment. I surely didn't need it to unload pumpkins at grocery stores, but because of it I can *choose* to unload pumpkins. And that's the wonderful difference. (There are plenty of fine things to do without a degree, but it will always open a few more doors.)

Funny—I used to think the same kind of thoughts about my mother when I was a child. She had been a farm girl (like myself) who went off to the state university in 1912 and earned a degree. I used to watch her on the produce market, my heart aching, and think, "Oh, Mama, you are so much; you shouldn't have to work like this!" But she had that same secret pride in her accomplishment. She never flaunted her education, never mentioned it; but I know it sustained her through everything.

Well, I didn't start in to preach, but I remember the discouraging hours and wanted to assure you that they are not wasted, though often it seems the only reward for hard work is the work itself.

I wish I could say that I was one of those eager scholars thrilled by every course I took, fascinated with each bit of accumulated knowledge. The truth was that I found a whale of a lot of tedium and downright boredom to endure. The amazing thing is that you will rejoice ultimately in having disciplined yourself to that tedious work. (It's a kind of discipline seldom mastered by the guys who take an eight-hour job out of high school at $5.50 an hour.)

If the college-trained enjoy a greater success in life (as statistics seem to prove) it is probably not because of superior knowledge, but because they develop a higher degree of mental discipline.

So, good buddy, make the best of them, these college years. Don't try to kid me that it's all hard work. Remember, I was there, and I don't forget the good times either. Make a bunch of new friends, and stay there enough weekends in a row to really gain a perspective on home.

And on the long days and nights when the tedium is "getting to you," remember that you are not alone. The spirits of all of us who labored through it are there with you. We love you and we value your labor.

Hang in there!

Silver Anniversary

I knew I was going to marry him the night I met him. All the vibes were right. He was a bachelor farmer belatedly finishing a college degree. I was an "old maid teacher" withering in a country school. He danced like Fred Astaire and held his fork like a gentleman.

Paul and I had never met, but our parents had graduated from college together and farmed in neighboring communities. We were in apples, they in potatoes; and we both classified as truck gardeners.

Paul never did ask me to marry him, though in a mad, impetuous moment (I remember the precise spot) he asked me if I would consider becoming engaged to a farmer.

He was a boy to set a mother's eyes gleaming; our pedigrees matched. It wouldn't do to indicate full approval. No one, after all, was quite good enough for my mother's daughters. "She'll go out there in the country and those stubborn Germans will just swallow her!" (His parents had their reservations, too. My father had been cremated when he died some years before, a practice very rare at the time. The news got about in that conservative community and the Pentons were classified as a bit strange.) But Mother couldn't invent any really serious objections. He was a good Protestant boy and if there was "bad blood" in his lineage her sources couldn't document it. When we announced our plan to marry at Christmas, she snapped tersely, "I don't approve," as if she'd rehearsed the line for years. Only later did it evolve that it was Christmas weddings she didn't approve.

Twenty-five years afterward I'm willing to agree that Christmas weddings are an abomination. Anniversary celebrations get all mixed up with tinsel and ribbons and church programs. But matching the pedigrees, checking the bloodlines, harmonizing the professions (archaic observances by today's antiestablishment standards) emerge as laudable approaches to marriage, especially for mothers-in-law. It's more often your son-in-law than your husband who ends up "honoring, comforting," etc., in sickness and in health.

Yes, we are a "perfect pair." He likes to get up early; I like to stay up late. He is punctual to a fault; my fault is that I am never punctual. I'm always cold; he's always hot. He likes football; I like poetry. He is musical; I can't read a note. I'm a liberal; he's a conservative. I'm a romanticist; he is a pragmatist. We've got something going for us night and day, and we've got all avenues covered.

From our common backgrounds came a set of common values and a mutual respect. With these guidelines we hammered out the compromises. Long before it was fashionable, my husband helped me in the house. He wanted to live in order, something my bookish life hadn't schooled me for, so he helped me achieve it. My mother's example had taught me farm work so I pitched in and helped him outdoors. We were already "programmed" when the women's movement emerged.

He gave me the freedom to pursue enthusiasms he didn't share, and cultivate friends to augment them. (With three sons he didn't have to leave the house to find cohorts to share his pastimes.)

But we had common interests, too, beyond our sons and our farm business. We both enjoyed foreign languages and the well-turned English phrase. We enjoyed swimming, skating, skiing. We had a wealth of loyal friends from childhood and we worked hard at maintaining ties with friends who passed through our lives and moved on. We valued our community, our church, and our families. I venture to say that we even enjoyed our battles royal—in retrospect. They were always open secrets.

We put priorities on what seemed to be incongruities—frugality and "living it up" while we were young enough to enjoy it. We scrimped on clothes and cars and household goods and took outside jobs so we could blow our money on ski trips abroad. Our silver anniversary doesn't seem to call for any milestone voyage to paradise.

We figure we've been rowing back and forth for twenty-five years.

The fragrant spring blooming, the luxurious summer shade, the fall abundance long had gone. The orioles built in the apple tree no longer; the apples that happened were sparse and uncared for; most of the limbs were dead and bare. I have a warm memory of the children playing on the swing that hung from the north bough, or in the expanse of sandpile that evolved there naturally. I remember satisfying September breakfasts in its breezy shade long ago in that sweet lull after school starts, before harvest begins. One branch framed itself in the casement window of my upstairs bedroom, the first visual impression of the morning. A fine spring day indeed when you opened your eyes to that pink-white blush against blue sky.

The apple tree had been my constant delight as it shaded the back door, a link to my childhood and the apple orchards of home, my barometer of the seasons as I learned housewifery in the tiny kitchen on the southeast corner of the house.

One limb and then another fell. The heart of the broad trunk rotted away but tenaciously the tree stood, a gnarled specter of its former self. The linden sapling we planted to replace it was twenty feet high and becoming cramped.

Reluctantly I said it time after time: "Don't you think you ought to get rid of that tree?" And with a similar reluctance Paul ignored me time after time.

This afternoon a chain saw sings outside the old kitchen. Teddy splits with an ax the section his father saws; Orrin picks up brush and rakes leaves and bark. The apple tree is gone.

The babes who played beneath it do men's work in clearing it away. A great pile of kindling mounts through the afternoon beneath the window of a new kitchen on the northeast corner.

The old apple and the old kitchen have passed simultaneously. I will never have to gaze from my kitchen window upon the place where it stood. My new kitchen opens on other vistas. Perhaps Paul sensed how lonely I would be with that void and its memories. Perhaps that's why he stalled until now. Perhaps it was he who feared the loneliness.

A fire burns on the hearth of our new kitchen, the first fireplace of our lives. I've wanted it since I was a small child reading "Little Polly Flinders sat among the cinders warming her pretty little toes."

Paul carries in a few logs from the clearing operation out back, moves the screen and lays one upon the embers. I seat myself in a rocker to enjoy a cup of tea as the afternoon dies with the year.

The dry apple catches fire and leaps up in characteristic hot flame. I prop my feet upon the hearth and am warmed by the realization that old pleasures sacrifice themselves to new.

LIST OF ESSAYS

HOUSEHOLDING

AGAINST THE GRAIN

CENTERING

NOSTALGIC ROSE